[redacted]

RADICAL ACTS OF JUSTICE

RADICAL ACTS OF JUSTICE

How Ordinary People Are Dismantling Mass Incarceration

Jocelyn Simonson

THE NEW PRESS
NEW YORK
LONDON

Published in the United States by The New Press, New York, 2023
Distributed by Two Rivers Distribution

ISBN 978-1-62097-744-6 (hc)
ISBN 978-1-62097-807-8 (ebook)
CIP data is available

The New Press publishes books that promote and enrich public discussion and understanding of the issues vital to our democracy and to a more equitable world. These books are made possible by the enthusiasm of our readers; the support of a committed group of donors, large and small; the collaboration of our many partners in the independent media and the not-for-profit sector; booksellers, who often hand-sell New Press books; librarians; and above all by our authors.

www.thenewpress.com

Composition by dix!
This book was set in Fairfield LH

Printed in the United States of America

2 4 6 8 10 9 7 5 3 1

Contents

Introduction

On a September day in 2018, more than 250 people gathered at a rally in front of the Cook County Criminal Court in Chicago. Banners read "Abolish Money Bond. End Pretrial Detention" and "Money Bail Is Ransom." Another banner featured the words "Free Them All," with a painting of a figure running out of Chicago's jail, through a swirl of color, and into the arms of family.

The rally took aim at money bail, known in Illinois as bond—a tool of the criminal court in which someone can be held in jail while still presumed innocent if they cannot afford the amount of bail money set in their case. The speakers at the hour-long rally had a specific demand of the judges and prosecutors inside the courthouse: that they follow a year-old court order requiring that judges stop detaining people in jail for unaffordable bond amounts. Despite this court order, more than 2,500 people remained detained in Cook County Jail pretrial. Those gathered at the rally condemned this as a form of ransom targeted at Black and brown communities in Chicago. But the crowd also had a larger message: End all pretrial detention. Free them all.[1]

The Chicago Community Bond Fund—one of a growing number of groups that have been established to pay the bail of people who can't afford to do so themselves—co-organized this rally with more than fifty groups from around the state, with the goal to end money bail. Also in the crowd were organizers from more than thirty bail and bond funds from around the country, visiting Chicago as part of a national network of bail funds.

Lavette Mayes,[2] an organizer with the Chicago Community Bond Fund, spoke into the microphone and to the rally's crowd, telling her own story of pretrial incarceration. Mayes had been arrested for the first time in her life while still in her nightgown, charged with aggravated battery after a fight with a family member. With bond set well beyond what she could afford, Mayes spent 571 days in Cook County Jail. Mayes described how she lost her housing, her business, and nearly lost custody of her children during that time. She had the crowd repeat after her: "Surely, we can do better than this." Mayes was released only after the Chicago Community Bond Fund helped pay her bond. Otherwise, she would have spent more days, and perhaps years, in jail while still legally innocent. Mayes said to the crowd, "When you incarcerate the mom, you incarcerate the whole family."[3]

The Chicago Community Bond Fund has been posting bond for strangers since 2015, freeing hundreds of people with the help of both paid staff and more than one hundred volunteers. The bond fund grew out of years of local organizing, when groups came together in 2014 to gather bond money for fellow organizers during protests against police violence. The organic collective soon grew into a formal bond fund aimed at bailing out people caught in the criminal system and sitting in jail because of their race and poverty. After paying their bail, the Chicago fund connects people to local services and organizing hubs, and the fund collects the stories and experiences of their group to provide a bigger picture of the communal devastation occurring via pretrial incarceration. Some people whom they free, including Mayes, join the bond fund in its work.[4]

When a group such as the Chicago Community Bond Fund gets together to raise money and post money bail or bond for strangers, they do more than free people who would otherwise remain jailed for their poverty. They also make a statement through that action: do not jail these people in our name; *we* are the community, too. The recent rise of community bail funds has coincided with the emergence of the Movement for Black Lives. While there were five or six active bail funds in the United States as of 2015, this number grew steadily and then surged in 2020, when millions of people donated to bail funds during the uprisings that followed the killings of George Floyd and Breonna Taylor. As of 2022, close to one hundred community bail funds operate throughout the United States, most of them members of the National Bail Fund Network. The Bail Project, a national revolving bail fund, has staff posting bail in more than two dozen cities.[5] And informal collectives of people posting bail in their communities pop up regularly. In each case, groups of people are freeing people from jail by using a tool of the criminal system itself: money bail.

The longstanding work of bail and bond funds can result in tangible political victories. In Illinois, for example, in 2021, after six years of organizing in coalition with other groups, the Chicago Community Bond Fund celebrated the signing of an Illinois law that will end money bond in the state.[6] But the power of bail funds goes beyond policy. To pay money bail via an organized community bail fund is a collective assertion of power over a judge's decision to hold someone in a cage because of their poverty. Bail funds tell us that incarceration does not make everyone feel safer; that freedom can mean community safety too. And they tell us this by working within the system, by using the written rules of criminal procedure to build their own power in opposition to that system.

Collectives of ordinary people intervene in the criminal system using other tools of criminal procedure too. Across the country, groups of "courtwatchers" sit in the audience section of criminal courtrooms to demonstrate support for the accused, their presence secured by the constitutional right to attend public criminal proceedings. They use social media to let the public know what everyday courtrooms look like from their point of view: prosecutors criminalizing poverty in the name of "the People" by asking for bail for a woman accused of stealing formula to feed her baby; a judge, consumed by prejudice, laughing at the idea that a nineteen-year-old Black woman is truly a college student with an exam the next day, and sending her to jail. As courtwatchers sit in rows wearing matching T-shirts, they send a message through their collective presence in the courtroom: we are the people too, and we do not think the incarceration of our neighbors makes us safer. They shift power away from the elite actors at the front of the courtroom and toward the swelling collective in the back. By telling the public about what they see, courtwatchers send a larger message about the violence of everyday courtroom proceedings. When they do that, they embody the potential to look outside of criminal courthouses for justice.

In other courthouses, members of "participatory defense hubs"—families of people who are incarcerated or charged with crimes—work together to intervene in criminal cases. They dissect the available evidence in detail and prepare biographical videos and photographic essays that humanize the person charged with a crime. A photo album, put together collectively by a hub, forces a judge to appreciate how a twenty-six-year-old Latino man parents his children day in and day out. When the camera is passed from hub member to hub member, it captures ordinary acts, such as changing a diaper or a preschool pickup. A photo essay can serve various functions in the courtroom, and one that is generated collectively—by Latinx and Black people whose families are also being criminalized—can have a resounding impact. As hub members gain expertise in criminal procedure, they can seize control of the narrative, shifting understandings of what the "community" thinks about whether justice requires the incarceration of a father who may have also engaged in a "criminal" act. Once again, power shifts as people organize for change together using the available tools of the courtroom.

Some collective defense campaigns happen at a bigger scale, including campaigns for criminalized survivors of violence, coordinated by groups such as Love & Protect and Survived & Punished. These defense campaigns—often organized by and on behalf of Black, Native, and Latinx women and gender non-conforming people—raise money, pack courtrooms, and plan protests. As they do so, the organizers connect the plights of criminalized individuals to systemic problems with the use of the criminal law to address interpersonal violence. As a working group of Survived & Punished NY, a local chapter of the larger network, wrote in a 2021 zine: "Criminalization, prosecution, and incarceration inherently spreads the violence, rather than solves it."[7]

Collective contestation of the criminal system goes beyond the courthouse and into the state house, the city council, the town meeting. In Los Angeles, as the pandemic swelled around them in mid-2020, fifty grassroots groups convened by Black Lives Matter–Los Angeles surveyed tens of thousands of Angelenos about their priorities for their city budget and led virtual participatory budget meetings with 3,300 more local residents. They developed an alternate budget, a "People's Budget," that recommended that just 1.64 percent of general funds be dedicated to law enforcement, compared to the 54 percent that the city had proposed be allocated to the Los Angeles Police Department. And they proposed a new budget category, "Reimagined Community Safety," which would include funds for restorative justice and other services outside of the criminal system.

These organizers exposed the wide gulf between the city's view of how to spend the people's money and the people's view of where their taxes should be spent: on housing security, on free transportation, on direct aid to poor people. After a presentation in front of Los Angeles City Council, the Council voted to cut the Los Angeles Police Department budget by $150 million. This was just a small fraction of the police department's overall budget, and in future years that budget would rise again. But the People's Budget was revelatory in a different way: it required elected officials to imagine ways of providing safety beyond the standard go-tos of policing and incarceration. This public, collective contestation over the meaning of safety outlasts any individual budget fight.

These collective tactics—bail funds, courtwatching, participatory and collective defense, People's Budgets—are not new. For hundreds of years, people have gathered together to free people from the violence of the state, whether it was packing courtrooms in support of people being held under the Fugitive Slave laws in the nineteenth century; the multiracial, nationwide efforts to participate in the defense of the "Scottsboro boys" in Alabama in the 1930s; or the creation of a bail fund in the Women's House of Detention in New York City in the 1970s, spearheaded by radical Black and Latina activists but done in support of and alongside all criminalized women.[8]

People coming together and employing these and other techniques today are indebted to this history. But there is something undeniably new happening. Each of these tactics, or forms of collective action, has grown exponentially since 2014, both in geographical reach and in public engagement. These methods of communal resistance lay bare the paucity of justifications for mass criminalization and mass incarceration. Because so many ideas about punishment and safety are ingrained in our popular understandings of justice, it is hard to make the large shifts—both conceptual and material—that would push us toward transformative possibilities. This active grassroots resistance to the criminal system helps transform ideas about "the people," "public safety," and "justice" that uphold the system as we know it, ideas that have allowed mass criminalization and incarceration to continue in recent decades despite the growing realization of their reach and devastation.

When people join together to contest ideas of justice and safety through tactics that include bail funds, People's Budgets, courtwatching, and participatory defense, they open up for debate the contours of ideas that we usually take for granted: that prosecutions and prisons make us safer than we would be otherwise; that our public officials charged with maintaining "law and order" are carrying out the will of the people when they arrest, prosecute, and imprison; that justice itself requires putting people in cages. Most fundamentally, these movement interventions are forcing us to ask whether we can continue to imprison Black, Latinx, and Native people at disproportionate rates and still call what we do "justice." They redefine the concept of justice itself: perhaps justice is when the state provides communities with what they need to support each other and keep each other safe. Perhaps safety means freedom, not incarceration.

The United States currently finds itself in a period of extensive backlash against leftist social movements of all kinds, including opposition to the rising call to reduce the reach of the criminal system and to abolish or "defund" the police. The backlash is not limited to traditionally conservative areas or groups. Many "blue" states and cities in democratic strongholds increased, rather than decreased, funding for police and jails in 2021 and 2022, following the uprisings in 2020. A "public safety" candidate and former police captain, Eric Adams, was elected mayor in New York City, running on a platform that not only equated police with safety, but also vowed to support and increase their funding—and followed through on that promise while reducing spending on public education and other services.[9] In 2022, voters in San Francisco recalled their "progressive" prosecutor Chesa Boudin.[10] Some state legislatures have passed laws restricting the ability of cities to reduce police funding, and others have attempted to curtail the work of bail funds.[11]

But this is only half of the story. These same years find grassroots coalitions winning political fights for decarceration too. Some states and cities are passing bans on prison construction. Some are ending money bond.[12] Some are reducing spending on jails or police in favor of spending on non-carceral public health initiatives.[13] These anti-carceral wins may not be lauded in the mainstream liberal media, but neither were most civil rights movement of the past.[14] And each of these wins emerges from decades of organizing, as well as from the energy and ideas developed in smaller groups, including bail funds, participatory defense hubs, and courtwatching teams. This is how change with respect to the politics of the criminal system happens: slowly, through ideological battles born of and sustained by struggle.

Today, it is in everyday acts in courthouses and legislative chambers that we can locate the collective energy, care, and radical thought that unearth transformative ideas that are not going away. And bubbling beneath the surface of these collective acts lie bigger questions and possibilities. Angela Y. Davis, Gina Dent, Erica Meiners, and Beth Richie, each a longtime thinker deeply embedded in abolitionist organizing, together remind us that looking only at the popularity of slogans such as "Defund the Police" misses the bigger, long-term ideological picture, the "immense gains and ruptures offered by the language of social and political movements."[15]

This book begins by laying out the reigning ideas of justice, safety, and "the people" that constitute an ideology of criminal prosecution against which many grassroots groups push. It also describes how collective action can be a form of democratic participation by contesting these dominant ideas. The next three chapters tell the stories of people joining together to engage in specific tactics of resistance within courthouses: bail funds (Chapter 2), courtwatching (Chapter 3), and participatory and collective defense (Chapter 4). These stories come from all over the country; I have been personally involved in quite a few. In Chapter 5, these groups take us outside of the courthouse and into the world of local, county, and state budget fights. They take the adage, often attributed to Rev. Martin Luther King Jr., that budgets are moral documents, and they make that moralizing a collective enterprise. Chapter 6 brings these radical acts of justice together, as many of these groups have done, to see how they force an ideological fight over meanings of justice and safety, a fight that unearths transformative possibilities.

This is a book about certain tactics of groups of people resisting mass incarceration in their neighborhoods, counties, and states. What unites these collective acts are the ways that they intervene in the workings of the criminal system, and in particular criminal courts, by using the tools of the system—a kind of political jiu jitsu that turns the force of the state against itself. These are not the only forms of collective action in the face of mass incarceration—from voting and serving on juries, to protests, riots, and civil disobedience, to mutual aid and collective care outside of the state, social movements today are engaging in a vibrant array of effective strategies and experiments.[16] And the tactics described in this book are not static or perfect; they shift and change over time as organizers experiment with them and sometimes even move on from the tactics or from each other. But what makes the tactics that this book explores important is that, at our moment in history, they bring with them vital, collective ideas about what is wrong with mass incarceration, and, through their actions inside of the system, point toward how we can dismantle it.

RADICAL ACTS OF JUSTICE

1

Justice, Safety, and the People

When I was a public defender in New York City, it was common for judges, clerks, and other courtroom players to refer to individual assistant district attorneys (ADAs) as "the People," as in, "Would the People like to request a lunch break?"; or, if an ADA was not visible in the courtroom, "Are the People in the bathroom?" The 2017 movie *Roman J. Israel, Esq.*, includes a scene in which Denzel Washington, playing an awkward defense lawyer, enters a crowded Los Angeles criminal courtroom in which an ADA has just referred to herself as "the People." "People," says Washington's character. "What people? There's no people, there's just you making a bullshit career-climbing offer, let's admit it." The movie's doomed antihero highlights the absurdity of a practice that has come to seem normal: an individual referring to herself as "the People" inside a courtroom full of the poor people of color she is prosecuting. Are these people accused of crimes not "the people" too?

I referred to the prosecution as "the People" on the record on more than one occasion when I was a defense attorney, even as I resolutely condemned the language outside of the courtroom. This was in part because I felt the need to maintain relationships with ADAs in order to negotiate for my clients, nearly all of whom were poor Black and Latinx Bronx residents. But that is only a partial excuse. The language of "the People" seeps into everyday courtroom practices, written motions, and case law—and can be heard at the beginning of all twenty-two (and counting) seasons of *Law and Order*, in which the voice-over intones that "the people" are represented by two "important groups": police and district attorneys. The term comes to seem ordinary. And it comes to seem true: prosecutors are elected officials, and so they must represent the people. People accused of crimes are not part of "the People," part of the public that matters. And when groups gather to support people accused of crimes or to resist incarceration, those groups are not part of a good or neutral public, but rather something else—something reactionary, something biased, something outside the workings of justice.

In many ways, our approach to public safety depends for survival on this limited notion of which "people" matter. Whether or not prosecutors are literally called "the People," as in the customary case caption, "the People v. the Defendant," it has come to seem natural that we entrust local prosecutors to define and render "justice" on behalf of the general public. Or, to take another well-known line from *Law and Order*, this one spoken by Assistant District Attorney Jack McCoy, for prosecutors, "justice is a by-product of winning."[1] Justice, from this prosecutorial angle, means finding and punishing individuals who have committed wrongs or engaged in disorderly behavior. Prosecutors deliver public safety by removing those individuals from society, labeling them as criminal.

These are not universal definitions or understandings of "justice" and "safety," but they dominate the American criminal courtroom, either because they are taken for granted or because they are questioned in silence. These concepts of safety, justice, and "the people" together constitute an ideology—a worldview that captures our thinking and serves to uphold and disguise a system of oppression. One central danger of ideologies is that, in seeming to describe the present accurately, they inhibit our ability to imagine and seek out large-scale and even transformative change. When an ideology upholds an unequal or racist system, this becomes especially problematic.[2]

While the concept of justice may be an abstract ideology, what many call the "criminal justice system" is a highly tangible series of institutions and array of actors that control policing, supervision, criminalization, and punishment using the criminal law.[3] Real people are subjected to this state violence: surveilled, stopped and frisked, strip searched, put in handcuffs, taken from parents, put in cages, forced into an ankle monitor or a drug treatment program. Real material resources are put into the political economy that drives and maintains the work of these actors and institutions.[4] And real people are killed, whether by police, from the traumatic toll of criminalization, or via the death penalty.[5] But to make this real state violence legitimate requires a set of ideas that justify it, sustain it, and make it seem an inevitable state response to harm and disorder.[6]

In discussing the way we internalize ideologies, organizer Paula X. Rojas writes of the "cops in our heads and our hearts," pointing to how organizers in the United States internalize systems of oppression. This is a metaphor heard frequently in left-leaning organizing meetings and workshops, where facilitators might, for example, ask a participant whether an initial response to a problem or tactic might come from the cop in their head and heart—whether they are assuming, without thinking about it, that it is police and punishment that can solve the particular issue at hand. Picking up on this metaphor from Rojas in the context of abolitionist organizing today, writer and organizer Mariame Kaba has said, "The prison and the police are in our heads and hearts, therefore th[e] system is naturalized in a way that makes it almost impossible for folks to step back and think that it wasn't always like this."[7]

In the legal academy, critical scholars often dissect the language of the criminal system and connect it to the legitimacy of the system. They analyze the ideas of "violence," "justice," "expertise," "safety," "criminal," "felon," victim," "harm," and more—each term carrying with it baked-in assumptions about the purposes of criminal law and punishment.[8] Even thinking of the institutions of criminal law as a "system" can be limiting, confining what we measure and how we conceive of success.[9] Underlying each of these terms is a broader ideology of white supremacy, one in which, for example, a fear of violence is associated unconsciously with the image of a lone Black man. This "condemnation of Blackness" extends to other people of color, and it also fuels the operation of the entire criminal system, including, ironically, the criminalization of millions of white people.[10]

Challenging ideological language has been a central part of the collective struggle against the American "justice system" for decades. Incarcerated organizers in the 1970s who formed labor unions and bail funds and led prison rebellions simultaneously critiqued the concepts of "rehabilitation," "criminal," and "violence" that were used to keep them caged.[11] Angela Y. Davis, Gina Dent, Erica Meiners, and Beth Richie, explaining the focus on ideological language employed by the thousands of people who came together in 1998 to form the abolitionist collective Critical Resistance, write, "One of the explicit goals of Critical Resistance was to generate new vocabularies and new theoretical strategies that might propel scholars, artists, advocates, and organizers toward bolder critical engagements with prevailing ideologies of law and order."[12]

A central insight of organizers and scholars alike is that the words and principles we use to frame our criminal laws and procedures in turn shape the cultures of our precincts, courthouses, prisons, and other sites of interaction between state actors and the public. Although these principles are not always explicit or uniform, they constitute the ideas and assumptions that run beneath the operation of the criminal process and legitimize the status quo.[13] They are the cops in our heads and our hearts, and noticing them can help unsettle them.

Thinking About Safety and Justice

Since 2012, the Ella Baker Center for Human Rights in Oakland, California, has been organizing the Night Out for Safety and Liberation, a series of events held on the first Tuesday in August each year, replicated in dozens of locations around the country, from Orlando to Atlanta, Houston to Chicago. At these events, people gather in public community spaces for block parties, voter registration drives, teach-ins, rallies, legal clinics, dance performances, bounce houses, and food. Organizers ask people to think about what makes them safe, and to share the answers on sticky notes, posters, and social media under the hashtag "#SafetyIs." A search for this hashtag leads to hundreds of descriptions of things that make people feel safe, ranging from schools and hospitals, to health care and housing, to community gardens and basketball games.[14] Notably, no responses equate safety with prison or jail.

Organizers plan the Night Out for Safety and Liberation for the first Tuesday in August because on that same date, the Department of Justice spends millions of dollars to put on its own version of an event promoting safety. Called the National Night Out Against Crime, the event was originally organized by private "community watch" groups in the 1980s and is now sponsored by police departments themselves. The National Night Out Against Crime features police officers joining cook-outs, soccer games, and block parties in an effort to create "partnerships" between police departments, local community organizations, and neighborhood residents. The idea of safety at these events is clear: through getting to know police officers better, residents will create relationships that will allow them to prevent and "fight" crime together. The mayor of Houston explained his city's National Night Out in 2021 this way: "Together with law enforcement, your neighbors can become your allies against crime, and together we will improve the quality of life in our city."[15]

These dueling events—the Night Out for Safety and Liberation and the National Night Out Against Crime—illustrate an on-the-ground ideological battle over the meaning of safety. In 2021, as Houston's mayor celebrated police officers as allies, across town the organization Grassroots Leadership hosted its Night Out for Safety and Liberation event in the city's Fifth Ward, with booths around the organization's parking lot featuring food, art making, a bouncy house, legal clinics, voter registration, and COVID-19 vaccinations. Dianna Williams, an organizer with Grassroots Leadership in Houston, explained at a virtual panel, "You have to change the narrative. People have for so long always dialed 911 for everything. So we have to take time, talk to the community, and say, Hey—we are working toward finding alternatives [to the police]."[16] Zach Norris, then the executive director of the Ella Baker Center, writes that "the point of our . . . event is to reimagine safety from a broader perspective, a more holistic one. We want people to get to know others in their community and build relationships and compassion. . . . We believe that this is what leads to greater safety, not suspicion of one another."[17]

The long-term organizing of groups such as Grassroots Leadership and the Ella Baker Center have helped unsettle the claim of police departments that they are the ideal providers of public safety. These organizations have done this not just through Night Out events once a year, but also through year-long organizing and policy work. The Ella Baker Center, for example, has since 1996 worked in California to close youth prisons, push for sentencing reform, and sponsor programs that include restorative justice circles, job training, and policy fellowships for incarcerated people. And Grassroots Leadership in Texas, founded in 1970 by former Student Non-violent Coordinating Committee member Si Kahn, connects its Night Out parties in Houston and Austin to its other work—running participatory defense hubs, training formerly incarcerated people to be organizers, and joining coalitions to shift funding away from jails and immigration detention centers and toward education, housing, and other services. Organizers with both the Ella Baker Center and Grassroots Leadership connect each of these projects to their visions of public safety. And they are just two of scores of groups throughout the country that are organizing around the idea of reimagining what safety means.[18]

These approaches represent an ideological struggle over the meaning of safety, but the "law enforcement" understanding remains dominant: the state's responsibility to promote safety becomes a responsibility to create the best forms of policing and "criminal justice." This conception of safety underlies the rise of mass criminalization and mass incarceration during Democratic and Republican administrations alike,[19] and it remains with us today, even as groups around the country actively question and contest it.

In criminal courtrooms, this dominant understanding of

safety is simply taken for granted. Federal and most state bail laws, for example, allow judges to set bail in the name of public safety, whether it is to safeguard "the safety of any other person or the community," to "protect the health, safety and welfare of the community," or any number of similar phrases.[20] The message often goes unquestioned: incarcerating someone pretrial can protect public safety. Politically, if a politician is asked for their views on bail reform and says, "I believe in public safety, first and foremost," the implication is similarly clear. It is unlikely that they are thinking of the safety of the incarcerated person and their family, or of the harms that might ripple outward from even a day of incarceration. Instead, to believe in public safety is to believe in incarceration.[21]

Justice, like safety, carries with it multiple meanings, whether construed broadly or focused on the context of an individual instance of harm. Some may feel that justice calls for punishing an individual who has caused harm; others may want to think about what could have prevented the harm, about what the survivor of harm needs, or about what the person who harmed someone needs to live safely in the future. In a criminal courtroom, however, justice typically means a conviction and a punishment. Ironically, this often means that the harm will continue, reinforcing the idea that justice via prosecutions remains necessary.

A curriculum packet put together by Santera Matthews from Project NIA, a grassroots organization that works to end the criminalization of young people, lays out understandings of justice that contrast with the criminal court understanding. *Two Sides of Justice* describes three different categories: punitive justice, restorative justice, and transformative justice. The existing criminal system represents only the first of these—punitive justice, or the idea that the state should punish people for their actions, especially when those actions cause harm.

In contrast, restorative justice concentrates on those who were harmed and "seeks to return circumstances and communities to the situations they were in prior to the harm"; while transformative justice looks more broadly at transforming the structures and conditions that led to the harm in the first place.[22]

Grassroots organizations around the country are currently trying to live out the ideals of restorative and transformative justice. Decades of work by groups including Impact Justice in California and Common Justice in New York have shown the power of restorative justice for adults and young people who have engaged in violent acts. And experiments in all areas of the globe demonstrate how people can set up methods of community accountability that respond to and prevent harm collectively under the mantle of transformative justice, whether by building the capacity to help people meet immediate needs after there has been harm or violence, or by developing community-based strategies to prevent harm. Unlike the purely individualized notion of justice inside a criminal courtroom, these alternative understandings of justice begin and end with community.[23]

The People v. the People

The idea that prosecutors are "the People" normalizes the concept that prosecutors define the parameters of justice and safety in criminal court. The United States Constitution provides a relatively expansive view of "the people," whether it is "the People" of the Second or Fourth Amendments or the "We, the People" of the Preamble.[24] Criminal law narrows this democratic ideal. In the context of an individualized system of punishment in which "defendants" are defined as the problem, "the People" becomes a stand-in for the collective, for society, in direct opposition to criminalized individuals: the People v. the defendant. The idea of "the People" assumes that all victims of harm want to prosecute and incarcerate those who harmed them. In fact, however, surveys of survivors show that many prefer to hold those who harm them accountable through options other than prison.[25] Use of the phrase "the People" also implies equal participation in the democratic process that led to the prosecutor or judge's election, in the face of widespread evidence that the people most directly impacted by the criminal system have the least political power. "The people" does powerful ideological work.

Legally speaking, a prosecutor's claim to represent "the people" is not clear-cut. Even when they are elected, prosecutors have a series of ethical duties that include, for example, the mandates to abide by constitutional rules and to use their individual discretion in deciding which cases to bring. The American Bar Association standards of professional conduct say, "The primary duty of the prosecutor is to seek justice within the bounds of the law, not merely to convict." The standards do not define "justice," though they do say that a prosecutor must "serve the public."[26] If this feels circular, that is because it is: prosecutors have a duty to seek justice, but they get to decide what justice means.

Now imagine that instead of prosecutors having the only claim to defining justice, other representatives of "the People" emerge. A group of people pays bail for a stranger after a judge has set bail in the name of "community safety." Another group wears shirts that say "Protect Your People" while they help those accused of crimes to prepare for their bail hearings. Another group gathers outside a courthouse with the names of people who have died inside the local jail, holding banners that say, "Not in Our Name." A coalition of many groups spends hundreds of hours collectively bringing forth a "People's Budget" with its own definitions of how the state can provide justice and safety. Now the criminal courtroom and the legislative chamber become sites of collective struggles, struggles in which "the people" can be located on both sides of the "v."

Audre Lorde famously said: "[T]he master's tools will never dismantle the master's house. They may allow us temporarily to beat him at his own game, but they will never enable us to bring about genuine change."[27] This idea is often invoked in legal scholarship as an inroad to asking whether legal fights can be a method of transformative change when law is the source of oppression.[28] Critical race theorists, in particular, have opened up rich debates on this question. In one seminal article, Kimberlé Crenshaw argues that claiming legal rights can be usefully destabilizing, even within an oppressive system: "Powerless people can sometimes trigger . . . a [legitimation] crisis by challenging an institution internally, that is, by using its own logic against it."[29]

The collective interventions that this book describes use the legal logic and language of the criminal system—the master's tools—against that system. They do this through action, commandeering the tools of the system to support people caught inside of it through otherwise routine procedural acts such as paying bail or participating in a sentencing hearing. When done collectively, by traditionally excluded groups and in opposition to the system's dominant ideas, these communal acts raise foundational questions that call into doubt the legitimacy of the system itself. This is what makes these acts radical—literally, getting to the root of things: people who ordinarily are not in charge of legal interpretation work within the system to live out a new definition of "the people," recasting the concepts of safety and justice so that those ideas can no longer support the status quo.

One of the arguments of this book is that these collective tactics are most powerful, and most radical, when they are done as contestation—what in democratic theory is known as agonism. People engaging in agonistic acts take an adversarial stance toward practices and ideologies of institutions in power, but do so through engagement with those institutions.[30] This means constantly contesting the ideas of the criminal system, but doing it using procedures and laws already in place. Groups that engage in this kind of collective contestation of the criminal system set up a new ideological struggle—the people v. the people—where the collective stakes of criminal punishment are on the table.

I stress the concept of agonism in democratic theory to underscore that these radical acts of justice are inherently *democratic* acts. To many, it is counterintuitive to say that the answer to the problem of mass incarceration is more democracy. After all, it is democracy that led us to lock up more people per capita than any other nation; again and again, people voted for politicians who ratcheted up the use of policing, prosecution, and imprisonment to solve social problems.[31] Many who care deeply about reducing the scope of the criminal system believe our focus should be on shifting authority into the hands of social scientists or public policy "experts," who can resist the tendency of the public to always turn to criminal punishment as a response to harm. One problem with this approach is that it is hard for these fixes to lead to large-scale change if the elite experts are still operating under the dominant concepts of justice and safety.[32] When social movements engage in collective contestation within the criminal system, they expand sources of expertise to include experiences of incarceration, of family members' incarceration, of enduring constant police surveillance, or of living in neighborhoods whose political power has been decimated by the criminal system.[33] They embody a different understanding of what it means to say that the people are in the courtroom.

Legal theorists, and in particular critical race theorists, have long highlighted the powerful legal thought that emerges from collective action by oppressed groups.[34] Building on this work, Lani Guinier and Gerald Torres developed the concept of "demosprudence" to explain how new legal and political understandings emerge from the actions of social movements.[35] Many of Guinier and Torres's central examples of demosprudence look back to the civil rights movement of the 1960s. They point, for example, to when organizers Fannie Lou Hamer and Bob Moses led an all-Black alternative delegation, the Mississippi Freedom Democratic Party (MFDP), to the 1964 Democratic National Convention in protest of the all-white delegation that Mississippi's Democratic Party had sent. The MFDP's presence disrupted the workings of the convention and reached national audiences when Hamer testified on national television about her experiences with voter suppression. The MFDP exemplified how long-term organizing can build power—and ideas—that challenge ossified legal understandings. Or, as organizer Bob Moses said to the MFDP delegates, "We're not here to bring politics to our morality but to bring morality to our politics."[36] Hamer, Moses, and the other MFDP organizers refused an offered compromise from the Mississippi Democratic Party to seat some delegates at the convention, because they were not there to secure a seat at the table, but rather to transform the structure of the table itself.

The long-term work of the MFDP entailed a sustained, collective reclaiming of the legal and political idea of the demos itself: who is worthy of voting and of deciding how the state should run.[37] Guinier and Torres argue that it is thanks in part to this battle of ideas, acted out through collective struggle, that President Lyndon B. Johnson signed the Voting Rights Act in 1965.[38] This is an ideological battle that predates the 1960s and continues to play out today. It is seen, on the one hand, in the increasingly mainstream debates over whether people with criminal records or non-citizens should be able to vote, and, on the other, in the emaciation of the Voting Rights Act itself by federal courts, or, more dauntingly, in the continued suppression of the Black and Latinx vote in the name of "voter fraud."[39] Clearly the Voting Rights Act did not end the material fight over the vote or the ideological struggle over who counts in the polity, but it is because of on-the-ground organizing and collective ideation from groups such as the MFDP, and their contemporary counterparts who organize Nights Out for Safety and Liberation, that these fights even continue today.

The organizers and activists whose struggles this book describes are also engaged in a long-term ideological fight over which people matter. Bail funds, courtwatching groups, and participatory defense hubs bring their ideological fight to a site of state domination—the criminal courthouse—that holds itself out as a place of justice. When they do so, these groups are bringing morality to the politics of the criminal system, and doing so in a way that centers the people most directly affected by mass incarceration and mass criminalization. At each point, their collective participation within the criminal system forces a destabilizing question of whether a criminal system focused on individualized punishment can *ever* be compatible with democracy.

Over time, the contours of the collective strategies change as groups work through internal disagreements and push forward into new tactics altogether—for it is not any one tactic or tool that is the answer, but rather the organizing and thinking behind it. When these same organizers join coalitions focused on state and local budgets, they enter legislative chambers to demonstrate that there are ways other than punishment for the state to provide justice and safety in their communities.

Like the slow work of registering voters in Jim Crow Mississippi, engaging in these radical acts of justice again and again ultimately adds up to a more expansive understanding of democracy, generating transformative concepts for the legal and political battles ahead.

2

Community Bail Funds

It was Martin Luther King Jr. Day in January 2020, and the pews of the Bible Way Baptist Church in West Philadelphia were filled with activists, neighborhood residents, and state and local legislators. A microphone was set up in front of the church's pulpit, with a large banner displayed behind, the artwork featuring a picture of a Black woman standing with her arms in the air, fists raised, and the words "Free Our Mothers / Uncuff Our Communities." Philadelphia District Attorney Larry Krasner was in the front row. Spectators who could not find seats stood on the side. They were there for a "People's Hearing on Bail and Pretrial Punishment."

One by one, speakers came up to the mic, most using first names only because they had open criminal cases. One man, Derek, told the crowd how, a year earlier, he had been living in an encampment on Emerald Street after an eviction from his apartment. One night, a police officer grabbed him and searched him, and then "started going through my tent, through all my property." When Derek questioned the officer, "Can you do that?," the officer replied "Watch what I can do," and arrested Derek. "That night I went to jail. I had no drugs at all, and [they] charged me with manufacturing, possession, and intent to deliver." Derek was brought to the police station and soon appeared, via video, before a bail hearing officer. He had no criminal record or history of warrants. He was released, and went back to his tent at the encampment, where he saw the same officer again. The officer said, "Didn't I arrest you?" and immediately arrested him again, with the same fabricated charges. This time, the two-minute bail hearing did not go as well. The bail commissioner said, "Weren't you just here last night?," and set Derek's bail at $10,000. Under Pennsylvania law, this meant that Derek would stay in jail for the duration of his criminal case unless he could pay 10 percent of that amount, or $1,000. The legal purpose of the payment was, in theory, to make sure that Derek returned to court and complied with any court orders while the case was pending.[1] Derek told the crowd that the $1,000 "might as well have been a million." He said, "By the second night [in jail,] I felt hopeless. That is what jail does. It breaks you. It beats you down. It isolates you. . . It makes you feel worthless. . . It's not a place for human beings."

To his surprise, Derek was released from jail after just a few days. At first, he did not know how his bail had been paid. Speaking at the People's Hearing, Derek said, "I saw this name on the bail receipt, Malik Neal—and that shook me, I didn't know a Malik Neal . . ." As he said the name, Derek pointed to an audience member sitting in the church's pews—Malik Neal, the co-founder and executive director of the Philadelphia Bail Fund, which had paid Derek's bail after receiving a call from his aunt.

The People's Hearing that day was co-sponsored by two sister bail funds, the Philadelphia Bail Fund and the Philadelphia Community Bail Fund, along with other community groups.[2] Both bail funds were founded in 2017, and both use a revolving pool of money to free people who are jailed because of their poverty. When a fund bails out strangers, the bail money they pay for people is returned to them—often minus a fee—when the criminal case is eventually resolved, assuming that the person returns to court. The group is then able to post bail for others using the same funds. In Philadelphia, the two funds coordinate their work and join in coalitions together for events such as the People's Hearing.

Money bail—also known as bond in some states—is meant to be a way to release someone charged with a crime while ensuring that they return to court at a future date and do not engage in "criminal" conduct while the case is pending. The idea is that someone will return to court because they do not want the bail money to be confiscated, or, if they use a commercial bail bondsman, for that bondsman to claim possession of a loved one's money or property used as a deposit or collateral. Recent studies reveal, however, that this incentive is a fallacy; in practice, money bail has been shown to provide little or no additional incentive to return to court or avoid rearrest.[3] When bail in any amount is set in criminal court, the reality for a poor or working-class person like Derek is that they may spend months, or years, enduring the violence, tedium, and isolation of jail while waiting for their case to be resolved, at high risk of losing their jobs, their homes, and even their children.

Although the Eighth Amendment to the Constitution states that "excessive bail shall not be required," this does not equate to a constitutional bar to setting money bail beyond a poor person's reach. And so, at any one time, more than 400,000 people are imprisoned in jails in this manner throughout the United States, incarcerated without being found guilty of anything just because they cannot afford the amount of bail or bond in their case,[4] in some states as little as $25 or $50. The number of people incarcerated pretrial has more than doubled over the past fifteen years, even as incarceration has otherwise begun to decline, and the racial disparities of pretrial detention are glaring: 43 percent of people held in cages until their cases end are Black, although Black people make up only 12.2 percent of the population. Similar disparities apply to Latinx and Native people.[5]

For people trapped in concrete cages reeking of excrement and under perpetual threat of violence, the incentive to plead guilty is strong. Studies repeatedly show that people held in jail pretrial are more likely to be sentenced to prison time, and to serve longer prison sentences, than people who are released. They are also more likely to be arrested in the future.[6]

Bail funds interrupt this process. In Derek's case, his public defender told him that he would need to plead guilty to be released from jail. He refused to plead guilty to fabricated "facts" that came solely from the sworn words of his arresting officer. By paying Derek's bail, the Philadelphia Bail Fund made it possible for Derek to fight his case effectively. After being released on bail, he soon found an apartment, was able to be with his mother when she was sick, and found a job with Pathways to Housing, an organization that had helped him when he was houseless. At the People's Hearing, Derek pointed to Malik Neal and said, "None of that would have happened if you hadn't bailed me out."

Nearly a dozen other people testified at the People's Hearing in January 2020, each describing how either the Philadelphia Bail Fund or the Philadelphia Community Bail Fund had changed the course of their case, and their life. A young Black man, Walter, described how he had been arrested at the age of seventeen. His bail was set, via video screen, at $52,000, and he was caged in an adult jail for nearly a year, until the Philadelphia Community Bail Fund paid his bail. Walter, now a youth organizer, said that this changed the outcome of his case. "Instead of years in state prison, I was given a sentence that allowed me to be home with my family and doing the important work that I am still doing to keep my people out of the system." Paulina, a Black woman in a hijab, stepped to the mic, describing how the Philadelphia Community Bail Fund had paid bail for both her son and her brother. Paulina said that all the court saw when setting bail was that "these were two young Black men." The court didn't take into account that "they are [also] two young Black men who are loved, supported, and missed."

Community bail funds aim to live out a new understanding of safety, one in opposition to that advanced by the criminal system. By using money collected from small donations from hundreds—sometimes millions—of people, bail funds and bailouts demonstrate that the idea that "jail does not keep us safe" comes not from a few renegade activists, but from a solid, broader community. Collective money and collective work together birth a collective vision, a "people's" vision, of safety without incarceration.

When the two Philadelphia bail funds organized, along with other groups, the People's Hearing on Bail and Pretrial Punishment, their goal was, in part, to push elected officials to make promises. At the end of the hearing, one councilmember stood and said that he would demand immediate oversight; a state legislator promised more funding for public defenders. And the Philadelphia district attorney, Larry Krasner, said, "We do need to end cash bail," and promised that he would push for more data on bail and pretrial detention.

But the goal of the hearing went beyond direct communication with politicians. It was also to lay claim—a "people's" claim—on how to define and measure the impact of money bail on the community. In recent years, hearings had been held in both the state and city legislatures to consider reforms to bail procedures. Bail fund organizers had testified at those too. On this day, though, the hearing was on different terms. Malik Neal and Christina Matthias, a board member of the Philadelphia Bail Fund, explain, "As the title suggests, the purpose of the hearing was to shift power away from politicians to where real power lies: with the people."[7]

In Philadelphia, the district attorney is not formally known as "the People," but DA Krasner would often use the term, and would later title his book, published in 2021, *For the People*. In contrast, at the People's Hearing, the identity of "the People" was clear: individuals who had been incarcerated because of their poverty and their race, as well as their friends and family. These people were all Black, all poor enough that they could not afford hundreds of dollars on a moment's notice. And they all had a concept of justice in which to be held in a cage because of inability to pay bail was counter to the will, and the safety, of their people.

The National Bail Fund Network

Malik Neal describes the Philadelphia Bail Fund as having two origin stories. The first is personal. When Neal was in college, his father was incarcerated in Philadelphia because he could not afford $50,000 in bail. Neal remembers feeling helpless as his father sat in a cage for two years until the case was eventually dismissed, teaching Neal that "the presumption of innocence, or at least how we talk about it, really means nothing if your skin is Black and your bank account is empty." The second origin story is a collective one: Neal co-founded the bail fund with three other organizers who were active in a coalition against building a new local jail, seeking to broaden their fight against the intractable hold of the criminal court system on their neighbors and communities in Philadelphia.

These personal and collective foundations complement each other, representing what gives a community bail fund its initial power: a fund counters, on the one hand, the isolating experience of people devastated by pretrial detention with, on the other, a collective experience of freeing strangers in the name of a different vision of community safety, one aligned with freedom rather than cages.

When the Philadelphia Bail Fund was founded in May 2017, it joined a growing constellation of bail funds and bailout organizations that had been spawned in the previous decade. The trend arguably began in 2007, when the Bronx Freedom Fund launched in New York's poorest borough, in partnership with the Bronx Defenders, a public defense office. In Queens, New York, a coalition of community groups formed the Lorena Borjas Community Fund in 2009, an all-volunteer group working to pay or raise money for bail for transgender women of color, many of them profiled as sex workers.[8] This was followed by the Massachusetts Bail Fund in 2011, spearheaded by social worker Norma Wassel and a small committee of volunteers, the majority of whom were also social workers. Then, 2015 saw the founding of the Chicago Community Bond Fund, born from Chicago-based organizing against police violence, as well as the Brooklyn Community Bail Fund. Others followed the next year, some based in particular cities and some focused on entire states: from Nashville, Tennessee; to Durham, North Carolina; to Colorado; to Milwaukee, Wisconsin; to Minnesota; to Seattle, Washington; and back to Connecticut on the East Coast.[9] These community bail funds began to meet and exchange ideas and strategies, eventually under the umbrella of the National Bail Fund Network.

Around the same time that these new community bail funds began to flourish, Black-led grassroots organizations also began to engage in large, targeted bailouts, such as the Black Mama's

Bail Outs, a coordinated set of actions to bail out women in honor of Mother's Day. During the first Black Mama's Bail Out event, in 2017, groups bailed out more than one hundred women and caregivers in nineteen different cities. Photographs and videos from that day show activists greeting Black women with hugs, flowers, and support at the exit doors of local jails. A woman in Charlotte, North Carolina, says through tears: "I can't believe it, you don't even know me, and you came to me . . ."[10] The Black Mama's Bail Out actions were conceived by organizers on the ground, including Mary Hooks, then the co-director of Southerners on New Ground (SONG), a member-based organization led by women and LGBTQ+ people. Hooks has explained, "in a spirit in which our ancestors bought each other's freedom, we said, 'we can do that and remind ourselves of what we've done for each other before.'" Emerging from the first Black Mama's Bail Out actions in 2017 was the National Bailout Collective, which coordinated Mother's Day and other bailouts for more than four years, and continues to inspire ongoing bailouts. The National Bailout Collective also provided fellowship and leadership opportunities for Black women and others whom they bailed out—to "create a national community of leaders who have experienced incarceration."[11]

The Philadelphia Community Bail Fund began as a Black Mama's Bail Out in May 2017 and soon transitioned to a year-round non-profit organization dedicated to supporting the leadership development of those they bail out. The group continues to bail out Black mothers each Mother's Day. Veronica Rex is a Black mother whom the Philadelphia Community Bail Fund freed in early 2019. After attending a community dinner sponsored by the bail fund, Rex became a volunteer and helped with that year's Black Mama's Bail Out. She also became deeply involved with Mothers in Charge, a participatory defense hub connected to the bail fund. As Rex explained in a podcast interview, "We had gifts for all the mothers: roses, little snacks and things when we got them off the van [from jail]. . . . I was able to be a part of that, which really felt good."[12]

The Tucson Second Chance Community Bail Fund also developed out of the first Black Mama's Bail Out in 2017. Under the leadership of attorney Lola Rainey, the Tucson chapter of Black Lives Matter raised money and bailed out one Black woman in their first action. This sole act of paying bail generated movement energy, and funding, that the volunteers had not expected. Lola Rainey continued the work, transforming the single action into a long-term bail fund, one that for its first four years was run entirely by volunteers. In 2020, the Tucson Second Chance Community Bail Fund received a grant that allowed it to pay staff, including Lola Rainey's daughter, Tiera Rainey, a long-time organizer who became the fund's new executive director. Tiera Rainey, looking back, reflects on this momentum: "It blossomed and turned into something far more substantial than we could have ever dreamed about."

Around the country, bail fund formations slowly grew into permanent, sustainable organizations. Leaders from community bail funds and the Black Mama's Bail Outs came together in July 2017 at a leafy, bucolic conference center in Tarrytown, New York, for the first convening of the National Bail Fund Network. There, representatives from fourteen organizations from around the country shared stories, strategies, and frustrations. On the first night, the organizers listened to a keynote speech from Mariame Kaba entitled "Free Them All: Ending Bail and Pre-Trial Detention as Abolitionist Praxis." Pilar Weiss, the founder and director of the National Bail Fund Network, remembers the energy generated in those first days, during which organizers realized, "My special challenge is actually a challenge shared by other people." I was at the 2017 conference, having recently begun writing about and working alongside bail funds, and I listened as organizers debated those challenges, such as how to spend their limited resources; whom to bail out; and whether to collect data. These questions had no quick or easy answers, and approaches to them varied widely.

For example, bail funds must decide whether and how to support the people whom they bail out. Approaches can range from minimal assistance, with rides to court and reminder phone calls, to providing a wide range of social and charitable services, such as drug treatment and job referrals for individuals with pending cases. Other funds focus instead on involving people in organizing and leadership development. These choices have implications not just for the day-to-day operation of a bail fund, but also for its place within the larger ecosystem of reform and social change. Being able to discuss these questions with other bail funds across the country at the first national conference was energizing, not because all bail fund organizers agreed on the best approach, but because there was a sense that the choices they faced were collective ones.

One particularly robust debate centered around whether and how to collect and share statistics about the criminal cases for which funds post bail, statistics that could help demonstrate the absurdity and cruelty of money bail itself. In 2015 and 2016, for instance, the Bronx Freedom Fund, Brooklyn Community Bail Fund, and Massachusetts Bail Fund all reported publicly that, over multiple years, over 90 percent of the people for whom they posted bail returned to court.[13] In the Bronx, it was 97 percent—a statistic that, they argued, "challenges the popular political notion that money keeps clients coming back to court."[14] Bail funds often combine those numbers with the stories and personal testimonies of people whose cases, and lives, change because they can be free pretrial—stories such as those at the People's Hearing in Philadelphia. By 2017, some bail funds had found that politicians grab on to these numbers as they push for bail reform. In New York City, leaders of all three branches of government—the mayor, the city council speaker, and the state's chief judge—named the Bronx Freedom Fund in speeches or statements about bail reform or about the need to close Riker's Island.[15]

At the same time, some bail fund organizers at the 2017 gathering were beginning to worry that the collection of information such as appearance rates could legitimize, rather than disrupt, the criminal system. To measure success by the system's terms—high appearance rates, low rearrest rates—is, in some ways, to cater to the logic of money bail itself, which justifies caging people based on efficiency and "public safety." Organizers within the National Bail Fund Network considered whether it might be more powerful to construct new ways of measuring or accounting for community safety and justice, whether through numbers, stories, or the building of new forms of collective care, even for those whom many consider dangerous. There was a sense that bail funds had the potential to act out a different form of community justice, one that might point a way forward to a world without money bail or pretrial detention at all.

By 2018, the National Bail Fund Network had grown to thirty-three funds. New national bailout campaigns also began to emerge, such as the Believers Bailout, a group that works in partnership with community bail funds around the country to conduct targeted bailouts during Ramadan each year in conjunction with political education sessions in Muslim communities.[16]

The national network's 2018 gathering took place in Chicago, where bail fund organizers from around the country joined the Chicago Community Bond Fund as it co-led an enormous rally outside of the criminal courthouse that called to end money bond in Chicago. The rally marked the one-year anniversary of a local court order that had claimed to end pretrial incarceration because of unaffordable bond. The Chicago Community Bond Fund knew from its daily work that judges had not followed this order; the fund had paid more than $300,000 in bond to free over sixty people from jail or house arrest after the order went into effect.[17] As part of the Illinois Coalition to End Money Bond, the bond fund had also monitored the court order through a courtwatching program and confirmed that the court system had not lived up to its promises.[18]

The rally harnessed this knowledge, combining forces with groups doing anti-carceral organizing around the city. That same year, the Chicago Community Bond Fund also wrote a report calling for the local sheriff's budget to fund "Communities, Not Cages," and took part in a lawsuit challenging the incarceration of people who should have been released on electronic monitoring after their bonds were paid.[19] Participating in the Chicago rally highlighted for the national gathering how a bail fund could, in just three years of existence, become part of impactful city- and state-wide campaigns for change. Tiera Rainey of the Tucson Second Chance Community Bail Fund remembers this national gathering as "life-changing," both in generating strategies for the Tucson fund, and with respect to her own personal analysis regarding the intersection of bail funds and resistance to the entire criminal system.

In 2020, the growth of bail funds accelerated under the twin pressures of the COVID-19 pandemic and the nationwide uprisings against police violence. Dozens of new bail funds and bailout formations sprung up, some organizing within hours to collect money and bail out protesters. And donations to bail funds spiked; more than three million individuals donated within a matter of weeks after mass protests began, and more than ten million individual donations came in by the end of the year. By 2021, the National Bail Fund Network consisted of more than ninety-five standalone community bail funds; at one point at least one hundred additional formations of people collectively were posting bail for protesters.[20] On top of this, the Bail Project, a national revolving bail fund, worked to post bail in twenty-eight different cities.[21] This rapid evolution, from 2015 to 2021, signaled a revival of an approach to organizing for freedom in which relatively modest acts of using established bail procedures became a form of collective resistance to jailing people based on their poverty, as well as collective resistance to incarceration itself.

A History of Radical Bail Funds

Bail funds have existed sporadically in the United States for decades, if not centuries. Informally, community groups and churches have long had a practice of passing a hat to collect funds to help people with bail and legal defense.[22] In 1920, just months after its founding, the American Civil Liberties Union created a short-lived "radical bail fund" to free union organizers, political protesters, and people accused of communism. And in the 1940s and '50s, the Civil Rights Congress operated a bail fund to aid people charged in politically motivated prosecutions, especially those accused of communism under the second Red Scare. The Congress's president, writer Dashiell Hammett, famously served five months in a federal prison because he would not reveal the names of the funders of the bail fund.[23] The last half of the twentieth century then saw a variety of bail funds emerge in short-lived forms—including those to aid political causes, such as the civil rights movement, and those formed in partnership with local governments trying to reduce their jail populations.[24]

In the 1970s, bail funds also began to emerge in which the

organizers focused not on political prisoners or causes, but on incarceration itself. A 1975 abolitionist handbook, "Women Behind Bars," published by Resources for Community Change, listed bail funds operating in Rochester, New York; Boston, Massachusetts; Chicago, Illinois; and Portland, Oregon.[25] And in 1980, the American Friends Service Committee published a "community bail fund organizing manual," written by longtime activist and later director of The Sentencing Project, Marc Mauer. The manual describes the formation of the Washtenaw Community Bail Fund, in Ann Arbor, Michigan, in 1974, and develops a series of questions and best practices.[26]

The closest predecessor to today's community bail funds—aimed at incarceration broadly—may be the Women's Bail Fund, active in New York City in the early 1970s. The fund was formed under the leadership of radical incarcerated organizers inside the Women's House of Detention, a jail located in Greenwich Village. These leaders included Joan Bird, Angela Davis, Denise Oliver-Velez, and Afeni Shakur. The bail fund organizers formed committees in each jail corridor, and those committees determined which women the fund would bail out. Many women were there for bail as low as $25. They were targeted for sex work, for their gender, for their poverty, for their race, for their sexuality, for their politics, and usually for a combination of these. The organizers communicated their decisions to feminist groups on the outside, who followed their lead as they put the bail fund into action.[27] Davis later recalled in her work on the genealogy of abolition feminism, co-written with Gina Dent, Erica Meiners, and Beth Richie, that "the organizing and collective decision-making among the imprisoned women was especially important because those who got out on bail committed to raising funds for the bail campaign after their release."[28]

Judith Clark was an active member of the Women's Bail

Fund on the outside. Having served time in jail in Chicago, and having been in the House of Detention when the bail fund kicked off with a demonstration on December 20, 1970, Clark knew firsthand both the horrors of jail and the power of inside-outside organizing, in which people who are incarcerated organize in partnership with those who are free. Clark was also close to Afeni Shakur, who was instrumental in the fund's founding. By mid-1971, Clark was living in New York City and attending regular meetings of the Women's Bail Fund, which often took place in living rooms with children present. The group members went to women's dances, theater events, classrooms, and other gatherings to solicit donations for the fund. Clark explained to me, "The idea was to have something that you're concretely asking people to do. . . It was a vehicle to say: when you're thinking about women's liberation, we have to look at how white-centered that movement is and recognize that Black and other women [of color] are actively involved in organizing, including inside prisons. It was a way to bridge that gap." For those who gathered regularly for Women's Bail Fund meetings, Clark reflects, it was at those meetings that a core group was able to "integrate anti-racism and internationalism into their feminism," deliberately taking the lead from Black and Puerto Rican organizers on the inside.

Angela Davis, Judith Clark, and others involved in the Women's Bail Fund in the early 1970s draw a line directly from that work to forms of intersectional feminism today, as well as to bail funds and bailouts happening fifty years later.[29] Judith Clark, seeing bail funds growing around her in her contemporary organizing, reflects that the power is the same: "If you involve people at that level of concrete work, they get a picture of the system and realize that the problems are systemic."

In her opening remarks at the 2021 National Bail Fund Network virtual gathering, network director Pilar Weiss made a similar connection, stating that today's abolitionist bail funds find their inspiration "in terms of building power and resisting [the] state [from] Black liberation bail funds and queer bail funds that were started by people in those movements who were resisting the state and resisting state repression. They said, 'This bail fund is both going to free people and be part of working toward liberation.' So we always want to hold that."[30]

When the Community Posts Bail

Despite this deep history, just fifteen years ago few people beyond these directly impacted organizers were aware that community bail funds or bailouts could or did exist. This was true when, in June 2009, Christopher, a twenty-year-old Latino immigrant, walked into a Bronx criminal courtroom on his appointed court date, at the appointed time. Just four days earlier, Christopher had been charged with two misdemeanors and released on $3,000 bail—meaning that someone had paid that amount of money as a guarantee that he would return to court. Judge Ralph Fabrizio, a former assistant district attorney in Manhattan, was presiding over Christopher's case on the day that he returned. On the case file in front of him, the judge saw that Christopher was designated as indigent, having stated in an interview with pretrial services that he did not have a job or the ability to pay a lawyer. When Judge Fabrizio witnessed this poor man walk into the courtroom on his own, in his own clothes rather than a jail uniform and handcuffs, the judge declared loudly to the courtroom: "He says he never worked, has no source of income. . . . [W]here is the money coming from?"

Under New York law, money bail, when it can be set, must only be in an amount necessary to "secure court attendance."[31] In Christopher's case, this ostensible purpose of bail had been served: he was standing before the court, and, on top of that, there was no allegation that he had engaged in illegal activity in the interim. But from the system's point of view, this was not how things were *supposed* to work. For poor people accused of crimes, bail in fact serves as a means of incarceration, a means of leading people to plead guilty, a means of sustaining the mass processing of poor people of color through local criminal courts. Rather than accepting Christopher's appearance in court as a good thing, Judge Fabrizio was determined to find out how Christopher was able to be free and safely home after bail had been set outside of his personal financial reach. The judge soon learned that the bail had been paid by the Bronx Freedom Fund. Judge Fabrizio fumed, especially once he learned that the same fund had been paying bail regularly for other poor people of color charged with misdemeanor crimes in the Bronx, freeing more than 130 people in just under two years.[32]

Judges, when setting bail for an indigent defendant, know full well that bail will serve to incarcerate the defendant for the remainder of their case. Judge Fabrizio's actions in the Bronx demonstrate this clearly. Other times, the casual comments of judges on the record crystallize this fact. A person who was bailed out by the Philadelphia Bail Fund, for instance, reported in 2018 how he had watched through a video screen as a public defender, prosecutor, and bail commissioner had discussed how much bail to set in his case. "I told [the bail commissioner] I was unemployed. They were negotiating about my bail. The commissioner said, 'I'm going to make it $100,000. He's not working, so he can't pay it anyway.' That's word for word—I won't forget that."[33] For much of American history, this has been the norm: a widespread judicial practice of deliberately setting unaffordable bail.[34] A series of studies by law professor Caleb Foote in the 1950s, for instance, documented that judges set bail to "break" crime waves, give defendants a "taste of jail," or otherwise "protect the community."[35] By the 1970s, it was fairly common knowledge—tacitly understood—that many judges set unaffordable bail with the purpose of caging someone still legally presumed innocent.[36] Even more than this, pretrial detention is central to the very functioning of the system as a way to secure guilty pleas and institute punishments before convictions.

This is why, when Christopher walked into Bronx Criminal Court a free man, in his own clothes rather than a jail-issued jumpsuit, he created an instant rupture in the workings of the system. The Bronx Freedom Fund, by posting bail for a stranger, had eviscerated the judicial power to incarcerate someone pending trial via exploitation of his poverty and his race. Judge Fabrizio did not order Christopher incarcerated in that moment, but he proceeded to investigate the workings of the Bronx Freedom Fund and presided over a series of hearings about the legality of Christopher's bail. Although Christopher remained free, the result was that the Bronx Freedom Fund was shut down as a violation of the state's insurance laws.[37] The fund was able to reopen three years later, but only after lobbying led the New York State Legislature to pass a law creating a new classification of "charitable bail funds" in 2012.[38]

Although Judge Fabrizio shut down the Bronx Freedom Fund because of state insurance laws, the judge made clear in his written decision that his initial concern was something different: the "apparent lack of any relationship" between Christopher and the bail fund.[39] In contrast, he described Christopher's mother, who was regularly in court to support Christopher, as demonstrating "traditional, independent family ties."[40] (In New York, "community ties" is a legal term meant to promote release of people who have family members, housing, or steady employment that might make them more likely to return to court. In practice, it excludes the most marginalized people from release.) The implicit contrast that Judge Fabrizio made in his decision is a crucial one, between "traditional" community ties, such as family members in court, and the community ties that a bail fund *creates* though the collective act of posting bail for a stranger. This alternative notion of community goes beyond family and touches on something larger: a community of people bound together by a larger belief in the injustice of pretrial incarceration.[41]

This focus on community has direct legal, and constitutional, dimensions. In the leading Supreme Court case on bail and pretrial detention, *United States v. Salerno* (1987), the Court states explicitly that a judge must balance an accused person's interest in liberty against the larger community's interest in safety. Writing for the Court, Chief Justice William Rehnquist said that a decision to set bail and then detain someone accused of a crime before conviction does not violate due process if a legitimate government interest, such as "preventing danger to the community," outweighs the sole factor on the "other side," an "individual's strong interest in liberty."[42] This was, and is, a standard legal understanding: a scale of justice with two competing sides, one for the "community," and one for the accused—assumed tacitly to be guilty and dangerous, and assumed explicitly to have interests diametrically opposed to the community and shared only with immediate family. The Supreme Court has never held that it is unconstitutional to hold someone in jail because they cannot pay the money bail set in their case, but, increasingly, constitutional challenges in lower courts based on doctrines of Due Process and Equal Protection are requiring judges to engage in just such a balancing test, with the community on one side and a person labeled a defendant on the other.[43] And today, the vast majority of state bail statutes use the word "community" when explaining how and when a judge may set bail in the name of public safety.[44]

When a bail fund posts bail in the name of the community, it rejects the premise of Justice Rehnquist's scale, and of these statutes, in which the community and the accused are pitted against each other in a balance of interests. According to the counter-logic that emerges from the work of a bail fund, liberty becomes more than an individual interest—it becomes a communal interest. Perhaps community safety can mean someone traveling by subway rather than being shackled to a seat in a dilapidated Department of Corrections van, someone able to help feed and dress their children rather than leaving them in the hands of other caregivers, or, worse, the state. And, at the register of public health, whether we are in the throes of a pandemic or not, it is true that to free people from the petri dishes of jails and prisons helps stop the rapid spread of contagious and deadly diseases, and in the process helps keeps everyone healthier, both inside and outside of jail.[45]

It is not just that the "community" may want people to be free, but also that incarcerating people via money bail *hurts* entire neighborhoods by extracting wealth from communities that are targeted by the criminal system. For example, in New York City alone, in 2017 approximately $28 million in wages were lost because of money bail, money that people detained in city jails pending trial would otherwise be earning in their jobs if free. During that same year, people in New York City accused of crimes—and their families—paid more than $268 million to private bond companies to secure their release. This does not count the tens of millions of additional dollars paid to the criminal court system through direct money bail, and the exorbitant fines and fees that accompany criminal prosecutions.[46] As Devren Washington, a co-founder of the Philadelphia Community Bail Fund, described this phenomenon at the People's Hearing, cash bail and pretrial detention "turn[] into generational trauma, it turns into generational poverty . . . something that our communities are still dealing with, born out of a legacy of slavery."[47] Given this collective impact on poor people, and especially on poor Black, Native, and brown people, the organizers at the National Bailout Collective call bail and pretrial policies the "Black Codes of Bail": the policies and procedures that punish Black people and other marginalized populations on a communal level, much like the restrictive Black Codes passed in the South at the end of the Civil War.[48]

The spectacle of Judge Fabrizio bristling with anger at a poor Latino man's freedom reveals the power of a group of people gathering together to bail out a stranger—not because they know the person, but because they are exposing the paucity of the concepts of community ties and community safety that the criminal system and the media take for granted. These acts reveal something about the system, and they also speak to the larger public. Lola Rainey, the founding executive director of the Tucson Second Chance Bail Fund, explained in a podcast in 2020, "We're asking the community to take a harder look at how the system works . . . to come to terms with the idea that caging people does not make us safe. What does make us safe, is investing in people."[49]

Beyond Exchanging Cash for People

During her six years as the executive director of the Massachusetts Bail Fund, Atara Rich-Shea paid bail or supervised someone paying bail more than 4,000 times—4,138 times, to be precise. As Rich-Shea learned quickly when she began the job in 2015, the seemingly simple act of posting bail for a stranger can be tedious and demoralizing, even when it results in freedom.

At the Massachusetts Bail Fund, the vast majority of employee and volunteer time is spent laying the groundwork to pay bail. Most referrals come online from attorneys or family members of people whose bail has been set beyond their ability to pay. After receiving a referral, bail fund staff can spend hours in conversations with attorneys and family members. If family members are contributing to a bail, they must coordinate that transfer. If people they hope to bail out have warrants, sometimes from other counties, the staff need to scramble to learn more and clear them up. Bail fund staff must communicate with the jail to double-check that the bail is entered in the system correctly; sometimes bail fund staff will find, for instance, that the bail has been entered in the system in a higher amount than that set by the magistrate.

The Massachusetts bail system becomes especially byzantine after this point. In order to pay bail, someone must physically appear at a jail or police station, which at many jails requires that someone get into a car and be driven by a corrections employee to the right building. Once there, an official must notify the bail magistrate or commissioner who initially set bail in the case, as that person will need to personally receive the bail. It can then easily be six to eight hours, sometimes more, waiting in a small room for that particular commissioner to appear to collect the bail.[50] As Janhavi Madabushi, who took over for Rich-Shea as the executive director of the Massachusetts Bail Fund in 2021, describes it, "We're sitting . . . waiting for the bail commissioners to arrive, so that they can count our money in person and fill out whatever paperwork they have to fill out." After more waiting, "We sign the papers and exchange cash for people, which every time is just as gross as you think it is."

Part of this feeling of disgust comes from the professional face that bail fund staff and volunteers must show toward officials who hold peoples' freedom in their hands: the corrections officer at the bail desk; the driver at the jail; the police officer at the door; the person at the records department; the bail magistrates and commissioners. Rich-Shea says, "You have to be polite, you have to figure out a way to make them like you. [But] you hate everything that they're doing! The better you are at getting a carceral institution to do what they are supposed to be doing in a way that gets more people free, the more it weighs on you."

Posting bail looks different in every courthouse and every jail throughout the United States, but it is slow and difficult work everywhere. As a result, it is easy for bail fund players to feel as if they are a part of the system they are trying to dismantle, helping make it run smoothly rather than throwing a wrench in the works. This runs up against the mantra of nearly every fund: that they want to "work ourselves out of business."

Indeed, many bail funds worry that, if they are seen as making reasoned decisions about the "safest" people to bail out, the work of the funds will seem to fix any errors in the setting of bail: if the judge or magistrate set bail in an amount above what someone can pay and the person should actually be free pending trial, then the fund steps in to fix the problem. When a bail fund publicly celebrates the number of people who return to court or who do not get arrested while free, the fund affirms the ways that the system itself measures success—measurements that are themselves part of the ideology of the system.[51] This all might, in the end, legitimize the institution of money bail by lending credence to the idea that some people—most often poor people and people of color—are deserving of pretrial detention, and that such detention can be justified by misleading worries of possible future "crime" or not returning to court.

Bail funds worry that legitimation can happen along other dimensions of bail reform too. For instance, the success of bail funds can focus reformers too narrowly on the oversimplified demand to end money bail. This can lead, for instance, to an increase in pretrial detention as judges often use risk assessment instruments to decide who should not be offered bail at all but detained instead. These risk assessments bake in neutral factors that are actually proxies for race and marginalization.[52] Focusing on money bail alone can also lead to reform measures that increase punishment and social control by replacing jail with electronic monitoring, mandatory supervision, or other forms of punitive surveillance.[53] As Pilar Weiss said to the National Bail Fund Network at its 2021 gathering, without constant attention to these dangers, "we know the system will just shape shift, and we'll be in this endless whack-a-mole where we [removed] one kind of bail but they added a different kind of detention, or a different kind of surveillance."[54] This fear of legitimation is not new. Angela Davis discussed a similar fear when it came to the Women's Bail Fund in the early 1970s, writing in her autobiography: "The problem was to prevent the bail fund from becoming just another service organization to provide bail for women inside, much the same way as lawyers are provided by Legal Aid."[55]

Bail fund organizers recognize these dangers. The challenge, along any dimension of legitimation, becomes to maintain a stance of collective contestation that forces questions about the system, that builds power toward other conceptions of justice and safety. In 2020, the executive directors of four bail funds—the Connecticut Bail Fund, the Colorado Freedom Fund, the Chicago Community Bond Fund, and the Massachusetts Bail Fund—wrote together of this need to "mov[e] from ending money bail to demanding freedom."[56] Bail funds work to maintain this stance of collective resistance in different ways. Some bail funds call out the dangers of bail reform directly. In Chicago, the Chicago Community Bond Fund has consistently opposed not just pretrial detention, but also electronic monitoring and pretrial services. Their 2018 report, "Punishment Is Not a Service," for instance, critiqued the pretrial services agency in Chicago for imposing harsh and punitive conditions when releasing people without bail.[57] In Pima County, Arizona, a 2021 report by the Tucson Second Chance Community Bail Fund used information gleaned from Freedom of Information Act requests to challenge the county's misuse of new "evidence-based" risk assessment tools. The title of their report made its message clear: "Pretrial Injustice: How the Pima County Judiciary Is Using Pretrial Risk Assessments to Cage People."[58]

Sometimes, the danger of legitimation leads bail funds to cease posting bail altogether. Both the Brooklyn Community Bail Fund and the Bronx Freedom Fund stopped posting bail in criminal cases after the 2019 passage of bail reform legislation that ended the use of money bail in some cases. The new law left a pocket of cases for which it was tacitly assumed that bail funds would pick up the slack—indeed, those became the only cases for which they could post bail under the charitable bail fund law. In a public statement, the Brooklyn Community Bail Fund asserted that because its mission was "to abolish money bail and pretrial detention," it would stop paying bail out of a concern that, with recent bail reform legislation going into effect, "revolving bail funds in New York may now be used to perpetuate money bail." They wrote, "Dismantling a system requires that we explicitly be in tension with it. . . . We would no longer be a community bail fund fighting for the end of pretrial detention if we were to be an extension of the state."[59] Ending the tactic of money bail did not end the organization—although it did undergo a name change, to the Envision Freedom Fund. Instead, their work began to focus on paying immigration bond, on organizing the Court Watch NYC program, and on fighting bail reform rollbacks in New York State.

In the face of these challenges, bail funds cultivate momentum by connecting their work freeing people to broader efforts to build power and resist the carceral state. For funds such as the Chicago Community Bond Fund that are born from local organizing against police violence or other faces of the carceral state, the connections to coalitions and campaigns are ever-present. Other funds find coalitions in their counties or states. Many cultivate organizers and leaders from among the people they bail out. Funds also run mutual aid projects for people both inside and outside jails and prisons, such as the Connecticut Bail Fund's #SurvivingInside campaign. Launched in 2019, the campaign calls attention to the plight of people who are already sentenced, via both a weekly radio show, "Resilience Behind the Walls Radio Show," and by running a commissary fund to help people meet essential needs such as toiletries and money for phone calls to loved ones.[60] And in many places, bail funds work in partnership with courtwatching and participatory defense groups doing work in the same criminal courthouses. In city after city, county after county, community bail funds and bailouts build out their presence as part of vibrant networks of groups, often led by directly impacted and incarcerated or formerly incarcerated people, to build power and push for change.

Bail fund leaders report, repeatedly, that it is through this combination of personal connection and coalition work that they have kept up the energy of their bail funds and built up what they feel is power in relation to this system. Rich-Shea says that during her tenure at the Massachusetts Bail Fund between 2015 and 2020, she felt energized each time that partnerships increased and coalitions expanded. During these years, the stance of the bail fund toward the people it bails out also changed, shifting away from the use of its own "risk" assessments of who is deserving of bail or likely to come back to court, and toward a model of trying to pay bail for as many people as possible. The motto of the bail fund became, simply,

"Free Them All." Rich-Shea, who now advises bail funds around the country, reflects that "a lot of bail funds came to being non-judgmental bail funds through being judgmental bail funds: We're birthed abolitionists." In Massachusetts, this shift came, Rich-Shea believes, from the everyday work of freeing people—both its joys and its frustrations—while in community with other local struggles. While in coalition with others, the ethos became, "We can be the underwriters for freedom, for these people and organizations and partners. That is our power."

Bail Funds and the COVID-19 Crisis: We Lean In and Bring the Change

Jails have always been places of violence, fear, isolation, and death. Although states do not keep official statistics, a Reuters investigation found records of 7,551 people who between 2008 and 2019 had died in jails throughout the United States, dying from suicide, neglect, botched health care, brutality, or a combination of these. At least two-thirds of the incarcerated people who died were in jail pretrial, before any conviction or plea.[61] But in 2020, the stakes rose. In the first six months of the COVID-19 pandemic, more than forty of the fifty largest clustered outbreaks of COVID-19 in the United States occurred in prisons or jails. The COVID-19 case rate for incarcerated people was 5.5 times higher than that of the general population in the United States.[62]

While those who were able retreated inside their homes and learned how to use Zoom, bail fund staff and volunteers around the country ventured outside to post bail, to meet with magistrates, to transport people home. And they were parts of coalitions trying to call attention to the public health crisis inside jails and prisons. The Chicago Community Bond Fund, for example, put out a statement calling for decarceration at Cook County Jail as early as March 6, 2020, well before the country was in a larger panic.[63] Within weeks, the Chicago fund had joined other local organizations in drafting a letter with a list of demands for government officials; created an extensive call-in campaign to local officials; and helped coordinate a socially distanced "solidarity caravan"—a protest of cars driving by Cook County Jail, local ICE headquarters, and the local juvenile detention center. In a statement in support of this caravan, the bond fund wrote, "When we say #FreeThemAll we mean no one should be stuck on the inside waiting for an almost inevitable infection and possible death from COVID-19. We mean incarcerated people . . . are a part of our communities, are experiencing this pandemic alongside those of us on the outside, and that our survival is dependent on their survival."[64]

And then came May 2020, and the murder of George Floyd by Minneapolis police officer Derek Chauvin. Coming on the heels of the March 2020 death of Breonna Taylor in Louisville, Kentucky, killed in her bed by police officers executing a no-knock search warrant, these events ignited the biggest mass protest movement in U.S. history. Quarantined in their homes, people followed calls on social media to donate to funds that bail out protestors. In Minneapolis, for example, the Minneapolis Freedom Fund reported receiving more than nine hundred thousand donations, totaling more than $31 million—and that was all in the first week of June.[65] In places where there were not already bail funds, new ones formed—some aiming to become permanent community bail funds, and some more informal, makeshift funds to contend with the crisis at hand. Pilar Weiss estimates that nearly two hundred formations of people were actively posting bail in 2020; donations to these funds, combined, likely exceeded $100 million by the end of the year.

These bail funds and bailouts scrambled, both to pay bail

and to redirect funds to grassroots organizations doing other important work, especially Black-led mutual aid–related organizing. During this time, in Denver, the executive director of the Colorado Freedom Fund, Elisabeth Epps, was gassed and shot in the leg with a rubber bullet by police officers while protesting. Bruised and limping, she still drove to post bail for someone the next morning, and the day after that. She posted bail not just for protesters but for people across Colorado subjected to the bail regime, which the Fund refers to—as do many other funds—as "ransom." In a tweet on June 4, 2020, Epps posted a receipt for five dollars from Denver's criminal court, writing:

> Once again, in addition to thousands of dollars in higher bonds, yesterday Colorado Freedom Fund paid another $5 ransom. FIVE U.S. DOLLARS. Imagine a city willing to pay ~$100/day to cage someone over $5 cash bail. No need to imagine. Denver does it.[66]

Four days later, Epps wrote that the fund had paid a $50,000 ransom for a Latina woman. In the interim, the fund's co-director, Eva Frickle, described paying so many ransoms that her credit card company put a stop on her card.

For new bail funds formed in the wake of the COVID-19 crisis and the 2020 uprising, there was at first little time for reflection and instead only the urgency of action and intervention. But funds that had been operating for longer brought to the table both their practical experience and the political analysis they had developed through their collaborative work. Less than three years earlier, Epps had spent twelve days in jail herself, accused of assaulting a police officer. During that time, she had bonded with the other women in jail and left with what to her was an inescapable conclusion: "Not one of those women needed to be there. Their misery did not make anyone safer."[67] After founding the Colorado Freedom Fund, Epps kept a constant hand in local- and state-wide political battles over police and court reform; indeed, in between posting bails nearly every other day in June 2020, she played an active part in pushing the Colorado State Legislature to pass a police accountability bill in the middle of the pandemic. And in 2022, Epps pulled an upset victory to become a state legislator herself, winning a highly contested primary against a moderate Democratic opponent and then decisively winning a Colorado House seat in November 2022.[68]

During the second half of 2020, the work of the Chicago Community Bond Fund also accelerated significantly. By October 2020, the bond fund had paid over $2.5 million to free 310 people. In addition, they joined a coalition to pay a $400,000 bond in Kenosha, Wisconsin, to free a nineteen-year-old Black survivor of sexual violence. The fund supported partners in lawsuits to decarcerate during the pandemic, successfully pushing for a local resolution to decrease the sheriff's budget by $25.9 million and invest it in community resources instead. They continued to help coordinate protests for decarceration. In early 2021, the Chicago fund celebrated a victory when years of state-wide organizing as part of the Illinois Coalition to End Money Bond led to the passage of a new bail reform law that will end the use of money bail in the state.[69] And the bond fund now posts bond both for those incarcerated and for those who are put on house arrest and electronic monitoring in lieu of jail, as "electronic monitoring turns people's homes into jails."[70]

Legislative victories in Colorado and Illinois were bittersweet, coming as they did in the midst of both uprisings and mass death, which disproportionately affected communities of color and people directly impacted by the criminal system. But the victories also provided fuel for exhausted organizers pushing to put the donations to bail funds from people across the world to good use, in the service of both individual freedom and systemic change.

More broadly, the national attention to bail funds brought a new valence to public debates around bail and jail. While bail funds had for nearly a decade been bringing national attention to the cruel absurdity of incarceration for poverty, now this attention went a step further: people were donating to bail funds in solidarity with a protest movement focused, at its heart, on the police killing of Black people. To sit at home and make a donation to a bail fund was an opportunity to think about how police violence might be connected to bail, and to incarceration. The bail fund moment opened up some eyes to the continuum of violence that begins with police violence against Black, Latinx, and Native people, and leads not just to notorious deaths like those of Floyd and Taylor, but also to countless stops, arrests, jailings, and imprisonments—and to the broader violence of the carceral state.

With these conversations raging on Twitter, in newspapers, and on the street, it was inevitable that backlash would follow. The Minnesota Freedom Fund endured a near-constant barrage of attacks in the press and on social media that questioned how the fund was spending the tens of millions of dollars in new donations in June 2020. Groups backing the Trump presidential campaign delighted in running TV advertising spots displaying the mug shots of people it claimed had been freed by bail funds and gone on to engage in violent acts (the connection, they claimed, was that a tweet from Kamala Harris on June 1, 2020, had encouraged donations to the Minnesota Freedom Fund).[71] Then, in the wake of the 2020 uprisings and the rise of donations to bail funds, legislative backlash against bail funds themselves developed in the following years. A law passed in Texas in 2021 instituted burdensome reporting requirements for bail funds and gave sheriffs authority over their operation.[72] A 2022 law in Indiana curtailed the work of bail funds through registration fees, limits on cases for which bail funds could pay bail, and limits on which groups could post bail in the first place.[73] Many other states tried to replicate these laws, though they were often unsuccessful.

The Massachusetts Bail Fund faced especially fierce backlash to its work. This came to a head when, in August 2020, the *Boston Globe* published multiple articles about a person whom the Massachusetts Bail Fund had freed who was charged with kidnapping and rape three weeks after being bailed out. The public outrage at the Massachusetts Bail Fund came from every direction. The Boston police commissioner, William Gross, declared the fund a "detriment to the community"; the state's attorney general, Maura Healy, announced that her office would investigate the fund; and the Boston district attorney, Rachael Rollins, called the posting of bail "the act of a coward."[74]

The organizers at the Massachusetts Bail Fund held their heads high. After all, backlash is an indicator that collective resistance is working, that the tension is there. The anger expressed by these officials clearly came from someplace deeper than sadness over accusations aimed at one man. These state actors were feeling a challenge to the workings of their system, to the connections being made between police violence, protests, and incarceration.

The scandal also led to conversations among social justice organizations in the Boston area that were struggling to figure out how to respond to the hubbub. The Boston Area Rape Crisis Center, a fifty-year-old organization supporting victims of sexual violence, spoke out against the Massachusetts Bail Fund when its leaders first learned about the case.[75] After conversations with organizers from the bail fund and allied groups, however, the Center revisited and revised its statement. In September 2020, it released a new statement, saying, "In hindsight, [the Center] regrets that our original statement placed undue responsibility on the Massachusetts Bail Fund. The bail fund was not responsible for [the man]'s actions. [The man] was. And secondary responsibility lies with a series of systemic failures in our criminal legal system that are all too common." The rape crisis center questioned whether the criminal law can bring justice for survivors of sexual assault, especially those who are Black, Indigenous, and People of Color. And they advocated, instead, for "sexual violence prevention in homes, schools, workplaces, prisons, and all public spaces."[76]

This public reconsideration of the purpose of the bail fund—and the emerging critique of the criminal system itself—reflected hours of private work in which organizers were in careful conversation with each other. The result demonstrated how renewed attention to bail funds around the country has generated unprecedented conversations about the best ways for the state to promote safety and support people—both people who harm and people who have been harmed, recognizing that they are often the same people.

Backlash to bail funds around the country became an opportunity for bail funds to show publicly that even people who may have harmed others are deserving of freedom. Fred Ginyard, who began his job as an organizer at the Philadelphia Bail Fund in the middle of these fights, told me, "[We're not] saying people are saints. We're steeped in reality. We know bad things happen. . . We're not telling you not to be angry at the person who hurt your family member. We're not telling you not to seek accountability. . . . We *can* say: there's a cycle of violence and harm that's happening in our communities. And we need to take every opportunity to break that cycle. Bail is a part of the cycle. So how do we break it? And then what's the next part of the cycle that we break?"

In March of 2021, the Massachusetts Bail Fund posted their highest bail amount ever, $100,000, for Mattie, a Haitian-American woman accused of abandoning her newborn child directly after giving birth in Boston. The bail fund did not post the $100,000 lightly, or quickly. Instead, the fund approached Families for Justice as Healing, a local participatory defense hub, as well as the National Council for Incarcerated and Formerly Incarcerated Women and Girls, which is based in the Boston area, and Black and Pink Massachusetts, a volunteer-led organization that supports and organizes alongside LGBTQ+ and people living with HIV/AIDS. Together, they posted a "coalition bail," sharing the cost and organizing together on behalf of Mattie. This case was unique, implicating overlapping issues: Mattie is a Black woman, an immigrant, who lived in poverty, who appeared to have a then-undiagnosed mental illness, and who was accused of harming a newborn. Janhavi Madabushi, the executive director of the Massachusetts Bail Fund, told me that this presented an opportunity to "do something that shows people that when Black women are criminalized, we come together to support them and protect them."

The four groups drafted a collective statement ahead of any newspaper coverage. These organizers explained: "Along with our incarcerated loved ones, we are reimagining a world that responds with care and support to crisis. We are building what different looks like and freeing people along the way." They listed the ways that the criminal system fails their communities: by failing to invest in education, housing, or health care; by responding to harm and trauma with more harm and trauma via policing and prison; by medical neglect during a pandemic.

Grounding their work in their own identities as formerly incarcerated people, as women of color, or as abolitionist organizers, they ended with the following:

> We won't be silent as the state continues to arrest, prosecute, and incarcerate Black women who are battling to survive poverty, trauma, and mental illness. We do not accept the tragic outcomes this system produces as the only possibility for us. . . . We have been shackled and lived on prison bunks. We have survived violence and our loved ones have too. So we know to not turn our backs on each other and instead, we lean in and bring the change we know is possible.[77]

The Massachusetts Bail Fund posted Mattie's coalition bail on the same day that the organizations released the collective statement. For what seemed like the first time, local news coverage was not entirely one-sided. Channel 7 News Boston displayed a picture of, and read from, the groups' collective statement on the 7 o'clock nightly news. Even the most sensationalist news stories quoted from the statement, naming the organizers' claim that the criminal system fails to promote community safety when it does not address trauma or mental illness.

I spoke with Madabushi a year later, in early 2022, when Mattie's case remained open. It looked as if the case were heading to an eventual trial, the outcome uncertain. In the meantime, though, Mattie has remained free. Families for Justice as Healing provided housing assistance, including six months of rent. Madabushi estimates that they speak to Mattie in some form every other day. As a result of this support, Mattie has been able to focus on working with her attorney and on getting much needed services. And, unsurprisingly, Mattie has returned to court, despite not paying her own bail.

Madabushi and the other organizers supporting Mattie continue to be careful with the broader message they believe this work is sending. They are wary of the tension, identified by Angela Davis fifty years ago, between supporting people with collective love and becoming a service provider that legitimizes the system. As with the back-and-forth with the Boston Area Rape Crisis Center, Madabushi says, "We are in conversation with people about what it means to believe in freedom unequivocally, while maintaining that people need supports and care systems that have not yet been created." By supporting Mattie, and by freeing thousands of others, the Massachusetts Bail Fund is carefully living out what that kind of care might look like. The answer is not, they believe, that the criminal system should provide these kinds of services via pretrial supervision while a case is pending, but rather that we should be living in a broader system in which these resources are available to those who need them, outside of the criminal system. Had Mattie had secure housing, mental health services, and other supports while she was pregnant, there might never have been any harm in the first place. Madabushi asked, "What can we do that holds this person in a different way than how we've been doing it in the past?" This question became, for these organizers, a way to "bring the change we know is possible" by living out a different understanding of freedom, safety, and community, even if it is still done in the shadow of the bail system that we have now.

3

Courtwatching

Reverend Alexis Anderson sat against a wall in a small room in East Baton Rouge's 19th Judicial District Courthouse. The courthouse's modern façade is marked by rows of tall windows—an architectural claim, possibly, over the visible nature of the justice doled out inside.[1] But the tiny space into which Rev. Anderson had squeezed had no windows. She sat behind a court commissioner and two court employees, the strongest light coming from one of the three computer screens in front of them. Elbows nearly touching, the four saw a man's face appear on the center screen. Rev. Anderson could see enough on the blurry video to know that he was a Black man sitting on a bench in the local jail, and from his voice and gray hair, she guessed he was likely at least in his sixties. Rev. Anderson watched as the commissioner informed the man via the video feed that the commissioner would now set money bond in the man's case. The commissioner did not look at the screen, but at a sheet in front of him that Rev. Anderson would later learn listed suggested bond amounts.

Sometimes, the man on the screen looked at Rev. Anderson herself, whose presence, and chair, were new to him. The commissioner did not let the man on the screen speak, but the commissioner did listen to whispered words from the clerk. And then the commissioner stated a number: one thousand, the dollar amount of bond that the man on the screen would have to pay to be released.

The man on the screen tried to speak, but the commissioner stopped him, telling the man that he could only answer two questions: one, can you afford a lawyer; and two, can you afford your bond. The man on the screen said "no" to both questions. Following directions, he spoke no more. A hand reached out to direct him out of the camera's eye, and then the next face appeared.

This face was younger, though still a Black man. The second man on the screen was asked the same two questions, answering no to each. The second man tried to speak, but the commissioner quickly silenced him: "No speaking, young man." Rev. Anderson watched the defeated faces of person after person on the video feed, arrested but not yet charged formally with any crimes, and not once did the commissioner take more than thirty seconds before determining the person's bond amount. She was stunned: "Here I was in this little room, the size of most people's closets—and there was no district attorney representation, there was no public defender representation, there was literally a judge, a clerk, and a man named Frank." (Frank, she learned, is the court employee in charge of the bond office.) In a matter of seconds, "lives are changed, and yet there's no accounting for all the players who are making things happen."

Rev. Anderson had come to the courthouse that morning in January 2019 with three other community members, in the first day of action for the newly formed Court Watch Baton Rouge. Court Watch Baton Rouge is a project of the East Baton Rouge Parish Prison Reform Coalition, a group made up of more than ten local organizations. Inspired after learning about courtwatching initiatives in other cities, Rev. Anderson and fellow coalition leaders had decided that to fight the violence of jail, they might need to go to the places where decisions are made to put people in cages in the first place. There, they hoped to observe, learn, share, and organize.

In addition to Rev. Anderson, the watchers on that first day of courtwatching included Linda Franks, another Black coalition leader; one white college student; and one white retiree on the coalition's email list who was looking for something constructive to do with her time. After the administrative judge begrudgingly allowed Rev. Anderson to enter the tiny bail hearing room—no member of the public had ever been inside before—the other three courtwatchers spread out through the rest of the criminal courthouse. They made their way into either the traffic courtroom or one of the many criminal court rooms contained within the large building. The courtwatchers sat down in pews, confronted with tableaus that might seem more court-like to fans of procedural television shows than the "bail closet" where Rev. Anderson was observing: rows of benches, armed court officers, a state flag hanging behind a robed judge at an elevated wooden desk. Despite these signals of justice at work, what the Baton Rouge courtwatchers saw from the audience was no less jarring: person after person in orange jumpsuit and handcuffs, physically brought before a judge for traffic tickets, unpaid fines, misdemeanors, or an occasional felony; each person told not to speak; each case considered for only a minute before the next person was brought in.

Rev. Anderson came to courtwatching after years as an outreach minister focused on working with poor Black families in Baton Rouge, most of whom had family members caught up in Louisiana's criminal system. Most recently, it was the death of twenty-seven-year-old Lamar Johnson, fellow courtwatcher

Linda Franks's son, that had led Rev. Anderson to co-found with Franks and others the East Baton Rouge Parish Prison Reform Coalition in January 2018. Johnson had been held in the East Baton Rouge jail after a routine traffic stop led to the discovery of a four-year-old warrant on a charge of writing a bad check. Four days later, he died in custody, before even appearing before a judge.

But for Rev. Anderson, Linda Franks, and those who had sat in court for family members in the past, the experience of courtwatching as a collective landed differently. They were not waiting in anticipation for one case of a person they knew well; instead, they were deliberately bearing witness to a parade of strangers, many jailed for poverty, all treated, in their view, as less than human. The courtwatchers saw judges chastise people for not paying their fees, fines, and bail; saw old men jailed on warrants for unpaid traffic tickets; saw teenagers in oversized jumpsuits, eyes down, afraid to move in the wrong way. They listened to the language of "justice" and "safety" spoken by attorneys and judges on the record. They heard people accused of crimes told again and again not to speak. And they emerged from the courthouse filled with a collective rage, screaming, as Rev. Anderson does, "Show me where a parking ticket has jack to do with public safety!"

Through the rest of 2019, members of Court Watch Baton Rouge appeared in East Baton Rouge's 19th Judicial Courthouse nearly every day that it was open. The court's state-mandated holidays, including "Shrove Tuesday" (better known as Mardi Gras), morphed from a day of rest or celebration into something more sinister: one more day of people waiting in cages to see judges after an arrest or a warrant. And the repeated threats that the courtwatchers witnessed in court—pay your fine or fee or bail, or else go to jail—added up to a larger question about how their Parish of East Baton Rouge funds itself.

Rev. Anderson, for her part, saw a system designed to "suck all of the life out of families," primarily Black families, through bail, through fines, through time in court. "They're there because they're poor and we have plucked every dime out of them. And now we need to use their bodies until there's nothing left." As Rev. Anderson continued to absorb the aggregate impact of what she was seeing month after month, what clicked for her was not just the violence and devastation, but also what she calls "the economic model": the way that caging and fines, fees, and bond combine to sustain the economic viability of the entire region, in part because of the jobs that the system provides (including in Rev. Anderson's own family: one sister was a corrections officer for thirty years, and one cousin is a state Supreme Court justice). Despite decades of advocacy and personal proximity to these interactions, not until sitting in a courtroom pew did Rev. Anderson feel a clear understanding of "the economic model" emerge. "And if we don't understand it, we're lost."

Rev. Anderson is not imagining these connections between everyday criminal prosecutions and the larger political economy of her home state. Louisiana has the nation's highest incarceration rate, as well as a higher rate of incarceration than any democratic nation in the world.[2] The racial disparities are as staggering as anywhere in the country. In East Baton Rouge in 2021, for example, Black and Latinx people made up 46 percent of the Parish's residents, and 80 percent of the jail population.[3] Even an advisory panel convened by Louisiana's Supreme Court described its own criminal courts, jails, and prisons as a "user-pay system" that collects hundreds of millions of dollars each year in fines and bail, not to mention charges for public defenders and other court costs, which in turn pay for the maintenance of the system.[4]

The 19th District Courthouse in Baton Rouge, for example, funds nearly all of its yearly $8 million budget to maintain its physical spaces with "charges for services," including court fees for people charged with crimes and traffic tickets.[5] All of this demonstrates what geographer Ruth Wilson Gilmore has dubbed "the prison fix": the forces of labor, capital, and racism interacting to make state economies seemingly dependent on the carceral state.[6] For Rev. Anderson and Court Watch Baton Rouge, it was regular visits to observe state actors in their local criminal courthouse—the "machinery of criminal justice" at work—that drove home for them the way these forces were interacting in their own parish.[7]

The Baton Rouge courtwatchers worked to share their observations and analysis with the larger public. They posted narrative videos on Facebook outside of the courthouse. Watchers called the two local bail funds when they saw bail set at unaffordable amounts. Sometimes they had more formal press conferences to share their outrage with what they had observed, bearing witness to communal violence. Or they took their knowledge into official spaces. Courtwatchers met with court officials about the availability of information on bail and bond in the courthouse, and testified in the state legislature regarding a bill that reduced, albeit modestly from forty-five to thirty days, what is known as "DA time," during which people can sit in jail for a misdemeanor arrest before formal charges of any kind are filed.[8]

For Rev. Anderson and her fellow courtwatchers, it was sometimes hard to know whether they were having an impact. One day in late 2019, as Rev. Anderson emerged from the elevator into the lobby of the courthouse, she saw a woman in the uniform of the cleaning company that the city contracts with to sanitize the courthouse daily. The woman pointed at the reverend, saying: "You. You. You!" with the word growing louder with excitement each time. Rev Anderson stopped still, nearly hit by the doors of the elevator. She asked, "Did I do something wrong?" The woman relaxed her mop in her other hand, telling the courtwatcher, "No. You all are changing things around here."

There were also small, concrete wins: courthouse officials agreed to meet with the group, and at their urging agreed to post information about bond hearings and bail funds at multiple spots inside the courthouse. Then, when courtrooms shut their doors to the public as the COVID-19 pandemic raged in April 2020, the courtwatchers were some of the loudest voices in meetings, successfully pushing for seventy-two-hour expedited arraignments.

As they continued their work, Court Watch Baton Rouge was following the lead, and seeking the advice, of dozens of organized courtwatching groups around the country. Volunteers with Court Watch NOLA, for example, had since 2007 been observing criminal court proceedings in New Orleans and publishing reports based on the data they collected while watching. Although a longstanding tactic of organizing in New Orleans and elsewhere, courtwatching began to take off in 2017, especially among groups fighting criminalization in their communities in the wake of the uprisings in Ferguson, Missouri; Baltimore, Maryland; and throughout the country.

In Chicago in August 2017, the Illinois Coalition to End Money Bond—made up of more than a dozen organizations throughout the state—began observing courtrooms to track the implementation of a new court rule requiring judges to set bond at affordable amounts. The year 2018 saw the founding of Court Watch NYC in January, "A Day in CA Court" throughout California in February, Philadelphia Bail Watch in April, and, in the fall, "What a Difference a DA Makes" in multiple counties in Massachusetts, which eventually melded into the organization CourtWatch MA.

Each of these efforts involved coalitions of organizations that together trained and organized volunteers to sit regularly in criminal courtrooms, document their observations, and report out to the public what they saw in court: bail hearings, arraignments, pleas, adjournments, returns on warrants, and the other everyday appearances that make up "criminal justice" in the post-trial world of plea bargaining.

By 2019, nearly two dozen organized courtwatching organizations or coalitions had formed across the country, from Memphis to Baltimore, St. Louis to Los Angeles. These groups created a growing list of resources to share with organizers interested in starting their own groups: sample forms and reports, organizing frameworks, virtual workshops, or, when possible, in-person trainings, something that Rev. Anderson and her fellow prison reform coalition members took part in when they went to New Orleans in 2018 to train with Court Watch NOLA.

Sporadic organized courtwatching initiatives have existed for decades, and likely for as long as there have been criminal courts. In Chicago, for instance, groups have monitored misdemeanor courtrooms since at least the 1970s, when the League of Women Voters initiated a courtwatching project in four Illinois counties.[9] Since well before that, activist groups such as the Communist Party and the Black Panthers have packed courtrooms in support of accused comrades in political trials. In the 1990s, a number of groups began to watch criminal court in support of prosecutions for domestic violence—demonstrating, among other things, that courtwatching is not inherently "pro-defendant."[10] The Fund for Modern Courts has been monitoring courtrooms throughout New York State on and off for decades.[11] And in New York City, more recent efforts have included the Prison Reform Organizing Project, which began a court monitoring project in 2013 to observe misdemeanor cases in criminal courts throughout the city, reporting on the effect of the city's policing policies on poor people of color.

But, as with community bail funds, the years 2017–2020 saw rapid growth in what is on its face a simple tactic: everyday people sitting in public criminal courtrooms observing the cases of people they've never met. This new surge of courtwatching had a diversity of groups and even of goals, but maintained a particular valence: to reclaim courtroom spaces as part of an effort to understand the practices there, document those practices, and, ultimately, push back against their very existence.

The People's House

Across the United States, criminal courtrooms are full of poor people, disproportionately people of color, sitting on rows of benches—or, if there is not enough room, standing in hallways—waiting for their criminal cases or the cases of their loved ones to be called. When I was a public defender working in the Bronx, I once heard a young Black boy ask his father as they walked into a crowded felony courtroom, "Daddy, are we in church?" My heart sank at the boy's question, as the superficial solemnity of a courtroom filled with people who looked like him met the tedium of the exchanges that the boy would find himself hearing once he sat down.

For the words coming from the judges, clerks, and lawyers were no sermons, nor even the hearings and trials that many have come to expect from the media's accounts of criminal court. In a New York City criminal courtroom, you might hear: "The People offer a 240.20 and community service."

"We have three bodies coming up." "Do you waive the rights and charges?" "The People consent to an ACD." "Case adjourned for motion schedule, time is excludable." "Case adjourned for discovery." "Case adjourned until the 180.80 date." "The People are ready." "Plea accepted. Mandatory court costs due in 60 days." In the world of plea bargaining, in which well over 95 percent of cases do not go to trial, these statements are the entirety of "criminal justice." There is nothing more.

Between these statements, there is waiting. So much waiting, even on a day with nearly a hundred cases on the calendar: waiting for the judge to be on the bench, for the prosecutors to have the right files, for the defense lawyer and defendant to appear—waiting that is then punctured by a blur of legal language. When I practiced as a public defender, between 2007 and 2012, the rules of Bronx Criminal Court forbid audience members who were not attorneys from reading or writing in courtrooms. If a teenager was reading a book for school, a court officer would yell at him or her to put the book away and face forward, to show respect—to listen to the words in the courtroom, as if those words carried important meaning.

The volume of violence in criminal court is easy to miss in the disappearing faces of people on screens, the bodies of people in handcuffs, or the clerks handing out pieces of paper listing the fine amounts people must pay to avoid being caged. Legal scholar Robert Cover, in an essay entitled "Violence and the Word," wrote in 1986 that "I do not wish us to pretend that we talk our prisoners into jail. The 'interpretations' or 'conversations' that are the preconditions for violent incarceration are themselves implements of violence."[12] Getting through a long day, for those who work inside courtrooms, requires forgetting rather than noticing the violence of the courtroom and its language. It is in these courtrooms that assistant district attorneys refer to themselves as "the People" with casual certainty, much as they would their own names. And it is here where court officers, judges, clerks, interpreters, stenographers, program representatives, and even defense lawyers rush through their days with an eye toward leaving as soon as possible, or, worse, joke around with each other in order to make the time pass while people wait handcuffed in dirty cells on the other side of the courtroom walls.

Enter courtwatchers. When people enter courtrooms as a visible collective, present not to wait for one case but to watch all of them, they disrupt the routine of forced, casual submission. They wear matching T-shirts. They come with pads and pens. They take up entire rows. They fill out forms to capture the details of what they observe. The disruption is apparent immediately. It may be a court officer coming up to question their presence. It may be the prosecutors or defense attorneys whispering to each other and looking back. Or it may be a clerk telling them bluntly that they cannot come in if they are not connected to an individual case: so accustomed to seeing only friends and family in the audience, court officials often believe it is against the rules for strangers to watch court, let alone groups of strangers. (They are wrong; the First Amendment generally guarantees a right to public access to criminal court, whether family or not.) Even when sitting quietly and following the rules—for most courtrooms do allow reading and note taking, and even the Bronx has changed that rule—simply to sit inside a criminal courtroom as a collective is to push back against the established power dynamics there.

The criminal system's actors are used to having an audience, but they are not used to being *watched*. It is hard to quantify the effect of courtwatchers' observation on the system they watch, but courtwatching organizers with Philadelphia

Bail Watch have given us at least a few data points. Their project emerged in 2018 as a joint effort of the Philadelphia Bail Fund and Pennsylvanians for Modern Courts. Philadelphia Bail Watch documents the happenings in the city's bail hearing room, located in the basement of the "Philadelphia Criminal Justice Center," the city's main criminal courthouse. The room contains rows of seats for spectators, with a glass wall separating the audience from the hearing itself. Like the bulletproof glass of a liquor store, the glass partition situates the audience members as potential threats to the safety of the hearings—even though the people accused of crimes themselves are not even present, but rather streamed in by video. Philadelphia Bail Watch observes these hearings on and off throughout each year. Between one and thirty people sit in the audience, taking notes on what the magistrates and lawyers say and decide.

Working with the bail fund, they also follow up with the people they see on the screens, whose bail is set by the magistrates in the room. As one person freed by the bail fund described in a Bail Watch report the experience from their side of the screen in jail: "I heard all the questions they asked me, but I couldn't hear when they were talking to each other. It was kind of hard to hear . . . and I was tired and dehydrated."[13] Using their own observations and reflections from people whose fates are on the line at the bail hearings, the watchers write formal reports and bring those reports back to the courtroom players: to meetings with the district attorney, the chief judge, the public defenders.

Once a year, these Philadelphia organizers conduct a twenty-four-hour courtwatching effort, usually close to the holidays in December. Being there for a twenty-four-hour period allows the organizers to compare the outcomes of the bail hearings during those twenty-four hours to the outcomes during the rest of the year. In 2021, organizer Fred Ginyard headquartered the twenty-four-hour effort at a hotel room across the street from the courthouse, so the courtwatchers would have a place to rest and snack between bail hearings. At least two courtwatchers attended every hearing, sitting in three- to four-hour shifts from 8 a.m. until 8 a.m. the next morning. They wore matching black T-shirts with a royal blue outline of the Liberty Bell and "Philadelphia Bail Fund" in orange letters on the front. As the day continued, and into the night, there was evidence that the magistrates—five different magistrates over the course of the twenty-four hours—noticed the courtwatchers. Two of the magistrates asked, through a microphone that broadcast through the glass partition, who the watchers were. Each time, the watchers replied, "We're just here to observe."

At one point, Ginyard observed the most comprehensive bail hearing he had ever witnessed: it took a full five minutes, as the prosecutor and the public defender debated whether cash bail should be set, naming specific things about the accused person who appeared on the video screen, debating his "ties to the community" and the importance of his criminal history. When the magistrate ultimately set bail, he put his reasons on the record. Ginyard gave a knowing look to his fellow watchers, who nodded back, amazed at what they saw as a performance for their benefit, the one and only time any of them had seen a bail hearing last more than a minute, or any of those arguments made. Ginyard said, "They put on a whole show . . . It was like an episode of *Law and Order*."

For the years 2018 and 2021, the watchers have been able to draw quantitative conclusions about the effect of their presence, scraping data from the First Judicial District's online portal and reconstructing the outcomes of bail decisions for every day of the year. (They were not able to get this data during other years.) In both years, the watchers found that during the twenty-four-hour action, magistrates set cash bail less frequently than they did on other days of the year. This meant that magistrates were *more* likely to release people with no requirement that they pay any money first, known as a release "on their own recognizance." In 2018, for example, of the ninety-seven people arraigned over the twenty-four-hour period, twenty-eight cases (28.9 percent) had cash bail assigned. According to a volunteer data analyst, this was the third lowest "cash bail rate" for a twenty-four-hour period in nearly a year. In 2021, the results were even more pronounced: during the twenty-four-hour courtwatch organized by Ginyard that included what they saw as an extended performance for their benefit, magistrates set cash bail in 25 percent of the cases in the courtroom. That 25 percent was not only lower than it had been during every other day of the year, it was *half* of the average rate of 50.1 percent.

The twenty-four-hour courtwatches in Philadelphia provide a rare quantitative account of something that all courtwatchers report feeling as they sit in the audience: they are changing the proceedings just by sitting there. In social science, this is known as the observer effect, or, relatedly, the Hawthorne effect: most basically, people change their behavior when they know they're being watched. Social theorists, including Michel Foucault, more pointedly examine how the act of watching can be a form of wielding power: in prisons, in schools, in hospitals, the architecture of observation by those in charge becomes a form of disciplining bodies, of domination through surveillance.[14] Social theorists have termed the turning of surveillance on those in power—watching the watchers—as "sousveillance," or surveillance from below. *Sous*veillance is a way to push back against the monopoly of those in power over information, technology, and control.[15] And courtwatchers model how sousveillance becomes even more powerful when done collectively, and when done at the very location of domination, such as a courtroom.

Courtwatchers aren't able to document all the details of how the system is operating; though technically open and public, courtrooms actively obscure what is happening within them. After sitting in her local municipal court, one volunteer for Court Watch LA in Los Angeles wrote on her reflection form: "Imagine watching a foreign language art film. It's all a blur. I maybe can capture a story, but not the specifics of the case. Or, if I get the specifics, [like the] case number, the story is obscured with jargon and information you can't process."[16]

It is not just the legal jargon. Most of the "justice" has happened elsewhere: a police officer has decided to stop and then arrest someone, a prosecutor has decided to charge in the name of the People, and a defense attorney has reviewed the case and, sometimes, talked to their client. Legislators have in the first instance created the laws that allow these decisions. Countless other employees have done their jobs: handcuffed, caged, and fed human beings; typed, written, and stamped court forms; cleaned the courtroom; printed rap sheets and docket numbers; conducted assessments of peoples' criminal histories, their employment status, their "ability to pay." All of this has been done out of sight of the public. But to call attention to this smokescreen is to reduce its power; to bear witness to the little that is said in each case adds up to something larger. In this way, one basic goal of organized courtwatching is to create the palpable power shifts that can flow from collective observation of those in power.

Courtwatchers also try to demonstrate solidarity with people standing before judges in handcuffs or appearing on video screens. Most basically, the observers make the silent argument that people accused of crimes are people too. Fred Ginyard told me that part of the purpose of a courtwatcher in Philadelphia's bail hearing room is "to ensure that the person on the other side of that screen—who gets told 'Don't talk,' and 'You can't ask questions,' and who gets ignored—knows that there are folks there to show that 'you can't ignore a human being that you've put on a screen to dehumanize. You can't ignore that, and we're going to let you know.' "

There are dangers in romanticizing observation too much.[17] Knowing that people are paying attention to your case may be uncomfortable for some people accused of crimes, even if it is done in solidarity. And courtwatching faces more intrinsic limitations. Communal observation cannot on its own cure unfairness, even if it changes the behavior of state actors slightly in the moment. Bearing witness to someone's being ordered into a cage does not make that outcome a fair one—and it can be a traumatic experience to witness the violence. Over time, officials may adjust to being watched. Transparency can legitimate and obscure what might otherwise be oppressive.

On its face, the performance that the Philadelphia courtwatchers observed when the attorneys and magistrate seemed to carefully consider and argue a case before them, might represent an ideal example of public justice. And yet, when the person went to jail after the magistrate set bail, the result did not become "justice," or at least not the courtwatchers' idea of justice, simply because the legal language of incarceration became momentarily comprehensible. Instead, the performance highlighted for the courtwatchers the absurdity of a system that can, on command, recite with feeling the arguments, reinforced over decades, necessary to justify incarceration.

At its most subversive, observation can cut through the obfuscation that legal language produces, undermining the legitimacy of the system that the language upholds. The benefit here does not come simply because, in the oft-quoted words of Justice Louis Brandeis, "sunlight is . . . the best disinfectant,"[18] but rather because the people opening the windows are the people traditionally shut out of the process of "justice." In those moments, "the People" are no longer just the assistant district attorneys; they are also the average people in the courtroom—people who do not approve of what the ADAs are doing in their name. As Rev. Anderson says of the courthouse in Baton Rouge: "When we enter, we consider it the People's House!"

Not in Our Name

In January 2018, more than one hundred curious New Yorkers entered a light-filled loft space in Brooklyn. As they headed toward the rows of folding chairs, each person was handed a yellow T-shirt with "Court Watch NYC" printed in large black letters, with the "o" replaced by a picture of a large eye. The volunteers took seats and were introduced to representatives from the three organizations collaborating on the new project: the Brooklyn Community Bail Fund; VOCAL-NY, a longstanding membership-based organizing group; and Five Borough Defenders, a collective of public defenders from organizations around the city. The projector in the front of the room displayed the Court Watch NYC logo, as well as its mission statement:

> At Court Watch NYC, we believe in community justice through community accountability. Our mission is to build a community movement to hold New York City prosecutors accountable to their promises to reduce

> inequality and unnecessary incarceration in our city's criminal legal system. As a result of community presence and pressure, we seek to shift court practices and culture. By building a movement led and owned by the people, we demand justice for all New Yorkers in a system that is all but blind.

This statement was not drawn up lightly. Organizers from the three organizations planned the Court Watch NYC launch for months. In their eyes, the coalition would have multiple goals, reflecting the varying priorities of the planning group. The most discrete goal was to target district attorneys in New York City by tracking whether the DAs' actions matched their "progressive" promises, including, in Brooklyn and Manhattan, to stop prosecuting most low-level turnstile jumping and marijuana cases. Rachel Foran, a key organizer of the project and then an employee of the bail fund, told me that from the beginning there was, in addition, a focus on building power: "There was this idea that if we train people and bring people in, then we'll build the movement toward more people wanting to end mass incarceration." And so the Court Watch NYC mission statement reflected these overlapping goals: using the word "community" four times, they named both a vision of system accountability and a belief that justice, as practiced, was "all but blind."

Among the audience members watching the January 2018 presentation was Jon McFarlane, a fifty-year-old Black man and lifelong resident of South Jamaica, Queens, who had read about the training on a legal listserv. McFarlane had time to give. He was retired, after an injury at his job at the United States Post Office as a data conversion operator (a fancy name for a data entry clerk, he tells me), where he was also a union representative. And he was intrigued by the idea of watching criminal court with others as a way of channeling frustration with a system that he knew well.

McFarlane had been prosecuted three different times over the course of his life, on charges ranging from misdemeanor marijuana possession to felony robbery. Although he did not emerge with a criminal record, McFarlane still bore the scars of prosecution: eight days spent at Riker's Island for one case because he could not afford bail; and five days spent at Vernon C. Bains Center, also known as "the Boat"—literally a floating jail—in the Bronx. One of his cases was a felony robbery charge, for which McFarlane returned to court at least once a month for eight months before the case was ultimately dismissed. (For most of those eight months, the ADA in his case did not reveal that they had in their possession phone records demonstrating that McFarlane was at home at the time of the robbery, records that would ultimately lead the ADA to dismiss the case.) Each time McFarlane came to the Queens criminal courthouse for his own case, he had to sit in the audience and observe other cases on the calendar while he waited.

Though decades ago, those hours of waiting were formative for McFarlane. He told me, "So you're sitting there watching other cases, wondering, 'How did his lawyer let him take a plea to that?' and even the circumstances of many of the cases were like, 'Whoa, that sounds like a violation of the Fourth Amendment, so why is she asking this eighteen-year-old Black defendant to plead out? . . . This doesn't make any sense.' " McFarlane remembers thinking that he wanted to get involved in changing things, but at that moment, at the advice of his mother, he focused on his own case. Still, the cases he saw stayed with him: "Through the years it was like a tumor that grew stronger in the back of my head."

Then McFarlane attended the Court Watch NYC training in January 2018. As he took a seat, McFarlane noticed that most, though not all, of the other future courtwatchers did not appear to be Black or Latinx, although the audience was multiracial. Many looked young, though one white woman in the third row had cascading gray hair. That made sense to him: most of the other people of color he grew up with had spent time in court for the cases of their cousins, friends, and children. Why would they want to come back? The eagerness of those in the room was a different story, perhaps in part because the launch was happening at a time when many relatively privileged liberals were energized after the election of Donald Trump in 2016.

A local political focus on bail and jail loomed large as well. Many New Yorkers first began to consider the harms of incarceration at Riker's Island after reading Jennifer Gonnerman's articles in *The New Yorker* about the 2015 suicide of Kalief Browder, who killed himself after spending three years at the city's notorious jail complex as a teenager, initially held when his family was unable to raise $3,000 for bail.[19] In 2016, heeding years of organizing against the jailing of poor New Yorkers of color, City Council Speaker Melissa Mark-Viverito vowed to close Riker's Island, a promise echoed a year later by Mayor Bill de Blasio.[20] Stoked by weeks of outreach from the Court Watch NYC organizers, an unmistakable energy—a "What is something that we can do now?" energy—filled the packed room. McFarlane was ready to be a part of it.

After the mission statement, the Court Watch NYC organizers continued the training with a primer on mass incarceration in New York, led by public defenders from Five Borough Defenders. The information was sobering, even for McFarlane, who may have experienced the system but did not always take a step back to consider its scope. As a colorful pie chart from the Prison Policy Institute showed, in New York State, approximately 88,000 people were locked in federal, state, local, or youth jails at any one time. This number did not represent the total number each year, though, as people cycled through the system at a breakneck pace. New York State's incarcerated population had been declining, but this was not true of the number of people incarcerated pretrial, which was steadily increasing as of the time of the training. For despite local attention to the death of Kalief Browder and the violence of Riker's Island, the notion of "bail reform" legislation had yet to take center stage in New York State, and district attorney promises to change their bail practices had yet to lead to noticeable change. It remained regular practice for people to sit in cages pretrial for months or years before resolution of their cases because they couldn't afford their bail. As another chart showed, the racial disparities when it came to incarceration were even starker than in Louisiana, especially for Black people, who constituted 16 percent of New York State's population but 53 percent of the people in the state's jails and prisons.

As the organizers continued, two large faces were projected on the screen: Brooklyn District Attorney Eric Gonzalez and Manhattan District Attorney Cy Vance Jr., accompanied by a list of recent promises they had made to change their bail and charging practices to be more lenient. Vance, for example, had announced earlier in January that his ADAs would stop requesting bail and instead consent to having the judge release people on their own recognizance in low-level misdemeanor cases, including shoplifting ("petit larceny"), trespassing, and marijuana possession.[21] Public defenders Zohra Ahmed and Ying-Ying Ma explained the power of these district attorneys over New York City's jail and prison populations, especially when it came to deciding whether to charge people with crimes, whether to offer plea bargains, and whether to request bail—if an ADA did not request bail, then a judge would rarely, if ever, set it, and the person would be released.

In the second half of the training, the organizers asked the volunteers to engage in a roleplay of what most arraignments look like: someone accused of a crime standing in handcuffs next to a public defender, who argues with the ADA over bail, followed by either a plea (with possible jail time and inevitable surcharges and fines) or a bail decision from the judge. McFarlane and the other watchers practiced filling out the Court Watch forms—checking boxes, noting ADA names, writing observations—after which they debriefed in small groups on what they saw. McFarlane signed up for a shift on the spot.

Within a week, McFarlane and three other courtwatchers entered the Manhattan arraignment courtroom together, pushing through the courtroom doors in a line, a caterpillar of yellow shirts and yellow legal pads. Before they could find a row with space for the four of them, an armed court officer stopped McFarlane: "Who are you here to see?" McFarlane responded, "Why are you asking?" and when all the officer could say was, "I'm just asking," they continued in, taking seats in the second row of the audience. The first row, reserved for attorneys and court personnel, was mostly empty. McFarlane leaned his pad on the back of the pew in front of him and began to take notes on the first case that they saw. The same court officer came up to McFarlane and asked him not to lean on the empty bench in front of him. McFarlane obeyed. But then the armed officer returned, saying, "Why don't you move to the third row?" Not wanting to push the subject, all four courtwatchers moved to the third row. McFarlane says that rather than feeling intimidated, he saw it as evidence that their presence mattered. "I felt inspired, like: look at us, yes, we're coming to observe you, . . . you *know* we're coming to keep an eye on you."

Court Watch NYC organizers hustled to process the

information they were receiving from watchers. They began with tweets. On January 24, 2018:

> Today in Manhattan court: ADA asked for $7500 bail on misdemeanor shoplifting case. Accused person's last warrant was from 1992 @ManhattanDA—why are your ADAs not following your new "bail reform" policy?! #EyesonDAs.[22]

Joan Vallero, a spokesperson in DA Vance's office, replied with four consecutive tweets justifying the bail request by noting that the accused person "has an extensive history w/multiple theft-related convictions."[23] Vallero's response was telling: in New York, bail can be set only to ensure someone returns to court; this particular person had apparently been charged multiple times, and, according to the defense attorney's statements, had not missed a court date in nearly thirty years. Vallero was, arguably, admitting that ADAs request bail for reasons other than those allowed by statute.

Immediate public responses like this showed the courtwatchers that their presence was having an effect. McFarlane explains, "It felt exhilarating. [Watching the ADAs,] I felt like *you're* the defendant now. . . . You're gonna say you don't care, but we know you do."

Responses to Joan Vallero's tweets from non-courtwatchers on Twitter soon followed ("Ridiculous!"; "Nonsense!"; "Such garbage. If someone had 21 misdemeanors probably means they need psychiatric help and/or services. All you can imagine is cages."). Although Vallero and other DA spokespeople responded to Court Watch NYC tweets for another week or two, they soon stopped. Court Watch NYC tagged individual ADAs in their tweets, and those ADAs soon deleted their accounts. Having initially thanked Court Watch NYC in the media for "keeping us on our toes," Vance's office instead made attempts to retreat from the scrutiny on social media.[24]

These first two weeks of courtwatching felt powerful for the Court Watch NYC organizers, as well as for watchers such as McFarlane who took part. Even as the ADAs retreated from scrutiny, or failed to respond to tweets, the watchers knew that the DA's offices were paying attention.

By the end of 2018, Court Watch NYC had trained more than one thousand watchers and watched hundreds of arraignment shifts in Manhattan, Brooklyn, and Queens. Many courtwatchers attended weekly happy hour check-ins to process what they were seeing—for while it may have been familiar to directly impacted people, including Jon McFarlane, to many of the courtwatchers it was the first time they were witnessing the violence of criminal court firsthand.

They particularly felt the harshness of the system in the low-level cases, where the charges themselves seemed on their face to come from poverty, yet resulted in incarceration because of unaffordable bail. But the courtwatchers also perceived injustice in the "violent" charges, potentially involving harm to others, where people were sent to Riker's Island or the Boat with the unquestioned assumption that the reciprocated violence of jail would fix things. One courtwatcher, overwhelmed by the sheer number of people—many with guns holstered to their belts—involved in putting someone in a cage, lamented, "It seems like the whole system is rigged against the defendant, who is fighting an army!"

It is one thing to know that nearly all people prosecuted in New York City are Black and brown, and it is another to see it. Even when observing people who were arraigned and then released, courtwatchers left their shifts angry, often channeling that frustration into blog posts. One courtwatcher watched an arraignment shift in Brooklyn in March 2018, comparing two different cases involving the prosecution of men of color for "petit larceny." In one, a man was sentenced to twenty days in jail for stealing yogurt; and in another, a man was sentenced to three days of community service for stealing undergarments. Rather than feel satisfaction at the second case, the watcher was dismayed by both, imagining the strain of having to return to court to do community service—and pay a surcharge—and "entrenching the already poor in ever deeper poverty."[25]

In this, the courtwatcher was noticing what sociologist Issa Kohler-Hausmann calls "managerial justice"—the way that the New York City court system surveils poor people of color in "Misdemeanorland" over time by requiring them to come back to court, usually multiple times, whether it is for future court dates, to do community service, or simply to pay the mandatory court costs that accompany every single guilty plea or conviction.[26] Overall, as they watched and analyzed the speedy processing of dozens, even hundreds of cases in each arraignment shift, what they saw mirrored the operation of the majority of criminal courtrooms and cases in the United States, what legal scholar Alexandra Natapoff describes as "an enormous, sloppy, shadowy world through which millions of Americans get rushed every year."[27]

Zohra Ahmed, then a public defender and one of the central Court Watch NYC founders, noticed that within the first year, the mood from courtwatchers was changing, even when they conducted additional trainings for new courtwatchers: "I never had to convince people that criminal court was problematic. . . . They were pushing *us* . . . to be more abolitionist than we had anticipated." From the trainings and debriefing sessions, "a shared language of opposition emerged:" Not in our name. We are the people, too. Or, as Jon McFarlane puts it, "If *you're* the People, then who the fuck am I? Who the fuck are we?"

In October 2018, Court Watch NYC issued their first major report, "Broken Promises: A CWNYC Response to Drug Policing and Prosecution in New York." Published in a zine-like format, the cover featured a drawing, made with colored pencils, of four people in yellow Court Watch shirts with a shared speech bubble reading, "Not in Our Name." The report contrasted the promises from both Eric Gonzalez in Brooklyn and Cy Vance Jr. in Manhattan to cut down on prosecutions for marijuana with the reality that the watchers observed: a clear pattern of continued prosecutions for marijuana and other drug-related crimes. As even district attorneys were starting to concede, the "war on drugs" falls at the feet of prosecutors as much as any other player. Even if a police officer arrests someone for possession of a joint, the DA has the clear power to decline to prosecute and to free the person immediately, no courtroom or arraignment required.

The "Broken Promises" report examined 233 drug prosecutions during July and August 2018—a fraction of all drug prosecutions, but the ones the courtwatchers were able to capture during their shifts. The report laid out clear racial disparities, showing in colorful graphs that not only were 85 percent of the people accused of drug charges that they had observed non-white, but also prosecutors were more than twice as likely to request bail for Black and Latinx people (67 percent and 68 percent of the time, respectively) than they were for white people (32 percent). And the courtwatchers gave examples: the same ADA requesting "time served" for a white man, but for a Black man requesting a drug treatment program with a ten-day jail alternative. "For two seemingly identical cases, the only difference we saw was the one we always see: that the person who got more leniency was White and the person who got more punishment was Black." After describing a different case, in which a Latinx man had bail set beyond what he could afford, courtwatcher Michelle L. wrote in the report: "The pain that the war on drugs causes was palpable in the courtroom, the pain that families and individuals are forced to bear in the name of 'public safety.' I wonder how prosecutors and judges can watch bereaved families and continue to support bail?"[28]

Court Watch NYC held a press conference and rally in front of the Manhattan Criminal Court when the report was released, wearing their yellow shirts and holding up signs that summarized the report's findings. Nina Luo, an organizer at VOCAL-NY who joined the project in mid-2018, remembers Vance's office sending a press person down to the rally, trying to speak to the reporters to refute the stories that were being read through a bullhorn. News reports, though, led with observations from courtwatchers—a *City Limits* article began with the details of four drug prosecutions from the report, and a picture of the Court Watch rally outside the courthouse.[29]

Reporters picked up on the clear premise of "Broken Promises": that to charge someone with a drug crime is a harmful act, even if they are released after they see the judge. Luo remembers a feeling of success on that day: "It was ultimately our narrative . . . a community account of what was actually happening." The success, for the organizers, was not that the ADAs necessarily changed their behavior, but rather that the courtwatchers were able to retell the story of how the criminal system works, generating their own collective counternarrative in which the violence of the courtroom was at the center, rather than the alleged bad acts of people arrested. As Rachel Foran remembers it, in the first year of Court Watch NYC, they were able to "tell a story that the . . . system will never tell about itself, which is, you know, the truth."

The Freedom to Listen

Court Watch NYC's goals of accountability, transparency, and mobilization mirror the Supreme Court's rulings about the importance of the audience in criminal court. The public right to observe criminal court proceedings emanates from two different provisions of the Bill of Rights. The first is an accused person's Sixth Amendment right to a "public trial," which, according to the Supreme Court, is meant to prevent political persecution via secret trials and punishments, represented by such practices as the Star Chamber in seventeenth-century England. In analyzing this right, the Supreme Court wrote in 1948, "The knowledge that every criminal trial is subject to contemporaneous review in the forum of public opinion is an effective restraint on possible abuse of judicial power."[30] Also at work is the First Amendment's freedoms of speech, press, and assembly—together, what former Chief Justice Warren Burger referred to in a 1980 case as the "freedom to listen." In a string of First Amendment cases that followed, the Court made clear that this right is meant to help the public keep a check not just on judicial behavior, but also on prosecutors and the police officers whose decisions lead to prosecutions.[31]

The freedom to listen, flowing from two different parts of the Bill of Rights, is one of only a few places in constitutional jurisprudence where community participation is intimately tied to the interests of individuals accused of crimes, reflecting an ideal of regular and meaningful audience interaction as part of a functioning system of punishment.[32] Observation is meant to have an effect not just on individuals, but also on the wider public's sense of what is right and what they should and should not do. It is meant to further democracy itself.

For some courtwatchers, though, the ideas that collective observation constitutes an "effective restraint" or will lead to "correct results" can feel like empty constitutional promises. In Manhattan in 2018, even as DA Vance's office clearly noticed the pressure from Court Watch NYC, the courtwatchers did not see different substantive actions follow inside the courtroom. This was frustrating. More pointedly, Philadelphia District Attorney Larry Krasner—himself a self-proclaimed progressive prosecutor—threw a physical copy of a Philadelphia Bail Watch report back at a courtwatching organizer who was meeting with Krasner alongside other activists to discuss Krasner's office's bail practices. The courtwatcher had handed Krasner a chart listing the results of 125 hearings observed between March 21 and April 14, 2019, showing that Krasner's office consistently asked for higher bail than necessary, directly contradicting the district attorney's public statements about cash bail.

Krasner had no interest in engaging with these charts and spreadsheets, and no qualms about demonstrating this by hurling the report back at the organizers. In a documentary about Krasner that aired on PBS, two of his top staff can be heard casually discussing their frustration with courtwatching for being "a Twitter thing" and "an activist thing."[33] The executive director of the Philadelphia Bail Fund, Malik Neal, reflecting on these incidents, told me sardonically: "They weren't really looking for critical feedback." It was responses such as this from Krasner, not to mention his choice to title his memoir *For the People*, that solidified organizers' sense that elite actors would continually resist outside accounts of the criminal court that disrupted the system's own measurements of success. This was one spark for the 2020 People's Hearing on Bail and Pretrial Punishment, discussed in Chapter 2, in which organizers from courtwatching, bail funds, and other groups packed a West Philadelphia church to spread their own account of the state of justice in their courthouse.

In Chicago, a 2017 courtwatching project by the Illinois Coalition to End Money Bond led the court system to begin to release its own data when it felt called out by the watchers. With that courtwatching project, the Coalition monitored the implementation of a new judicial rule that the groups had helped lobby for and consulted on, mandating that a judge could set money bond only when the person had the ability to pay the amount necessary to secure their release—possibly the first rule of its kind in the nation.[34] The courtwatchers sat in Chicago's criminal court every day for a month before and a month after the rule took effect, completing a total of ninety-three courtwatching shifts by forty-six volunteers. They saw mixed results flowing from the new rule.

Promisingly, the rate of pretrial release almost doubled, and the use of monetary bond dropped by half. At the same time, they reported that "even with these improvements . . . many people are *still* receiving unaffordable bonds and facing indefinite pretrial incarceration as a result." And the racial disparities persisted, a result, they argued, of the "historical injustices" that "will likely persist unless Illinois abolishes secured monetary bond in its entirety."[35] The coalition made all of the raw data they collected available on their website, accompanied by charts, statistics, and qualitative observations, modeling the openness they were demanding from the court system itself. As courtwatching organizer Sharlyn Grace told a reporter, "We shouldn't have to rely on the organizing and willpower of people to know what's happening."[36] The result was relatively swift: Chicago's criminal court began to release its own data online for the first time, clearly a reaction to the courtwatching report.

Reporting to the public on what happens inside courtrooms is particularly potent in the criminal legal system, which is notoriously bad at collecting or sharing information about the cases it processes. In 2021, Measures for Justice, a non-profit dedicated to unearthing data in the criminal legal system, released a report lamenting the absence of data at every point in the system, which "creates a landscape of unknowns and unknowables, and so the criminal justice system begins to look opaque, impenetrable, and, in a way, immovable as a result."[37] Non-profits such as Measures for Justice have helped collect and publicize some of these missing numbers; and the MacArthur Foundation's Safety and Justice Challenge has provided funding to localities to reduce incarceration, including by collecting and publicizing data.[38]

Data has a different quality, though, when it comes from organized courtwatching projects, which accompany the charts and spreadsheets with narratives generated from the perspective of, or in solidarity with, those directly impacted by the system.[39] When that happens, the system bristles. In New York City, one anonymous court official told a reporter in response to the "Broken Promises" report: "If they don't have the proper expertise or a law degree, how are Court Watchers fit to comment and critique individual court cases?"[40] Even the Chicago court system's speedy publication of its own data in response to the courtwatching report demonstrates the system's discomfort with data-driven narratives from those who would question the premises of criminalization.

Sitting peacefully in pews and collecting data is not the only way to bring political action into a courtroom, of course. Courtwatching organizers are well aware of the long history, and especially the Black radical tradition, of disrupting courtrooms. This trend is most closely associated with the behavior of people on trial themselves—the trial of the "Chicago 7," for instance, famously included outbursts and responses from the political activists on trial, as well as the brutal judicial response of binding and gagging Black Panther Bobby Seale for speaking in court.

Although courtroom "disorder" such as this often brought media attention, it was, even in the 1960s and '70s, far from ordinary. Appearing before a New York City commission on courtroom disorder, critical race theorist Derrick Bell testified that accounts of Black defendants disrupting proceedings were rare, and often exaggerated. More pointedly, as Bell later memorialized in a 1973 law review article: "Black defendants in criminal cases have *not* engaged in disruptive behavior, not because they lack provocation, but because nothing in their personal experience, and little in the history of the black man in America, provides them any hope for justice."[41] Bell believed that the experience of being a Black defendant led, instead, to sitting in court "not with thoughts of destruction, but with despair." The response from many court officials in the early 1970s, however, assumed that Black people accused of crimes, and their families, were itching to disrupt and disrespect court proceedings. This helps explain new rules, including the reading ban in the Bronx, and increasing numbers of armed court officers in each room and entrance. Courtwatching has been a response, in part, to this silencing of Black people in courthouses, as much as to the history of "disorderly" courtroom resistance.[42]

At the same time, the matching T-shirts and clipboards of courtwatchers may not be that different from the rows of black berets and leather jackets worn by Black Panthers in packed courtrooms during the political trials of the 1970s. Contemporary courtwatching—packing courts, observing cases, bearing witness, collecting and publicizing data—brings a different kind of resistance, contesting knowledge production in the carceral space through orderly presence rather than vocal outbursts. Fred Ginyard, after the twenty-four-hour bail watch in 2021 in Philadelphia, reflected, "For me as an organizer, I'm always . . . about the action, as I like to get loud. But I think part of what the courtwatch action has done for me is encouraged me to think about action differently. . . . Actions don't have to be aggressive. . . . [With courtwatching, we are] very adversarial in passive ways that shift the power dynamics in that room."

One thing that the constitutional jurisprudence swirling around "the freedom to listen" gets right is that collective observation of criminal cases can shift power relations in the context of our larger democracy. The freedom to listen can be the most powerful when it places the public on the side of the accused. This stands in contrast to the idea that has solidified in the public consciousness of the prosecution as "the People." Legally, it also rubs up against much constitutional criminal procedure, which flaunts individual rights—to counsel, to remain silent, to a jury trial—as guarantees of a fair process, while carefully limiting this fair process to one about individuals and not the system. (This is a central insight of Critical Race Theory.)[43] Courtwatchers sit in solidarity with the accused, but in a collective, systemic way as they amass information about cases in the aggregate. This can facilitate a different kind of democratic legitimacy than that envisioned by federal courts: not a legitimacy of the criminal system, but a righteous and necessary democratic battle between contrasting ideas, and measurements, of justice.

Not every courtwatching group takes this adversarial attitude toward producing stories, knowledge, and expertise. Sometimes they work alongside court actors. Indeed, courtwatching groups often disagree with each other about both how their groups should relate to the court system and how to articulate their movement's broader demands. Nor is an adversarial attitude toward the system an on/off switch; in Chicago, Philadelphia, East Baton Rouge, and elsewhere, even groups with a stance of resistance have met multiple times with public officials. Still, across the country, heading into early 2020, ordinary people were increasingly stepping into the space of criminal courtrooms in organized groups that, through their presence, questioned the courtroom's capacity for accountability or justice. These groups were refusing to take the system's understanding of justice as a given, and leaving changed from the process.

Going Virtual

And then came the devastation of COVID-19, which, in addition to raging through jails and prisons, led many criminal courthouses in March 2020 either to shut their doors to the public, shift to virtual courtrooms, or both. In Los Angeles, Court Watch LA was forced to go virtual only six months after beginning their courtwatching. Before the pandemic hit, the coalition of Los Angeles courtwatchers went to five different courthouses in the city, sitting in 17 different courtrooms and watching 133.5 hours of court time. In March 2020, however, when the municipal courthouses closed to the public, any opportunity for the public to listen or observe closed too. Court Watch LA organizers lobbied, alongside the ACLU of California and other local groups, for virtual access to court, and the court system began to provide spotty access to audio of court proceedings in early 2021.

And so the courtwatchers listened in from their living room couches or kitchen counters, knowing that Los Angeles's jail population of over sixteen thousand people was crowded into open dormitories, sleeping inches from each other, while the rest of the world was ordered to mask and social distance to save their lives. Criminal court itself was not virtual: people still had to appear in court for their own cases, even for the most low-level municipal charges. On February 6, 2021, for example, courtwatchers listened to a judge preside over the cases of two co-defendants—a married man and woman—in the Compton Courthouse, charged with Carson Municipal Code 5702(c), which criminalizes owning a house with "paint deterioration upon any buildings causing dry rot, warping or a lack of weather protection." The woman did not appear, and her husband told the judge the reason: she had tested positive for COVID-19. The man had been exposed to the virus, clearly, but without a positive test result was worried about receiving a warrant if he did not appear in court.

Rebecca Brown, then a legal fellow at the National Lawyers Guild focused full time on the courtwatching project, learned about the cases and wrote two matter-of-fact tweets from the Court Watch LA account: one stating the charges in the cases; another explaining that "this means that everyone in that courtroom could have been exposed yesterday."[44] The absurdity of criminalizing small things in the name of public health while still requiring people exposed to COVID-19 to come into court was not lost on the hundreds of people who engaged with the tweets within hours. Most expressed shock. One person retweeted the thread, along with, "How to spread Covid in the most petty, classist way possible . . ." Rebecca reflected: "Everyone's like, 'Why are people being brought into court for having deteriorating paint on their houses in the middle of a pandemic?' "

Courtwatchers were listening in Baltimore, too. Baltimore Courtwatch began observing bail review hearings in person in 2019. The collective was founded by two abolitionist organizers, Chris Comeau and Angela Burneko, who connected at rallies as part of a constellation of Black-led organizations in Baltimore pushing for decarceration and abolition. When Comeau and Burneko decided to start organizing around regular courtwatching in Baltimore's criminal courthouse, conversations with public defenders they knew led them to focus on bail review hearings, in which someone detained after an arrest has the ability to appeal a magistrate's bail or detention decision to a judge. These hearings rarely had an audience, and the system shared no data on what happened there. A small, committed group of members of their coalition observed the hearings, slowly learning the language of bail reviews, surprised and yet not surprised at the repeated denial of requests for freedom. As Burneko explained the experience to me, "You know it to be true and then you KNOW it to be true."[45]

When things turned virtual, Comeau and Burneko had to shift their practices. They began to organize small groups of watchers—listeners, really—to call in to the bail review docket every day. The vast majority of the watchers were college students with time to give, and Comeau estimates that about two-thirds of them were white. As the watchers listened in pairs, a third person would then live-tweet summaries of each and every case. As the pandemic raged on, this meant that between April 2020 and December 2021 (and continuing in 2022), Baltimore Courtwatch tweeted about hundreds, and then thousands, of cases. The result is an ongoing archive of the devastation of bail reviews.

Thursdays are the hardest days, when the bail review hearing court presides over "juvenile transfer hearings," which the courtwatchers refer to as "baby bail hearings," or the "baby docket." Again and again, the courtwatchers tweeted as judges reviewed, and usually affirmed, the caging of fourteen-, fifteen-, sixteen-, and seventeen-year-olds who had been ordered jailed with no bail set, so that there was not even the possibility that their families could pay bail for their release.

A typical November 2020 tweet, in the middle of a thread of cases: "CASE 2: another child whose case we've observed several times. He is awaiting sentencing on one charge and transfer hearing/trial on another. His attorney can't visit him to prepare for these court dates. [The child] has been in jail for two years. ASA Stock says state is asking for HWOB [held without bail], Judge Sampson orders HWOB."[46] Sometimes the voices of the children could be heard too. An April 2021 tweet: "Returning from break, waiting for Judge Taylor to return, a tiny, defeated child's voice is heard, 'I don't want to be here, they are just going to deny it.' "[47]

Comeau believes that virtual courtwatching, even if it is just listening, can for some people be even more radicalizing than sitting inside physical courtrooms. There is a particular kind of dissonance that emerges from sitting in one's own bedroom, next to a cup of coffee or a cat, and hearing distant voices stating numbers and acronyms that will end with someone in a cage during a deadly pandemic. In debriefing sessions, whether in simultaneous group chats or later group Zooms, Comeau saw courtwatchers processing the trauma of this dissonance. Even Comeau, already an abolitionist organizer, found that he had to process emotionally more than he thought he would. He told me,

> This confirmed everything I thought about the system. . . . The system is not capable of doing what we want. Maybe it can do what white supremacy wants, maybe it can do what capitalism wants, maybe it can do what patriarchy wants . . . but it can't protect communities. It can't keep people safe. And it can't provide any sort of justice in any meaningful sense, or what I would call justice. It is a machine that grinds people's lives to pieces and tears apart families and causes humans harm on a day-to-day basis.

It is listening to legal language in virtual bail review hearings that also, paradoxically, gives Comeau some hope. "It's all held up by like these ridiculous logics [and so] it's helpful to imagine a different world based on how ridiculous this stuff is. Like, if they can do *that*, we can do whatever we want."

There's No Repairing the System

In October 2021, well over one hundred people once again attended a Court Watch NYC training. Unlike the first training in a Brooklyn loft, nearly four years and 1,500 trained courtwatching volunteers earlier, however, this training was on Zoom. It began with the voice of Angel Parker, the new coordinator of Court Watch NYC, which in 2020 had transitioned to become a project of the Envision Freedom Fund (the new name of the Brooklyn Community Bail Fund).

Parker, in her yellow Court Watch shirt, introduced herself and gave some opening thoughts about the importance of courtwatching in the context of a deadly pandemic, and especially in the shadow of a recent string of deaths in New York City's jails. Although Court Watch NYC had stayed in operation throughout the pandemic, watchers had not done physical courtwatching since March 2020, sometimes because the courts had gone virtual (with no virtual public access) and sometimes out of concern for the health risk caused by adding further crowds to courtrooms. Instead, much of their activity involved creating zines based on data available online, or convening virtual working groups, including, for example, the "data investigations group" and the abolitionist study group.

In the fall of 2021, Court Watch NYC geared up to return to court in their matching shirts, aiming for the criminal courthouses in all five boroughs of New York City this time. Parker looked into her webcam and explained, "Anyone who's been following our work over the last few years has probably noticed that Court Watch has really changed our organizing philosophy. Our organizing in the courtroom has really challenged us to adopt an abolitionist praxis, as opposed to fighting for reforms. . . . We don't believe there is a progressive way to cage and torture people."

For forty-five minutes, the training focused on ideas to ground courtwatching: the prison-industrial complex, white supremacy, and the importance of community organizing against those forces. It was only then that the training turned to New York City's criminal courtrooms, taking the second hour to delve into how arraignments work and what the courtwatchers could expect to see and to record. Any subtlety about the possibility of pushing assistant district attorneys to be accountable to the people was gone, as the manual handed out at the training made clear: "As abolitionist organizers, we know that no matter who is leading the Manhattan DA office, it's that person's job to ruin lives, break up families, and cage our neighbors."

A few weeks later, Court Watch NYC joined a coalition of other local organizations for a Day of Action for Decarceration, with a particular focus on the need to decarcerate in New York City given the spate of deaths at Riker's Island and the city's jails during the pandemic: fifteen in 2021 alone. (Before the end of the year, it would be sixteen.) Over the course of the day, groups of courtwatchers gathered in four different boroughs of New York City. At each courthouse, watchers in yellow shirts observed arraignments for one hour, and then met coalition members for a rally on the courthouse's steps. It began in Queens, at 11 a.m., when Jon McFarlane joined two new courtwatchers, both white women, Rev. Rosemarie Newberry and Cassandra Ritas, inside the arraignment courtroom in Queens Criminal Court. It was a relatively slow day in court, but the courtwatchers were able to observe five arraignments before leaving to join the rally.

This was the first time that Rev. Newberry, a minister with the United Universalist Congregation of Queens, had ever been in a criminal courtroom; the pandemic had brought her into the world of courtwatching. Stuck at home, she found herself reading about the 2020 uprisings around the country in reaction to the death of George Floyd. She was especially drawn to learning about organizing in places such as Atlanta, Georgia, where people were fighting to use city funding for social services rather than jail. She began to read about the costs of mass incarceration and to watch webinars about abolitionist organizing.

Researching groups in Queens that were doing related work, Rev. Newberry was drawn to courtwatching because it was something concrete she could do in addition to her work with her own congregation. On her first day watching, Rev. Newberry was struck most by a father, sitting with a relative in the back row of the courtroom. The father could not understand what was happening to his son, who stood before the judge determining his bail. The son was released, but the panicked looks on his relatives' faces stayed with the reverend as she left the courtroom.

Rev. Newberry and Jon McFarlane joined a quickly growing group holding up a banner in front of Queens Criminal Court, displaying the names of each person who had died at Riker's and the Boat that year. The action came with a clear message: Decarcerate now. Rather than stand outside a jail, however, they stood in front of each of the city's criminal courthouses to underscore how the actions inside of those buildings were the ones that led to the violence of incarceration. Said one sign: "Judges who set bail have blood on their hands." Another: "Rikers = Death."

Members and organizers from a host of organizations took turns speaking into a bullhorn, punctuated by chants demanding decarceration and freedom. When Jon McFarlane took the bullhorn, he told the crowd: "Part of decarceration has to do with observing what goes on in these courts, specifically at arraignments. When you got this yellow shirt and you're in there, sometimes, not always, but sometimes, the judges think just a little differently about 'the defendant that's standing there in front of me.' "

The last speaker was Rev. Newberry, who offered a prayer to end the rally before the activists moved on to the next criminal courthouse, in Manhattan. She said:

> Oh heavenly Mother and Father of God, we stand by the rights of all humans to have a life where they get medical care, they have food, where they have housing, and where they can live their dreams. And we will march and yell and scream and watch these courts until we abolish the entire [prison] industrial complex. Amen.

Reflecting later, Jon McFarlane told me that he felt this prayer deeply, but thinks of its message not in the language of abolition—too unrealistic a term, in his mind—but rather in the language of destruction and rebuilding. His takeaway from four years of courtwatching echoes Rev. Newberry's call to take things apart. McFarlane says: "There's no repairing the system, the system was racist from the first brick, so how you gonna try to rebuild it? You can't rebuild it, you have to start over . . . [The purpose of] courtwatching is to show how racist and disproportionate the system for Black and brown people is, in the hopes of enough people looking and saying, you know, we gotta start this whole shit over."

4

Participatory Defense

Imani Mfalme-Shu'la identified herself as a "freedom fighter" from a young age. Her mother, Paula P. King Booker, was vice president of the local Knoxville, Tennessee, chapter of the NAACP. When Mfalme-Shu'la was a young girl, an investigation into death threats phoned to their home revealed that local Ku Klux Klan members were targeting Booker. Undeterred, Booker took part for decades in campaigns for desegregation and equal pay. Mfalme-Shu'la explains that, as a young girl watching her mother's resilience, she had a sense that "there were no limits to where you can take the fight" for equality and justice.

No limits, that is, until it came to the criminal system, a constant presence in her life. Four out of five of Mfalme-Shu'la's brothers spent time in prison. She remembers their absence as a continual silence in her home growing up. It wasn't just her brothers: "Everybody I knew was affected by the system." When Mfalme-Shu'la was in her mid-twenties, she was driving on a road on the east side of Knoxville with a friend when officers pulled her over and, with the excuse that they smelled marijuana, searched her car, finding a gun in the glove compartment. Mfalme-Shu'la was booked and charged with misdemeanor weapon possession. Even though her case was eventually dismissed—a judge found that the search of the car was unlawful—Mfalme-Shu'la was told to sign a piece of paper agreeing to forfeit her property. Mfalme-Shu'la followed directions and signed the paper. But she had a sense that something was deeply wrong about this, something connected to the way that police, courts, and prisons wove through her entire life, neighborhood, and the Black community in Oak Ridge and Knoxville. Although her gut told her that there were systemic problems with these experiences and those of other people of color in Tennessee, she "just did not know of any other way to do anything about it, except for hire the most expensive attorney and pray about it."

That changed in 2015, when Mfalme-Shu'la attended a free community training at the Knoxville Public Defender's office to learn about a practice called "participatory defense." At the time, Mfalme-Shu'la was in recovery from breast cancer, and her debilitating treatments had forced her to leave her job as a caretaker for people with mental disabilities. When Mfalme-Shu'la entered the room, the training was just beginning. Two women from Silicon Valley De-bug, an organizing group based in San Jose, California, were there as trainers representing the National Participatory Defense Network, which at the time included roughly a dozen groups engaging in the practice. Silicon Valley De-bug had been developing the concept of participatory defense for more than eight years, and the trainers were there to share their stories.

One trainer drew and wrote on a large flip chart set up on an easel, while the other told stories about how their group in San Jose, California, had been engaged in community organizing around criminal cases, in a "hub" of families and neighbors working together to understand and support people in fighting their cases. The trainers described the practice of participatory defense, a term that names "an instinct and not an invention," in which people collectively create agency in situations—criminal court cases—where they normally feel alone, even when they have well-meaning lawyers to guide them. The group might help dissect discovery documents, create a video or binder with sociobiographical information about the person accused of a crime, or any number of seemingly small interventions that, they find, have actual impact on the outcomes of cases. One of the trainers, Charisse Domingo, also said something else: that by changing outcomes in individual cases, over time, participatory defense hubs *could fight mass incarceration itself.* She argued that by building power among families and generating knowledge over time, they could actually push back against the system within which they were struggling.[1]

Mfalme-Shu'la listened, inspired but also dubious. She wondered to herself, "What is this sorcery that you're talking about?" She brought a notebook and wrote down the names of her brothers, as well as her friends with open cases, with question marks next to some of the names. "I was thinking back—my brothers, cousins, friends, *all* these cases, even in my case . . . wondering if we could have done this or that, or we *can* do this or do that." (Two of her brothers were still in prison at the time, and one was on probation.) Mfalme-Shu'la did not know most of the other people sitting in the audience with her, but she later learned that a few of them noticed her because of how furiously she was taking notes. As the training ended, Charisse Domingo asked the room for a show of hands of people who might want to participate in something like this in Knoxville. Mfalme-Shu'la raised her hand, as did others. A pastor at Knoxville's Tabernacle Baptist Church volunteered his church's basement for a meeting. "Let's do this now," Mfalme-Shu'la suggested.

Within a week, Mfalme-Shu'la and nine other residents of

Knoxville and its neighboring counties sat on folding chairs in the Tabernacle Baptist Church basement, resting their notepads on a white, T-shaped plastic table. Some came as members of local community organizations, including the NAACP chapter of the nearby city of Oak Ridge. And some, including Mfalme-Shu'la, came as unaffiliated community members. The group began by selecting a name: Community Defense of East Tennessee. Going around the room to discuss peoples' visions for the group, they soon discovered that one attendee, Eddie, had an ongoing criminal case. Eddie had been arrested while walking down the street in Oak Ridge County, on the sidewalk near a hotel. (The police officer later wrote down in the official report that he looked "suspicious.") The officers found no drugs or weapons on Eddie. Instead, his sole charge was "Resisting Arrest," for the way the officer claimed Eddie responded when two officers threw Eddie to the ground and placed him in handcuffs.

Hearing about Eddie's open criminal case during their first meeting, the group recognized a phenomenon familiar to them—a police officer making an arrest without cause in response to perceived disrespect or criminality, sometimes known as "contempt of cop."[2] The group decided to set aside their planning and jump in to practicing "participatory defense." They followed the method the trainers had described: on a flip chart on an easel owned by the church, they wrote down what they knew, and didn't know, about Eddie's case. They wrote down the allegations that the police were making, one by one. They realized that Eddie was missing official reports about what the police claimed happened. And, analyzing a map of the area, they wondered whether there was any surveillance footage from a hotel that sat less than a football field's distance from where police threw Eddie to the ground.

Eddie, Mfalme-Shu'la, and another Community Defense

member went together to a meeting with Eddie's public defender in Anderson County—as they knew from experience, it can be hard to ask even well-meaning attorneys questions about the case or about their advocacy. They came with more than a dozen questions they planned to ask the attorney, including if an investigator from the public defender's office could try to find witnesses or surveillance footage of the arrest from the nearby hotel. When they walked into her office, however, the attorney's first words to everyone but Eddie after "hello" were, "What are you all doing? You need to get out."

Banished from the lawyer's office, Mfalme-Shu'la waited for Eddie in the lobby. Yet, sitting there, Mfalme-Shu'la felt exhilarated. She knew that Eddie was prepared to hold his own with his lawyer. Mfalme-Shu'la had, in recent years, been going to local marches for Black Lives Matter in Knoxville. Those protests were energizing and made her think about structural racism in new ways. But, despite the words of the participatory defense trainers, it was only while sitting in the lobby of Eddie's attorney's office that she was jogged into realizing that she could play a part in changing results in the criminal system. She did not yet know that this intervention of Community Defense of East Tennessee *would* change the legal trajectory of Eddie's case—the case would be dismissed a year later thanks to video evidence from the nearby hotel to which Eddie alerted his lawyer. Still, Mfalme-Shu'la already felt power shifting, even as she sat there, knowing that Eddie had the right questions to ask and the support of the hub in his ordeal. "We can make noise, but then what? This was the 'then what.' This was the action item. This is the way to give power back to people."

Community Defense of East Tennessee continued to meet in the church basement one evening every week. For Mfalme-Shu'la and the other hub members, it was not always easy to create a sustained community of organizers; during their first year, there were a number of rifts among participants, including around how to center the perspectives of people of color and people accused of crimes; and how or whether to partner with public defenders. At one point, a member of the Oak Ridge chapter of the NAACP—a Black man who was also Eddie's ride from Oak Ridge to the meetings in Knoxville—decided to leave the group after a particularly contentious meeting. Among other reasons, the man had expressed concern about the group's embrace of the term "Black Lives Matter," thinking it too radical. Responding to these difficulties, Community Defense of East Tennessee drafted seven principles of unity, with a specific focus on centering families and recognizing the dangers of white supremacy. One principle stated, for example, "We understand the criminal [in]justice system is fundamentally rooted in and operates through violent state oppression, especially white supremacy, classism, and misogyny." And another: "As police and the growth of prisons in the country directly formed as an institution of slavery and racism, this group will unapologetically center Black and Brown liberation and power and this should be reflected in group leadership."[3]

With these collective principles, a steady group of regulars grew, and nearly seven years later, Community Defense of East Tennessee has rarely missed a Monday meeting. As the years progressed, the group slowly accumulated collective knowledge of the local criminal processes in Knoxville and its neighboring counties. People who joined the group with their own cases developed into long-term leaders. Hub members learned how to dissect police reports and how to put together "sociobio" packets—binders of sociobiographical information containing pictures and documents in a way that emphasizes the family, community, and general humanity of the criminalized person.

They learned which local drug treatment programs could most easily accept new patients. They developed partnerships with the Knoxville public defender's office, both in individual cases and in policy campaigns.

In 2021, the Community Defense of East Tennessee hub worked on more than fifteen cases alongside the accused and their families. These included situations in which the hub helped members advocate, via sociobio packets and investigations, for better plea bargains than initially offered by the prosecutor or judge; at least two cases in which the hub supported community members on probation who were trying to avoid jail for violation of conditions; and ongoing protests and packing of courtrooms during the trial of hub member Reggie, a U.S. Navy veteran found not guilty of aggravated assault of a police officer in a case where the officers brutalized him so severely that a tooth broke and his head required staples. A video shot on Mfalme-Shu'la's cell phone following the verdict shows six hub members, in masks, surrounding Reggie in a hug of celebration. The hub also concentrated on larger demands that year, such as a social media push to demand that the district attorney's office stop the practice of pushing for punitive plea bargains while the COVID-19 pandemic raged in the Knoxville County Jail.[4] At the end of every case, the hub engaged in a tradition passed down from the national network—on a whiteboard, they crossed off names as each case came to a conclusion, calculating the "time saved"—the difference between the initial sentence being threatened and the outcome of the case.

Mfalme-Shu'la remains the executive director of Community Defense of East Tennessee, as well as a trainer with the National Participatory Defense Network, which grew to dozens of hubs by 2022. Tennessee alone counts three active participatory defense hubs, including Free Hearts in Nashville and Concerned Citizens for Justice in Chattanooga. Mfalme-Shu'la is now the one who goes around the country giving trainings similar to those she received. Sometimes these trainings are virtual, and sometimes in person—one Las Vegas training gathered three potential hubs from the region for a two-day session. Mfalme-Shu'la aims to give others the same reaction that she had seven years ago: "[After] seeing my people being oppressed, this was a model that you could actually give someone power to face this system that has been destroying our families forever."

De-bugging the System

Silicon Valley De-bug began as a practice of community organizing for temporary tech and factory workers. In 2000, Raj Jayadev was a recent college graduate with a temporary job on an assembly line at a Hewlett-Packard factory. San Jose, the third-largest city in California, was at the heart of what was being branded as Silicon Valley's "new economy." It was then, and still is, a city whose residents are approximately one-third Latinx and one-third Asian American. Jayadev worked on the last leg of a global chain of labor that ended with the packaging of laser-jet printers; he would take each printer from the conveyor belt, check for parts and proper packaging, and return the printer to the moving belt. For Jayadev, the job was truly "temporary" in that he anticipated a different career; but Jayadev quickly realized that these jobs were the sole source of financial support for many families. Although Jayadev ended up being laid off within nine months—a relatively ordinary occurrence for a temp at the time—he started organizing with his co-workers around wages and job protections.

To Jayadev, it felt as if the people he saw struggling to support themselves and their families were invisible in the context of the hype around Silicon Valley at the turn of the millennium. With the help of Sandy Close and Kevin Western at Pacific News Service, Jayadev and other temporary workers began to write a collective column, "Young and Temporary," as part of the *Youth Outlook* newspaper run by the news service. The group met on Tuesday evenings at a Vietnamese restaurant, working with Close and Western to craft stories of their work and lives into columns.

Around the time that they published their first magazine, the group gave themselves a name: Silicon Valley De-bug. As Jayadev explains: "If you worked on a conveyor belt [or] assembly room–type situation, if . . . the product isn't working you call the De-bug Unit to inspect the product, to get to the root cause of the malfunction: to expose it, in order to fix it." To this group, the term was a metaphor so grounded in their experiences that it didn't need much discussion: by telling their stories, they were exposing the world, in order to fix it. Looking back now, Jayadev says, "Who gets to look into the machinery is a question of power. And then who has the audacity to be able to say that there could be something problematic about the machine, who has the wherewithal to look into something and expose it: that is De-bugging."

With the donation of a physical building space for its work, De-bug soon morphed from a focus on storytelling to an organizing model that aimed to provide people with what could meet their economic and creative needs. There was a meditation space, a printing shop, and youth programming. With these came protests for fair wages. In its first years, though, Silicon Valley De-bug's involvement with criminal court did not extend beyond throwing car wash fundraisers to help raise bail money for families with loved ones incarcerated pretrial.

Then, in 2004, the group worked alongside a family whose son, Rudy Cardenas, was shot and killed by an agent from the

California Bureau of Narcotics. The white agent claimed to fear that Cardenas, who was unarmed, would pull a gun on him.[5] Working with Cardenas's family, De-bug organizers led protests against overpolicing in San Jose and pushed for a public grand jury to consider the Cardenas killing. This led more families to come to De-bug when their loved ones were arrested, prosecuted, or held in jails and immigration detention centers.

At first, Jayadev and his fellow organizers responded to families who sought support with their loved ones' cases by convening separate meetings for each case. A "Justice for Rudy" meeting worked with Blanca, the mother of a different Rudy, who was charged in juvenile court with a serious crime but was developmentally delayed and required twenty-four-hour care.[6] A "Justice for Karim" campaign meeting focused on figuring out how to assist teenager Karim's mother, Gail, with Karim's juvenile court case while Karim was held in juvenile detention pending trial.[7] At one point, when the organizers found themselves having five different "Justice for . . ." meetings within one week, they decided to combine the five cases into one meeting. All of the families met together. They wrote the five names on a whiteboard and discussed each of the cases. They collectively brainstormed next steps on each case, and met again the next week. The cases varied: There was an adult with a "resisting arrest" case. There was someone looking for post-conviction relief, for a conviction twenty years earlier. And then there was Ceci Chavez, there asking for help understanding her father's immigration case while he was being held in immigration detention following a misdemeanor charge in criminal court.

They went one case at a time, seeing what was happening and how they could help. They used strategies that groups around the country, including Community Defense of East

Tennessee, would later emulate, such as sociobio packets and case investigations. They packed courtrooms. They saw sentences reduced, cases dismissed. And because all the cases were different, they were able to take in the big picture. Their knowledge, as a collective, accumulated.

As with bail funds and courtwatching, bringing multiple cases together allows hub members to see patterns over time. Gail and Blanca continued as members of De-bug's hub, working alongside parents who felt alienated from the juvenile cases of their children, just as Gail and Blanca had with their own children's cases. Ultimately, the hub became involved in challenging broader policies in San Jose's juvenile courts, including "three strikes" laws, as well as in working with court officials to facilitate parental involvement in juvenile cases. Other policy campaigns born of the practice of participatory defense soon followed. De-bug organizers joined a coalition successfully pushing for limits to Santa Clara County's cooperation with Immigration and Customs Enforcement. They gathered graffiti artists to meet with the local district attorney's office and convinced the attorneys there to change the way that they approached "vandalism" charges related to tagging and graffiti art. De-bug members have also testified in state and local legislatures in multiple successful efforts to pass laws reducing criminalization, including a slew of state sentencing reform laws.[8]

As they did the work of participatory defense over years and then decades, Silicon Valley De-bug organizers found themselves asked to do trainings for other groups around the country, and in 2016 the National Participatory Defense Network was founded to help that work along. The slogan of the national network became "Protect Our People," articulating a "people" separate from "the People of the State of California" and from other prosecutor officers who are criminalizing communities around the country in their names.

Each year brought multiple new local policy campaigns, both those leveled *at* the system and those that engaged regular people *in* the system. In 2018, for example, hubs from nine different counties throughout California became involved in pushing for bail reform and a reduction in pretrial detention, supporting a lawsuit in the California Supreme Court that challenged the constitutionality of the system of money bail in that state. The campaign, "A Day in Court in California," began with coordinated courtwatching throughout the state to monitor new bail reform legislation—a tepid bill that the groups feared would not lead to a substantial reduction in pretrial detention.[9]

When a California appellate court issued a ruling in the case, *In Re Humphrey*, the California hubs worked in partnership with the lawyers at Civil Rights Corps and public defender offices throughout the state to combine the courtwatching with political education. The *Humphrey* case was complicated—rather than hold that incarcerating someone because they cannot afford bail is always unconstitutional, the lower courts and eventually the California Supreme Court required case-by-case analysis of each person and situation.[10] But the legal changes felt significant to families; Jayadev remembers that people cried at a Silicon Valley De-bug hub meeting when they read parts of a 2018 appellate *Humphrey* decision out loud. The organizers felt "it shouldn't be just discussed by lawyers; this is a live possibility that people walking in a court need to know about." And so they held press conferences outside eight different courthouses and handed out flyers explaining how families could advocate for loved ones given the recent legal changes, including by demanding bail review hearings. They also worked with then–San Francisco public defender Jeff Adachi to draft a sample motion that groups could work together to fill out in individual cases.

When the *Humphrey* litigation came to an end in 2021, De-bug extended the "A Day in Court" practice of courtwatching to what they call "court doing." In partnership with the Santa Clara County public defender's office, they attend felony bail hearings and work with family members to explain the bail law and how their presence in the courtroom can be helpful. Using a form, hub members hustle to collect information from audience members that the public defender can then use to advocate more effectively—information that the lawyers rarely have or use in the rush of bail hearings. For people who do not have family in court, the attorney can tell the judge that De-bug hub members will serve as "community support": they invite those with pending cases to weekly meetings, connect them to needed services, and provide transportation to court if necessary.[11] If the judge's bail decision leads to pretrial detention, family members are invited to De-bug hub meetings to continue their fight. When De-bug and public defenders conducted a joint evaluation of cases before and after the "court doing" and community support interventions, the data revealed that reliance on set bail amounts dropped by almost half. The rate of no-bail release quadrupled.[12]

But these releases are not, themselves, the object of "court doing." The goal is not to become a permanent fixture of the system—Silicon Valley De-bug refused the county's request to apply to become a system-funded program of pretrial community support.[13] Instead, as with all of the hub's organizing, the aim is to combine collective advocacy in individual cases with the building of power to change public conversations and policies—in this case, shifting understanding around bail and pretrial detention, and around the broader criminalization of poor communities of color in California. As Jayadev wrote of the message of "court doing": "The future of pretrial justice is not pretrial detention or system supervision. It's Freedom and Community."[14]

In all that they do, De-bug's participatory defense practice has aimed to stay close to its roots as a community organizing strategy, a pooling of experiences and resources in an effort to build knowledge and power. They continue to say that they are "naming an instinct" of collective power-building in the face of the criminal system rather than creating something new. Organizing, a collective form of participation in political life, is in many ways the opposite of what it means to be accused of a crime. When you are prosecuted, your name is placed on the other side of the "v." from "the People" in the case caption. This symbolic isolation plays out in real life, as you are physically isolated from your family and the rest of the world while you wait to see a judge. You are encouraged to testify against any friends you were arrested with as part of plea bargains. You are otherwise told to remain silent, lest you jeopardize your case.[15]

Collective action is incredibly difficult within such an individualized system. There have been efforts, some even successful, to organize people with open cases collectively within the system; for example, some groups have experimented with "plea strikes"—coordinated efforts of people to refuse to plead guilty so that they might "crash" the system that depends on large-scale plea bargains to function.[16] Such efforts at plea strikes are exciting—the whole system hinges on isolation, so to undermine that is to undermine the system. But the barriers to such collective action are tremendous, and come with real risks of stiff penalties for those who turn down plea deals. These barriers underscore how deeply ingrained individualism and isolation are to criminal procedure and to the functioning of the system.

Participatory defense hubs, even in their simplest form—families getting together regularly to work on their loved ones' cases—push back against this isolation. Participatory defense hubs demand entry into legal spaces that are designed to be exclusionary. Power is built each time that a small thing changes because of this collective action—when a judge examines a binder of photographs of someone's everyday life; when an investigation prompted by a hub leads to proof of legal innocence; when a judge learns about an individual's family and community connections before deciding whether to set bail. And when a group such as Silicon Valley De-bug or Community Defense of East Tennessee connects individuals to a larger collective process, wearing shirts that say "Protect Our People," they are shifting power dynamics in complex but concrete ways that reverberate beyond the individual case.

In 2018, Raj Jayadev won a MacArthur "genius" award, which Jayadev thinks of as being less about him as an individual, and more "as a 'we' thing, a nod to the process that everyone has collectively contributed to." In hindsight, Jayadev often says that by staying outside of criminal courts in their early years, De-bug "relinquished collective community power at the time when it was most needed: when someone was stepping into Court and facing all the apparatuses of that institution."

Locating the Public in Public Defense

Within an individualized criminal process, a defense attorney should, in theory, be an antidote to the system's forced isolation. The 1963 Supreme Court case *Gideon v. Wainwright* is often considered a landmark of due process, requiring that states provide a lawyer to indigent people in most criminal cases. Because of this constitutional requirement, approximately 80 percent of people accused of crimes in the United States are represented by a public defender provided by the state. For those facing prosecution but unable to afford a lawyer, having an advocate on their side should help foster connection and understanding. Often this is the case; a good public defender will explain what is happening and work collaboratively with clients and their families to push for innovative outcomes and connections to needed resources. Perhaps most important, defenders can voice solidarity on the record and infuse the humanity of the accused into discussions both inside and outside of the courtroom. I certainly tried to do all of these things during the five years that I spent as a public defender in a relatively well-resourced office with a focus on "client-centered" and holistic advocacy.[17] This work can be rewarding and powerful.

But even having an excellent criminal defense attorney cannot counter the alienation inherent in being placed on the other side of the "v" from "the People." This is especially true for poor people of color facing prosecution. In a 2020 study, sociologist Matthew Clair examined the experiences of people represented by public defenders in Boston. Clair found that the judge and prosecutor rewarded silence and compliance in the courtroom, which was easier for privileged people who are accused of crimes and have the time, space, and resources to grow a relationship with their lawyers. In contrast, poor people of color accused of crimes tend to approach their cases and court appearances with either resistance or resignation to their powerlessness. The result is a set of relationships and legal results in courtrooms that "operate and legitimate taken-for-granted forms of race and class discrimination."[18] In another study, sociologist Nicole Gonzalez Van Cleve showed how public defenders perpetuate "the logics of racialized justice" by internalizing demeaning stereotypes and minimizing the agency of clients, even as those same public defenders would voice substantive critiques of the system.[19]

Counterintuitively, a focus on the right to counsel as a guarantee of fairness and connection can feed alienation by legitimizing the process: if someone has an advocate, then surely the fight must have been fair. But one advocate, no matter how zealous or well resourced, cannot counter the larger systemic forces—overpolicing, racial and gender bias, the criminalization of poverty—that lead someone to appear before a criminal court. And these structural inequalities become baked into the attorney–client relationship. As legal scholar Paul Butler argued in *Poor People Lose*, his critique of the right to counsel, "*Gideon*'s announcement of a right to counsel appear[s] to give the poor an agency in criminal justice that they actually do not have."[20] Parallel constitutional doctrines regarding someone's right to represent themselves *pro se* or to choose their own attorney only further this illusion of autonomy.[21]

Compounding the problems with the right to counsel is another dire reality: many public defenders are *not* zealous or well-resourced advocates. The Constitution does not require excellence. Courts have held, famously, that even a state-appointed lawyer who falls asleep during trial may not violate the constitutional right to counsel.[22] Many, if not most, public defender offices face severe funding restraints, resulting in high caseloads, meager case investigations, and lack of sufficient training and supervision.[23] Structural racism compounds these problems at every step.

Many criminal reform advocates meet the "crisis" of public defense with calls for more resources for public defender offices, including funding, training, and a focus on holistic advocacy. The goal is sometimes stated as seeking out a "fair fight" between the defense and the prosecution. As early as 1932, the Supreme Court described the plight of an indigent person facing trial in this way: "He lacks both the skill and knowledge adequately to prepare his defense. . . . If that be true of men of intelligence, how much more true is it of the ignorant and illiterate, or those of feeble intellect."[24] Emerging from this prototypical understanding is a dream of a well-funded public defense office in which experts assist helpless individuals as they navigate a complex system.

Participatory defense complicates this dream. By engaging in participatory defense or collective defense, people are regaining control over their own narratives in court, showing that the "feebleminded" have something to say alongside those with law degrees and who are accustomed to legal language. The public defense crisis becomes not about ignorant and illiterate people in need of help, but rather about a system that isolates ordinary people and strips their agency via seemingly neutral procedures.

Although not always articulated in constitutional terms, members of participatory defense hubs are engaging in what Lani Guinier and Gerald Torres call demosprudence, the ability of groups of people to shift legal meaning through new, collective understandings of their relationship to the state.[25] In the case of the legal understanding of the right to counsel, partnerships between hubs and public defender offices can facilitate the sharing of information and power that, in the words of Raj Jayadev, Janet Moore, and Marla Sandys, allows "people who face criminal charges, their families, and their communities to transform themselves from service recipients to change agents."[26] This is a sentiment echoed by groups such as the Black Public Defender's Association, which calls for public defense offices to center Black communities in their work.[27] The centering of community members, as practiced by participatory defense hubs, has implications for both the practice of public defense and its constitutional meaning. As Jayadev and Moore write, "By working with and assisting public defenders, or pushing them when they falter, participatory defense raises [constitutional] standards. Strengthening [constitutional] norms strengthens the right [to counsel]."[28]

An inherent tension exists between the institutional knowledge that public defenders bring to the table and the bottom-up knowledge that participatory defense hubs demand courts consider.[29] After all, public defenders are regular players in the courtroom and may have a better sense of courtroom dynamics than do hub members. If a sociobiographical binder or video is more likely to anger a particular judge than to push them toward a lower sentence, then perhaps it should remain outside the courtroom.

It is in part for this reason that some defense lawyers resist the interventions of participatory defense hubs, much as Eddie's public defender did in Oak Ridge when she refused to let hub members join their meeting. Resistance from public defenders is often subtle, manifesting less as overt hostility and more as a general ambivalence toward the interventions of the hub. Moore, Jayadev, and Sandys describe the resistance, and the clashing of different forms of knowledge and expertise, as a "productive tension," one that can perhaps push both public defenders and the larger public to a different understanding of what public defense can and should be when it is done in collaboration with directly affected families and communities.[30]

Some public defender offices welcome this tension. Many offices have jumped into partnerships with participatory defense hubs: they host trainings, refer families to hubs, and engage in public campaigns for reform led by hub organizers.[31] From the point of view of public defender offices increasingly interested in working alongside local grassroots organizations pushing for change, participatory defense hubs can become a way to combine individual representation with collective partnership.

Whether in stances of partnership or opposition, when participatory defense hubs bring their collective power to a case, they often achieve what even experienced public defenders might consider the impossible. Mfalme-Shu'la tells a story of one hub member in Knoxville, Daniel, who was facing a sentencing hearing for which his attorney told him incarceration was the only possible outcome, in part because the assistant district attorney claimed that Daniel was a dangerous gang member. Members of the local Black Lives Matter chapter had created a petition of people demanding leniency, attesting that they knew Daniel as a harmless person in their neighborhood. And the Knoxville participatory defense hub put together a sociobio binder containing a mental health treatment plan that hub members had worked with Daniel's mother to create. The binder also contained letters, from both close friends and relative strangers, members of the community who described Daniel as a familiar and welcome presence who would walk the local streets.

A video taken in the hallway outside the sentencing courtroom shows more than a dozen supporters from Community Defense of East Tennessee—a mix of races and ages—in a tight circle around Daniel, his mother, and his attorney, as Daniel's mother implored the attorney to ask for mental health treatment rather than incarceration. The lawyer stood and listened politely. In the courtroom, the lawyer's hesitation to use the binder to advocate for Daniel was clear. Mfalme-Shu'la remembers the offhandedness with which the lawyer presented the binder to the judge: "Well, judge, they want me to give you this."

Something then shifted: the judge flipped through the binder, and then told the crowded courtroom that he would have to stop the hearing in order to consider all of the information before him. The case was adjourned. This moment generated a swell of excitement for hub members, a small but concrete win: "We stopped him from going to prison!" The exhilaration of collective power swelled even more when, at the next court date, the judge sentenced Daniel to the very treatment plan that hub members had helped put together. The impossible became possible because these hub members refused to take the ossified power relationships in the courtroom as fixed, and instead used collective knowledge and advocacy to penetrate an exclusionary space.

Survived & Punished

The idea of collectively participating in an individual's criminal defense flows through another, parallel set of social movement strategies to organize alongside people facing the punitive arm of the state. This kind of collective defense involves groups that organize locally on behalf of individuals in ongoing cases, while connecting those cases to broader systemic problems. As Mariame Kaba, a national leader in this form of advocacy, has described such collective defense campaigns, they attempt to highlight how "our fates are intertwined and our liberation is interconnected." To do this, these collective defense campaigns—often organized by and on behalf of Black, Native, and Latinx women and transgender people—publicly frame cases "as emblematic of the conditions faced by thousands or millions who should also be free."[32]

Kaba herself is a co-founder of Survived & Punished, a national collective that emerged in 2017 from a constellation of Black-led collective defense committees for criminalized survivors of domestic or gender-based violence, including the Chicago organization Love & Protect. A few years earlier, the Free Marissa Now Mobilization Campaign and the Chicago Alliance to Free Marissa Alexander (founded by Kaba) had raised money for a national campaign to support and bring awareness to the case of Marissa Alexander, a survivor of domestic violence who was prosecuted in Florida for shooting a gun into the air to ward off her husband after he threatened to kill her. Alexander had suffered physical abuse for years, and at the time of her arrest had given birth to a premature baby only nine days earlier. Nevertheless, Alexander was convicted of aggravated assault with a deadly weapon after a judge denied her ability to put forth a "Stand Your Ground" defense under Florida law. Alexander was initially sentenced to twenty years in prison under the state's mandatory minimum sentencing statute.[33]

The Free Marissa Now campaign raised funds, public awareness, and political education around Alexander's successful appeal of her conviction, and included education materials—toolkits, zines, and teach-ins—to connect Alexander's plight to the larger problem of the criminalization of survivors, especially Black, Native, and trans women. A comparison to George Zimmerman's case, in particular, struck a national chord as public discussion of the racialized nature of "defense" and Black lives began to emerge: while Alexander was denied the ability to use a "Stand Your Ground" defense, George Zimmerman was able to use "Stand Your Ground" successfully at his trial, where he was acquitted of the 2012 killing of Black teenager Trayvon Martin. And the Free Marissa Now campaign continually connected Alexander's experience to other criminalized survivors; one widely distributed campaign poster had a long but potent tagline: "Stop the Legal Lynching of a Black Domestic Violence Survivor by Florida's Racist Mandatory Minimum Sentencing Laws."[34]

Survived & Punished is now a national network of groups engaging in organizing that includes collective defense campaigns, combining individual advocacy with national political education around larger issues of criminalization. Unlike a participatory defense "hub," a collective campaign group focuses in on one individual case and then works to connect that case to larger systemic critiques. In the 2017 toolkit "#SurvivedandPunished: Survivor Defense as Abolitionist Praxis," members of Love & Protect and Survived & Punished document dozens of such campaigns across the country for criminalized survivors, including Nan-Hui Jo, Bresha

Meadows, and Ky Peterson. The organizers emphasize the importance of the work for participants: "Survivor defense committees . . . can transform not only the lives of criminalized survivors but also those who come to their defense."[35]

And they stress that these individual stories—a woman who defends herself against an abuser, a transgender girl who uses force against a police officer trying to sexually assault her, or a young girl subject to sexual exploitation yet treated as a criminal—are representative of the larger problem of the criminalization of victims of violence. Studies show that between 50 percent and 95 percent of incarcerated women have been sexually assaulted or subjected to abuse by intimate partners. As legal scholar Leigh Goodmark has written, "In that sense, most incarcerated women are criminalized survivors."[36] No matter the form of prior trauma, organizers at Survived & Punished and Love & Protect stress that criminalization and incarceration are themselves forms of abuse and trauma, continuing rather than preventing a broader, structural cycle of abuse.[37]

Collective defense campaigns have existed for centuries. In the mid-nineteenth century, for instance, antislavery organizers, many of them Black women, joined together with abolitionist lawyers to support people captured and brought to court under the federal Fugitive Slave Laws.[38] Mariame Kaba sometimes begins a discussion of the history of defense campaigns in the early twentieth century by pointing to the decades-long multiracial campaign to defend and free the nine poor Black teenagers known as the "Scottsboro Boys,"[39] falsely charged with raping two white women in Alabama in 1931. Initially, the teenagers received weak legal representation (and sometimes none at all) and were sentenced to death before an all-white jury. Following these initial convictions, the Communist Party's International Labor Defense department led a much-publicized campaign to appeal the convictions. Over the seven years of the campaign—spanning multiple appeals, retrials, and even two successful and famous Supreme Court cases—members of the Labor Defense group and local leaders battled the case both in court and in public, through organizing, protests, and letter-writing campaigns. The multiracial coalition was often led locally by Black women, including Louise Thompson Patterson, who was one of the main organizers of a large protest in support of the Scottsboro teenagers in Washington, D.C. The League of Struggle for Negro Rights, of which Langston Hughes was for some time the vice president, was also heavily involved.[40]

The idea behind the nationwide, and at times international, campaign was not just to free the innocent men, but also to lay bare the racist underpinnings of the entire criminal system. The campaign compared the death sentences of the Black teens to lynchings, and, according to a number of historians, changed nationwide views about the criminal system in the South, especially among white southerners.[41] Langston Hughes's 1932 series of "Scottsboro" poems included his famous poem "Justice": "That Justice is a blind goddess / Is a thing to which we black are wise. / Her bandage hides two festering sores / That once perhaps were eyes."[42]

The organizers at Survived & Punished also highlight in their toolkit the national defense campaigns of women of color in the 1970s, including Joan Little, charged with killing a prison guard who had been sexually assaulting her. As with the Scottsboro campaign, these national defense committees had dozens of local chapters around the country and combined fundraising, protest, political education, and broader media pushes in their efforts to support the women.[43] Thousands participated in a national campaign for Little, led by a combination of Black Power, civil rights, and feminist groups, which ultimately led to her acquittal. As historian Emily Thuma has documented, all four of these campaigns made explicit, repeated connections between racism, classism, and patriarchy—what we think of now as intersectionality—and the larger problem of the criminalization of women who defend themselves in situations of gender-based or domestic violence.[44] Angela Davis wrote in *Ms.* magazine in 1975 about Joan Little's case, "All people who see themselves as members of the existing community of struggle for justice, equality, and progress have a responsibility to fulfill toward Joan Little."[45] It was with these and other related histories in mind that activists formed the national collective Survived & Punished, beginning at an Allied Media Conference in 2017.[46]

The legacy of this work can also be seen in the collective defense work of groups such as the Survivors Justice Project in New York, which works, among other things, on legal campaigns to free incarcerated survivors in post-conviction cases. Many core members of the Survivors Justice Project organized together for years when incarcerated in New York's Bedford Hills Correctional Facility, and now work to bring that sense of collective struggle to the individual cases of criminalized survivors today.[47]

Uniting all of these efforts, both participatory defense "hubs" and individual defense campaigns, is a focus on the collective force of strangers who support the accused while acting in solidarity with them, in the faith that doing this work for one person can lead to collectively generated critiques of the criminal system.[48]

Stand with Tracy

Tracy McCarter's relationship with Survived & Punished NY developed slowly. On March 3, 2020, McCarter stood before a judge in Manhattan's night court at her arraignment on a charge of murder in the second degree for the death of her estranged husband. The last forty-eight hours had been a blur. Arrested in her scrubs—at the time, forty-four-year-old McCarter worked as a nurse at Weill-Cornell, in addition to studying for a master's degree at Columbia University—she had been taken to a hospital, then a police precinct, and now the court, with little sleep between. McCarter's adult children, who lived out of town, were not present in the courtroom, but McCarter saw the flash of a camera as she was led in handcuffs before the judge, as well as rows of strangers sitting as spectators in the audience.

Although McCarter did not know her, one of these spectators in night court was Erica Bersin, a Court Watch NYC volunteer. Bersin had observed at least a dozen shifts for Court Watch NYC in recent months. In those prior shifts, Bersin had been appalled by what she describes as the "lack of humanity" throughout the arraignment process. One past incident stuck out to her in particular, when two court officers had dragged a Latino man in a hospital gown by his feet through the courtroom hallway, while two other officers walked by—"as if it was business as usual. Which it was." Despite these past experiences, from her seat in the courtroom pews Bersin could tell even before Tracy McCarter's arraignment began that McCarter's case was different: people were milling around the courtroom and whispering about the case; the judge; the assistant district attorney, Sarah Sullivan; and a defense lawyer held multiple off-the-record conversations at the bench; and a photographer lingered in the back of the room.

Bersin watched as McCarter's arraignment began. From the on-the-record statements of Sullivan, Bersin learned that McCarter was being charged with the murder of her husband, James Murray, and from the defense attorney's statements,

Bersin learned that there was a long history of alcohol abuse and domestic violence by Murray toward McCarter. The defense attorney stated that McCarter had been defending herself. It was McCarter who had called 911. When the police arrived, the nurse was administering first aid to Murray. Despite these statements from the defense, Bersin heard ADA Sullivan say that "the People" were demanding that McCarter be held without bail, calling McCarter a flight risk because she had been a travel nurse and her grown children lived in other states. (This was quite a stretch in reasoning: McCarter had lived in NYC for six years, no longer traveled for work, had a steady job in a New York City hospital system, and was attending a master's program at Columbia University.)

Bersin saw Tracy McCarter's knees buckle beneath her body upon hearing Sullivan's argument that she was a flight risk. Heeding the ADA's request, the judge announced that McCarter would be held without bail and sent to the jail complex on Riker's Island. Court officers escorted McCarter out of the courtroom through back doors, still in handcuffs, still shaky on her feet. In the hallway after the arraignment, Bersin confronted ADA Sullivan: "You know, I'm one of the people that you say you represent, and shame on you. I hope you never find yourself in this position." Sullivan turned away, unresponsive. That evening, Bersin began to reach out about McCarter's case to anyone she could think of, including Court Watch NYC organizers. Her email soon made its way to Rachel Foran, an organizer at Court Watch NYC who was also a member of Survived & Punished's New York chapter.

By 2020, Survived & Punished NY was a stand-alone affiliate of the national network of groups organizing on behalf of criminalized survivors. At the time, the New York group had approximately 130 people on their mailing list, and between 30 and 50 people active in the chapter's subgroups, which met regularly via Zoom. In addition to active collective defense campaigns, S&P NY had working groups doing research and advocacy—one group, for instance, organized mutual aid for criminalized survivors; another engaged in research around the funding of prosecutors in New York City. The chapter also published a newsletter, which featured the writing and artwork of criminalized survivors, as well as updates on the campaigns and fundraising efforts of S&P affiliates throughout the country.[49] When Rachel Foran heard about McCarter's case, she quickly wrote a letter to McCarter at Riker's Island, letting her know about the work of S&P NY and asking if McCarter would potentially be interested in their help.

Within weeks of her detention at Riker's Island, Tracy McCarter received letters from both Foran and Bersin, the Court Watch NYC volunteer. There was also a third letter, from a stranger who had seen McCarter at the Riker's Island legal library and wanted to date her. McCarter told me that her reaction, at first, to receiving these three letters at around the same time was to avoid processing or responding to them. She was withdrawn from the world, thinking, "Jail is weird. I just want to go home."

McCarter was held at Riker's Island for more than six months, just as the COVID-19 pandemic began to escalate in the city around her, and in particular at Riker's Island. Her stay at Riker's inflicted traumas on top of the trauma of Murray's death. McCarter told me, referring to the night Murray died, "More than that night, Riker's has caused me the most trauma."[50]

McCarter's pretrial detention also had ripple effects on her family, as incarceration so often does. McCarter missed the birth of her first grandchild, for which she had planned to be present as a nurse. Her daughter, Ariel Robbins, said in a podcast interview, "When somebody goes to jail or prison, the entire family goes to jail. [I never knew what that meant] until we experienced this as a family."[51]

Caged at Riker's Island, McCarter held on to the letters from Foran and Bersin, and as weeks went by, she eventually decided to respond. She felt her current attorney was not listening to her, and judges had continued to deny repeated bail requests. McCarter remained wary of offers of assistance from strangers, but considered, "Maybe they'll be able to help, because I don't know what else to do." She soon found herself on a call with Rachel Foran—in-person visits were curtailed during the pandemic—and McCarter learned more about the work of Survived & Punished NY. McCarter told me, "I realized quickly that these women were not how I might have prejudged them, and that they had knowledge that I needed."

Soon, with McCarter's consent, members of S&P NY formed a defense team to work alongside McCarter and her family on McCarter's case, meeting weekly via Zoom and other virtual platforms every Monday night for more than two years. McCarter's daughter, Robbins, regularly joined, and sometimes McCarter's mother did as well. When possible, McCarter joined in by phone from Riker's Island. Internally, the group spent time at their weekly meetings working through the legal elements of McCarter's case, making sure that McCarter and her family understood what was happening—something that McCarter's first lawyer was not helpful with.[52]

The meetings were structured: someone made an agenda that was shared ahead of time so that people could add to it; someone was the notetaker. There were no leaders, and roles rotated. To McCarter, it was essential to be in a space that centered Black survivors, as so much of her prosecution seemed driven by white "feminism," especially the stance of the lead ADA, who seemed on a mission as part of her role in the domestic violence unit. McCarter told me, "I've never felt so much distress and cynicism with feminism in my life." Her S&P NY team became a safe haven for open discussion about these reactions, as well as the connections of her case to the broader criminalization of survivors of domestic violence, and how this intersected with the marginalization of Black women in particular. Rachel Foran at S&P NY told me, "Tracy's self-determination is the center of everything we're doing."

The New York group working on the court case with McCarter simultaneously led an outward campaign for her defense and demanded her release, with the tagline "#StandWithTracy." Through Twitter power hours and other outward campaigning, as well as an article in the *Gothamist* by journalist Victoria Law, McCarter's case became part of the discourse around the emerging primary election for Manhattan district attorney. On September 10, 2020, Alvin Bragg—who would go on to become the new Manhattan DA—tweeted from his own account, "I #StandWithTracy. Prosecuting a domestic violence survivor who acted in self-defense is unjust."[53]

By this time, McCarter had secured new pro bono lawyers, with the help of Sanctuary for Families, a New York City–area provider for victims of domestic and gender-based violence. Finally, in the fall of 2020, a judge changed McCarter's bail conditions so that she was released into home confinement with an ankle monitor—unable even to walk her dog, but out of the continuous trauma of Riker's Island. From home, McCarter was able regularly to attend the weekly S&P NY meetings. McCarter's new lawyers were committed, experienced advocates, swiftly moving along her defense with the resources of three law firms (and eventually four) at their disposal. But conversations with her lawyers about the case were still sometimes overwhelming for McCarter, and her S&P team helped her navigate the relationships. McCarter explains this aspect of the S&P relationship, "It's still the weirdest and least comfortable thing for a person like me who [doesn't] ask for help, . . . *I'm* the person people come to for help; that's a much more comfortable place to be in my world."

The S&P NY team centered McCarter's experiences and expertise, and they pushed for public pressure with respect to her case. As Foran explained of their strategy, "Lawyers are a part of it, and op-eds are a part of it, but we also felt the power of the collective pressure" generated from virtual and physical courtwatching, from social media, from wearing matching red shirts that say "Stand with Tracy" at protests and in court. Foran told me, "We just believe that the only way she's going to win is if there is power behind her case and not just the fancy words, not just the media placements."

McCarter's S&P NY team entered 2022 hopeful that the election of Alvin Bragg as district attorney would signal a quick end of McCarter's prosecution. After all, Bragg had tweeted his support while on the campaign trail. These hopes were quickly dashed. Bragg refused to take a public stand, and ADA Sullivan continued to push the case toward trial. At one point, Sullivan would not consent to allowing McCarter to enter an out-of-state treatment facility during an acute mental health crisis. (When Sullivan did consent months later, the criminal court judge refused the request.) While McCarter's lawyers continually advocated for her within Bragg's office, the S&P NY team took the fight outside the courthouse. Monthly social media pushes reminded the public of Bragg's claim to #StandWithTracy. More than sixty organizations signed a March 2022 letter imploring Bragg to drop the charges. Thousands signed an online petition. Supporters in red shirts came to each court date. Eventually, Bragg's office filed a motion to dismiss the most serious charges if Tracy McCarter would consider a plea deal to a lower charge that would keep her out of jail. But even that compromise was denied by the judge, and by September 2022 McCarter's case remained headed toward trial.

As months dragged on, it became clear that the culture and procedures of criminal court would not bend easily in the face of overwhelming support for McCarter, including from inside the district attorney's office. Collective defense had helped McCarter survive, and had led DA Bragg to change his tune, but the organizing was no magic bullet in the face of the system. McCarter told me, "As a Black woman, I've spent most of my life making sure I'm not an offense. Speaking well, properly. [But this experience] changes how I view America. . . . I thought I could code switch, I thought I could fit everywhere, because I'm 'articulate' and educated and I'm not an offense. I learned that yeah, I am [an offense]. The system doesn't know what to do with somebody like me."

In November 2022, District Attorney Bragg finally took a stronger stance in McCarter's case in a letter to the court recommending a dismissal of the indictment. Bragg wrote that he had reasonable doubt as to McCarter's guilt: "I cannot in good consci[ence] allow a prosecution to proceed to trial and ask a jury to reach a conclusion that I have not reached myself."[54] Bragg did not explain how or why his conscience took nearly a year to emerge, nor why the case went on for two and a half years, but from the outside it was impossible not to view this emergence of doubt alongside the collective power of the S&P NY campaign.

In response to Bragg's letter, Judge Kiesel dismissed McCarter's indictment on December 2, 2022. In a written opinion, the judge described herself as "powerless" and leveled criticism at McCarter, her defense campaign, the media, and most of all the district attorney.[55] But the continued vitriol of the court toward McCarter could not undermine the legal fact of the dismissal. And, despite her efforts to the contrary, Judge Kiesel's opinion served only to highlight the collective power that the campaign to #StandWithTracy had generated over time. As Tracy McCarter wrote in a tweet reacting to Bragg's letter: "They thought they were building me a cage. Instead they were building me a pulpit."[56]

The Problem Is the System

Tracy McCarter reflected that before experiencing her own criminalization, "I had done mass incarceration protests. I knew what was wrong, and I felt like I gave my body to be out in public, a couple times. . . . But I didn't know what I could *add*." McCarter figured out that what she as an individual could add began by being part of a small community focused on one case—her own—while consistently connecting the work to larger systemic forces. Mariame Kaba refers to this side of collective defense as a "practice of abolitionist care," in which short-term, collective work to free individuals, done in partnership with those individuals, strengthens a broader, movement-based critique of the system.[57]

For the S&P NY team, the larger problem with the prosecution of McCarter was nothing less than criminalization itself. In June 2021, Sojourner Rivers, a member of McCarter's team, co-wrote with Taylor Blackston an op-ed in *Truthout* connecting McCarter's case and the upcoming district attorney's race in Manhattan. Rivers and Blackston noted that DA candidates claiming to want to help survivors of domestic violence—including future DA Alvin Bragg—were making promises of *more* prosecutions for domestic violence, "advocating for devouring the already austere New York City budget to build out the criminalization infrastructure." Rivers and Blackston wrote, "Any discussion about reforming criminal legal systems on behalf of survivors without mention of how these very systems are abusing survivors themselves is incomplete at best, and extremely harmful at worst. This is particularly true for Black, Latinx, Indigenous, queer and trans survivors who are rarely seen as 'real' victims by courts if they fight back, but are also killed at the highest rates when they do not fight back." Naming again the prosecution of Tracy McCarter, Rivers and Blackston argued that prosecutions against criminalized survivors should end, along with the criminalization of marginalized people more broadly.[58]

Blackston and Rivers argued that, rather than criminalizing survivors, the city should promote justice and safety by reducing the prosecutor's budget in favor of investment of noncarceral resources for victims of violence. Meanwhile, McCarter's S&P team was, week in and week out, living out their own understanding of community justice, through protests and court packing, organizing Twitter power hours, and the hard work of accountability and relationship-building within the group. This collective feeling of justice could come only through collaborative work—the "practice of abolitionist care."

5

People's Budgets

As bail funds, courtwatching groups, community defense campaigns, and participatory defense hubs grew in strength and number between 2015 and 2020, they increasingly expanded their organizing beyond the criminal courthouse. For example, as the Philadelphia Bail Fund entered its fourth year of operation, it began aiming to connect its bail payments, courtwatching, leadership development, and political advocacy to larger questions about how the city of Philadelphia promotes "community safety." In early 2022, fourteen Bail Fund members, a majority of whom were people previously bailed out by the fund, spread out to knock on doors and survey city residents about their thoughts and experiences with bail and with safety more broadly. They did not survey every neighborhood in the city. Instead, they hoped to target the neighborhoods that had been most impacted by money bail specifically, and the criminal system more broadly. Fred Ginyard, the Bail Fund's director of community organizing, explained to me, "Bailing folks out [is] not the end goal, [it's] the band-aid. If we're actually going to end cash bail in Philly . . . we had to intentionally create a space to support and develop leadership skills for directly impacted [people] and families, to create a . . . campaign based on their own experiences."

In order to figure out in which neighborhoods to conduct the survey, bail fund organizers worked with data scientists from the group Code for Philly to download daily criminal court dockets and analyze the relationship between cases where bail was paid and different zip codes in the city. They spent a year collecting and analyzing the data, which eventually showed that in 2021, of the more than $21 million that people in Philadelphia spent on cash bail, the burden of paying it fell disproportionately on just five of twenty-eight zip codes in the city. These five zip codes accounted for nearly a third of all bail paid in the city, and each zip code paid more than $1 million in bail over the course of the year. These neighborhoods, representing parts of North and West Philadelphia, are among the poorest in the city, with a federal poverty rate of between 30 percent and 41 percent. The bail statistics demonstrated how targeted policing and prosecution in neighborhoods of color enabled the court system to collect millions of dollars from the communities that could afford it the least.

Fred Ginyard explained that the bail fund entered the new survey project with a direct focus on working with people who were most directly affected by policing and prosecution. And so the Bail Fund organizers went door-to-door in these five zip codes, and ultimately collected survey results from 871 people. They asked about peoples' experiences with bail, and learned that 73 percent of survey-takers knew someone who'd had cash bail set in a criminal case; and a full 38 percent had themselves had a case in which bail was set. The survey questions also shifted beyond bail, asking, "What do you need to make your community safe?" and giving a series of possible choices. The number one answer to this question was "education & youth programs," followed by mental health and addiction recovery services, jobs and economic support, housing and food assistance, and community-based violence prevention programs. At the bottom of the list was cash bail, which only 17 percent of respondents believed makes communities safer.

The Philadelphia Bail Fund organizers collected this information into a report, "Ransom and Freedom: Ending Cash Bail in Philly," released in August 2022.[1] They also created an online portal where the public could view and analyze the raw data on bail scraped from the court system's website. And, going forward, the Bail Fund's goal would be to continue to make connections between the ways that cash bail extracts money from already poor communities of color, and the ways that the city itself chooses to spend, and not spend, its money keeping people safe.

In New York City, organizers participating in collective defense campaigns also began thinking about their advocacy in the context of the ways that the court system raises and spends its money. In 2020, a working group within Survived & Punished NY decided to focus its attention on learning more about budgeting within the Manhattan district attorney's office, with an eye toward making the budget a part of the upcoming elections for a new district attorney. This work felt in keeping with the group's central practice of organizing collective defense campaigns for criminalized survivors. For example, with the campaign for Tracy McCarter, a survivor of domestic violence being prosecuted for killing her estranged husband in self-defense, the Survived & Punished NY team began to think about how much money was being spent on prosecuting McCarter rather than on providing her and others with support and healing. The group found, through their research, that funding for the district attorney's office increased during the pandemic, including by a one-time allocation of $125 million from the city amid the 2020 uprisings, and by

$700 million a year from asset forfeiture funds—money and property collected as a result of law enforcement and prosecution. Survived & Punished NY's working group published a zine analyzing this budget, with an illustration depicting rolls of money going into a funnel, which fills a container marked "Prosecution, Prisons, Perpetual Trauma." Next to it, another container labeled "Healing, Justice, Community Safety" sits empty. The zine highlighted Tracy McCarter's story as an example of the harmful results of prosecutorial budgeting within just one county, connecting that one prosecution to a broader vision for how the city could be supporting survivors.[2]

In doing this work, the Philadelphia Bail Fund and Survived & Punished NY were following a deep history of movements connecting the geography of mass incarceration and criminalization to the way that the government spends its money. In 1979, for instance, the "Think Tank," a group of activist-intellectuals who were incarcerated in Green Haven Prison in New York State, began to theorize and study collectively the relationship between prisons, punishment, and the communities that they came from. Incarcerated thinker Larry White articulated an idea, generated amid prison rebellions in Attica, Auburn, and other state prisons in the early 1970s, that there was a relationship between state neglect in particular areas and the high numbers of people found in prison. Think Tank member Eddie Ellis had the idea to cross-reference census data with population information from other state agencies, leading the group to release in 1979 what became known as the "Seven Neighborhoods Study." This Think Tank study, generated with outside assistance from Dr. Kenneth Clark of *Brown v. Board of Education* fame, demonstrated that 75 percent of the people confined in the state prison system came from just seven primarily Black and Latinx neighborhoods in New York City.[3]

The Think Tank's proposed solution to the findings of the Seven Neighborhoods Study was to reallocate funds from the state's capital prison budget to education and economic development programs targeted at those seven neighborhoods. Led by five core incarcerated leaders—Larry White, Eddie Ellis, Cardell Shaird, Charles Gale, and Lawrence Hayes—the group spent the next fifteen years developing the idea that state underfunding and neglect of particular neighborhoods could not be separated from the money spent on, and isolation created by, prisons. At the same time, the Think Tank created educational programs and study groups inside state prisons that might push back against the abandonment experienced once people were released.[4] Eddie Ellis explained at a seminar at Green Haven in 1990, "When we look at the places to which we must return, we begin to realize that these communities have become so devastated with crime and drugs and violence, and mis-education, and a whole number of other things that leave precious little for us to return to. We understand that our futures are tied up with those communities." Once released, Eddie Ellis and others worked on state-wide initiatives to challenge prison construction and reallocate funding via alternative budgets.[5]

In New York State, a clear line of thinking and advocacy connects the Think Tank's work inside prison to later advocacy and research on both the geography of incarceration and the idea of divesting from the criminal system and investing in other forms of social supports. For example, in the mid-1990s Ellis himself was part of the Prison Moratorium Project's push to unite community-based organizations throughout the state to establish an "alternative budget," reallocating $900 million from prison construction to community-based resources and programs.[6] As scholars Omani Burton and Seema Saifee have each explored, the Think Tank's ideas were also the uncredited seeds of broader projects to develop the widely used concept of "million dollar blocks"—singular city blocks on which a prison system spends more than a million dollars to incarcerate people—as well as the concept of "Justice Reinvestment," which promotes shifting state spending away from prisons and toward other forms of preventing "crime."[7]

The work of the Think Tank is just one example of directly impacted people working together to analyze the relationship between the criminal system and the way that the state prioritizes its spending. The last fifty years have seen the growing use of local, state, and federal budgets as tools of analysis and organizing.

In 1992 in Los Angeles, for example, a negotiated gang truce led to a proposal for a "reconstruction" of Los Angeles, focusing in large part on its budgeting. The members of rival gangs focused not just on their actions toward each other, but also on how the city could do a better job of supporting the communities they were a part of. Their plan called for a $3.728 billion investment that would reconstruct the city through new infrastructure, health care, work programs, parks and recreation, as well as $700 million to transform the city's public schools. The Plan for Reconstruction demanded that these investments be accompanied by a reduction in policing and criminalization, and proposed a new patrol program in which former gang members, rather than police, would patrol their own neighborhoods. These demands were met with a promise: that, if the city acted immediately to move toward these goals, in return "the Bloods/Crips Organization will request the drug lords of Los Angeles . . . to stop drug traffic and get them to use the money constructively." The proposal famously ended with the words: "Give us the hammer and the nails, and we will rebuild the city."[8]

The city of Los Angeles did not change its budget in response to this document, nor did they decrease surveillance and criminalization (in fact, they did the opposite). But, as historian Elizabeth Hinton has documented, the generation of the budgetary document did change the outlook of those who worked collaboratively to create it. For much of their lives, their identities had been reduced to the labels of gang members and thugs—as of 1992, 47 percent of Black men and teenagers in Los Angeles were classified by law enforcement as gang members. After the negotiated truce, these organizers and former gang members developed new businesses, after-school programs, and job training and childcare services—only faltering when the city failed to follow through on its promises of investment in revitalization. Despite a lack of investment from the city, these groups developed gang intervention programs that continue successfully today.[9]

The 1990s saw other groups in California, such as Mothers Reclaiming Our Children, develop collective ideas about the relationship between austerity politics, criminalization, and violence. In writing about these fights, of which they were a part, Ruth Wilson Gilmore and Craig Gilmore speak of "the Budget as Battleground," meaning that, through budgetary fights, "the state is not only site and weapon, it is both adversary and, in a few corners at least, ally."[10] To make collective claims aimed at a budget—whether at the local, county, state, or federal level—allows a group to open up their demands beyond the criminal courthouse or the prison, to ask broader structural questions about where the state should concentrate its attention in the first place.

Using the budget as a battleground became a key organizing tactic throughout the United States as the Movement for Black Lives gained steam in 2014, 2015, and beyond. One of the key prongs of the Movement for Black Lives' first comprehensive policy platform, issued in 2016, was "Invest-Divest": "We demand investments in the education, health, and safety of Black people, instead of investments in the criminalizing, caging, and harming of Black people."[11] Organizing around this idea could be found throughout the country—from Atlanta to Baltimore, Orlando to Oakland, Houston to St. Louis, Durham to Chicago, Phoenix to Milwaukee, local groups made demands about their local budgets. Many coalitions connected their budgetary demands to the expansion of policing and criminalization, calling for the end to new jail construction or the removal of police from public schools.[12] State budget coalitions gained steam, too. In Minnesota, a state coalition brought a "United Black Legislative Agenda" to the statehouse, successfully advocating for investments in job training and development programs in 2016.[13] Maryland Communities United and Californians United for a Responsible Budget made similar pushes. As a 2017 report, written jointly by the Center for Popular Democracy, Law for Black Lives, and the Black Youth Project in collaboration with twenty-five community organizations, emphasized, in each place groups conducted their own research and concluded that "the choice to resource punitive systems instead of stabilizing and nourishing ones does not make communities safer."[14]

The influence of these decades of organizing around budget fights is clear both in the rise of the demand to "defund the police" in 2020 and in efforts such as the Philadelphia Bail Fund's 2022 survey on community safety or Survived & Punished NY's budgetary advocacy.[15] At least two threads of thinking continue from the Think Tank until now: one, that there is a direct connection between the political economy of the criminal system and the state neglect of poor, Black, and brown neighborhoods; and two, that including people directly affected by that devastation when generating data about these connections can help elucidate them. Mariame Kaba has said, "When I hear folks from the Movement for Black Lives . . . saying Invest/Divest, I smile because I know that that's Eddie

Ellis. And they don't know him, never met him. But he made it possible for us to think that thought, having learned it from somebody else before him."[16]

Budgeting for "Public Safety"

For a bail fund or courtwatching group, organizing around budget fights is an appealing way to extend their vision of justice beyond "criminal justice." Collective resistance inside of criminal courthouses is powerful, but it is in other government spaces—city halls, statehouses, and local legislative chambers—where these same groups can demand that their governments play a part in supporting forms of justice and safety that don't include punishment.

In particular, many groups have joined larger coalitions generating collective documents—"People's Budgets"—that bring together local community knowledge with large-scale thinking about government spending. In Nashville, ten organizations came together in the summer of 2020 to found a collective called the Nashville People's Budget Coalition.[17] One of the central organizations—Free Hearts—runs a local participatory defense hub; and another, Southerners on New Ground–Nashville, regularly engages in bailouts and courtwatch programs. With decades of organizing experience in their city, these groups came together quickly amid the protests following the deaths of George Floyd and Breonna Taylor. The Nashville People's Budget Coalition surveyed more than five thousand Nashville residents in the course of four days in June 2020, and released a report, "Invest/Divest: Building a Nashville People's Budget."[18] The report questioned the city's official budgetary category of "Public Safety," which allocated $362 million to the criminal system—well over the amount it budgeted for health care, social services, transit, and housing combined. Demanding a reversal of these trends, coalition members rallied and testified in city council in the summer of 2020; although the budget did not shift, the energy and attention paid to the way the city allocates money for "safety" did.

The Nashville People's Budget Coalition expanded its work in 2021, surveying nearly three thousand Nashville residents and conducting a series of monthly "People's Assemblies" around budget priorities. At People's Assemblies, a strategy developed over decades in places such as Lowndes County, Alabama, and Jackson, Mississippi, people come together collaboratively to debate and discuss local issues through a combination of small group discussions and larger debates.[19] The Nashville People's Budget Coalition also surveyed residents again, both online and through door-to-door canvassing. Coalition members asked residents, "What keeps your community safe?" in a few different ways. Despite what the organizers believe was a coordinated effort by police officers themselves to fill out the survey anonymously and choose maximum funding for the police, the results of the survey indicated that more than 80 percent of respondents would allocate less money to all three criminal system agencies than the city's current budget did. Survey-takers overwhelming wanted the city to reduce spending on policing and redirect that money toward affordable housing, infrastructure and transportation, non-police violence prevention and intervention, non-police first responders, property tax relief, social services, health and hospitals, parks, recreation, and libraries, metro arts commission, and education. Analyzing this data, Nashville People's Budget Coalition members wrote in a 2021 report, "The vision of 'public safety' undergirding Mayor Cooper's proposed budget is not the kind of public safety we deserve."[20]

The Nashville People's Budget Coalition was one of a growing set of groups coming together to organize around budgets in a holistic way. These coalitions looked not just at changing the criminal system or housing policy, but at the relationships between all forms of spending, much as the Think Tank and those involved in the Los Angeles gang truce had done decades before, and much as groups around the country had been doing with the Movement for Black Lives. They saw how organizers in Minneapolis used the energy from years of organizing around their state and local budgets to bring national attention to the demand to "defund" the police during the rebellion in the summer of 2020.[21] In Long Beach, California; in St. Louis, Missouri; in Lansing, Michigan; in Minneapolis, Minnesota; in Somerville, Massachusetts; and in Dallas, Chicago, and Los Angeles, 2020 and 2021 saw "People's Budgets" or "People's Plans" being developed and presented to local governing bodies.

In Dallas, Our City Our Future, a group founded in 2019 and led by women and gender non-conforming Dallasites, conducted community meetings in three districts to discuss the meaning of public safety for Dallas residents, and to ask how they might spend the $36 million that the Dallas Police Department was asking for in order to hire new officers. They collaborated on a 2020 Budget Report, demanding that the city rethink the 60 percent of its budget it devotes to so-called "Public Safety & Criminal Justice."[22] And in Chicago, facilitators from People's Budget Chicago spread out into thirteen neighborhoods to conduct "budget parties." In one exercise, participants gathered around a large, colorful game board and were asked collectively to distribute wooden tokens representing pieces of the city's budget into five categories. Facilitators recorded the results of these sessions: on average, most groups gave the most money to health, and the least to the carceral system.[23] The People's Budget Chicago used the ideas generated from playing the wooden board game, as well as the results of an online survey, to develop a people's budget in contrast to Chicago Mayor Lori Lightfoot's proposed budget, which increased police spending.[24]

In each case, these people's budgets pushed back not just against the relative distribution of money between the criminal system and non-carceral forms of support—housing, social services, education—but also against the budgetary categories that cities used to determine these distributions. This categorical fight was perhaps the clearest in Los Angeles. The People's Budget-LA coalition is a formation of more than fifty community-based organizations, many of which had been organizing around local and state budgeting for decades. These groups came together in 2020 to survey 24,426 people and engage 3,300 participants in a virtual town hall, from which they generated their detailed People's Budget.[25] The organizers asked residents how they would like to see the city's budget distributed, finding that participating residents wanted far less than the current 54 percent of city money spent on law enforcement, and far more of the budget dedicated to programs and infrastructure that promote stability and safety in other ways.[26] The People's Budget presented a new vision of categorizing city spending. Whereas the city's proposed budget gave 54 percent of its funds to law enforcement as "public safety," the People's Budget proposed that law enforcement spending be named just that—the budgetary category "law enforcement"—with only 1.65 percent of the budget, while a new category of "Reimagined Community Safety" would receive 25.06 percent of the budget, to be spent on preventing and addressing harm without the police through services such as restorative justice, mental health services, and violence prevention programs.

This proposed categorical shift drove home a choice

presented to the city council and the mayor in Los Angeles, whether to think of "public safety" as something that is only about policing, prosecution, and jails; or whether "public safety" was instead something that could be developed and protected in other ways, ways that the thousands of survey-takers were asking for. These were not merely abstract demands—the People's Budget listed a dozen possible models for violence prevention without policing, many of which had been subjected to rigorous studies that showed a reduction in incidents of gun use and violence.[27] And, as organizers were always quick to point out, keeping the police out of the equation reduces violence in other ways: the violence of police force, the violence of criminal courts, the violence of jails. There were also existing models right in their backyard: Los Angeles County had recently founded the Countywide Office of Violence Prevention, which works with community-based organizations on trauma-informed responses to violence and violence prevention programs.[28] And so, the choice was laid out to the city council in concrete and categorial terms.

Around the country, organizers from People's Budget coalitions brought similarly stark ideological choices into formal budget hearings and testimony. On June 1, 2021, dozens of members of the Nashville People's Budget Coalition testified at a city council hearing on their People's Budget. Many testified about the work of their own organizations to engage in violence prevention or provide after-school programs, many struggling to maintain programming with a limited budget. Gicola Lane, an organizer with Free Hearts and a participatory defense hub leader, described the work of Free Hearts and connected it to the demands of the People's Budget. She testified,

> We're organizing with families who go through the courthouse every day. Every day. We work on voting rights

> restoration. We're paying rent and providing utilities relief. We're bailing people out of these jails. We're going into juvenile [detention] and jails, helping with parenting classes and conflict resolution. We're building cooperatives. *None of which you all are helping us with. Not a dime.* . . . We are the people doing the work with the people who elected *you.*

Whether or not city budgets actually shift their funding in any given year, the groups that put together People's Budgets engage in public battles over ideas about local governance that would otherwise be taken for granted. Budgetary categories become engrained over time, their key words—safety, housing, education—standing in for an array of state functions. It has, until recently, almost always been the case that if a city council declares it will be funding an initiative for "safety," it will fund police programs, court reforms or court-based diversion programs, or improvements to local jails and other forms of surveillance. When movement activists create a new budgetary category, such as "Reimagined Community Safety," they are not just making a budgetary suggestion; they are presenting a contrasting ideological claim of how the government should go about providing safety and security. This claim takes on an additional dimension because it is being made by a group that is demanding inclusion, as the "people," in a system that they feel has excluded them. This collective idea of community safety can gain purchase even when it does not result in immediate budgetary changes—which was the case in 2020 in Nashville, Chicago, and Dallas.

In Los Angeles, for example, it's possible to trace rifts and changes in how the public thought about spending priorities after the first People's Budget presentation in 2020, which did lead the council to cut the Los Angeles Police Department budget by $150 million. Just three months after the first People's Budget presentation, a solid majority of Los Angeles residents voted for the passage of a referendum, "Measure J," which required that the city allocate 10 percent of future budgets to community investment and alternatives to incarceration that do not include law enforcement or courts.[29] For the 57 percent of Angelenos who voted for Measure J, the message that community public safety can lie outside of policing and prosecution had perhaps begun to sink in. Within a year, a federal lawsuit brought by county employee unions held Measure J unconstitutional; and then, in fall 2021, the city council vowed to allocate funding in a way consistent with the measure despite the lawsuit.[30] At the same time, the budget passed by the city council in 2021 *increased* police department funding. The budget had become a battleground.

The court dispute over Measure J illustrates the tremendous legal barriers that can prevent even successful initiatives to reduce local spending on policing. Many pre-existing state laws limit local government authority over their own budgets, whether by setting baselines for the funding of law enforcement or imposing duties on policing agencies. And new laws are proliferating. Since 2020, both Georgia and Texas have passed laws limiting the amounts by which cities can reduce their police budgets; and Florida passed a law providing for appeals and oversight of any reductions in local policing budgets. Federal government policy can also affect local spending on policing, through funding and other incentives to turn local governing priorities toward law enforcement.[31] With these legal and political barriers, organizers run up against the formal limits of community power. This means that People's Budget coalitions measure their success in slow, incremental work over time—work aimed at building power and shifting ideas just as much as at the budgets themselves.

Participatory defense hubs, courtwatching groups, and bail funds are often drawn to these collaborative budget fights because they take the alternative ideas of justice and safety out of the courthouse, thinking not just of the harms of criminal courts but also of new ways for the government to help people keep each other safe. Zohra Ahmed, a founder of Court Watch NYC, told me that engaging in organizing around budgets is a way to avoid the instinct to want to fix the courtrooms you spend hours sitting inside. Thinking about budgets "provide[s] for a wider conversation about what safety, security, health, looks like. [And] that's exciting, in the context of courtwatching, when you're narrowly tethered to court processes." Looking beyond criminal courts, perhaps the state *can* be a source of justice. This excitement builds when the work is done in the name of "the people," requiring us to take seriously the imaginations and demands of those most directly harmed by our carceral systems, especially Black, brown, and Native people: not because these budgets represent all people, but because they lay bare how the status quo privileges the ideas and input of only a subset of the demos, while excluding the ideas and opinions of the marginalized.

The Seattle Solidarity Budget

For much of the 2010s, the city of Seattle was a hotbed of organizing around local budgets. In 2012, for instance, a Seattle coalition formed to oppose the funding of a new youth jail in the city, working to stop a new tax levy for the new jail, as well as to push for a moratorium on new jail or courthouse construction. In July 2020, these organizers celebrated the city executive's announcement that the city would commit to closing the youth jail by 2025.[32] Local groups had also organized around other funding issues: for transportation, for climate infrastructure, for education, for services for the Indigenous Duwamish tribal community. When, in the summer of 2020, these groups came together to create one budgetary document—the Solidarity Budget—they had decades of knowledge and collaboration under their belt. Angélica Cházaro, a legal scholar and key organizer with the Solidarity Budget, explained, "We knew the answers, we had the reports. It was a question of bringing them together."

The Solidarity Budget coalition chose its name carefully. "People's Budget" was taken by a different local political group, and the organizers wanted a term that would symbolize how groups that had for decades been organizing around their own discrete issues would gather under one umbrella. The beginnings of the coalition developed via the groups Decriminalize Seattle and King County Equity Now, which presented a "Blueprint to Divestment" to the city council in July 2020.[33] The need to collaborate more broadly crystalized when Seattle mayor Jenny Durkan responded to movement pressure by making a promise to invest $100 million of the city's money in Black, Indigenous, and People of Color communities.[34] Organizers were dismayed to hear that the source of the $100 million would be, in part, a new revenue stream the city had previously promised would be spent on housing assistance, food vouchers, and other social services.[35] Suddenly, community-based organizations found that the promises of funding were pitting possible recipients of the money against each other. Cházaro remembers this frustration, and then the consensus that emerged by the end of summer 2020: "We're not going to allow them to play us against each other or fight with each other. Let's work together. That's where Solidarity Budget was born."

The Seattle Solidarity Budget coalition began by generating a "A Statement of Joint Principles," endorsed by more than seventy-five local community groups. The statement demanded that the city divest from policing and courts in favor of "invest[ing] in building self-determined, dignified, productive and ecologically sustainable livelihoods, democratic governance, and ecological resilience." Acknowledging the role of community-based organizations in budget battles, the coalition also made a commitment to "refuse to compete with each other for funding, when we know all our efforts are mutually reinforcing." They demanded that the city raise new revenue to meet the needs of the city during the pandemic and beyond. And, perhaps most centrally, they asked that the city involve people in marginalized neighborhoods in the budget process through expanding participatory budgeting—a process in which the government engages the public in generating budgeting priorities.[36]

Having experience with budget battles, the Solidarity Budget organizers were particularly wary of budget demands that simply asked for a movement of funds within an existing pie of money. They were aware of the history of "Justice Reinvestment" initiatives, for example, which in a number of states had reconfigured *how* money was spent on the criminal system, rather than diverting it *away* from the system and toward other forms of spending. Even when money is actually reallocated, a focus on saving money can feed into the austerity politics that promote limiting local budgets as much as possible, much like the "efficiency" mandates that lead to mass processing and plea bargaining.[37] On top of that, many cities use policing and local courts themselves as ways to generate revenue—through fines, fees, surcharges, and restitution in low-level tickets and misdemeanors; through civil asset forfeiture; and, of course, through bail and its associated fees. Reducing the footprint of the criminal system means that local, county, and state governments must find other ways to generate money.[38] As legal scholar Allegra McLeod has put it, "Meaningful decarceration will cost money."[39] The competition for the city's $100 million investment in communities of color in Seattle had brought this lesson home for organizers there. And so, part of the Solidarity Budget proposed revisions to the city's tax structure to make it more equitable and to generate more money for the city.

The Seattle Solidarity Budget coalition was thrilled when, in fall 2020, the city passed a budget that cut spending on police by $35 million and transferred some police functions, such as parking enforcement, to other city departments. In addition, the city council—over the mayor's veto—allocated $3 million to be used for community-led research around public safety. The money became the core funding for the Black Brilliance Research Project, a Black, queer-led group that originated within King County Equity Now and then became its own entity. LéTania Severe was a leading researcher with this project. A full-time firefighter with the Seattle Fire Department, Severe became involved when, during the COVID-19 lockdown in spring 2020, they attended a Zoom organizing meeting with King County Equity Now to see if they could find a way to volunteer during the pandemic. In addition to being a firefighter, Severe has a PhD in sociology and over a decade of data management experience. And so they joined the team, and, along with fellow researchers Shaun Glaze and Antonette Harmon, became a leader of the Black Brilliance Research Project.

Once the Black Brilliance Research Project secured the city funding, the work was on: a year-long process of training more than a hundred researchers, many of whom had no prior formal research training, and spanning out across the city to interview more than four thousand community members. The Project used a range of methods to collect information—from surveying thousands of residents, to conducting targeted focus groups, to creating storymaps, videos, and photographs depicting ideas about community safety. For each aspect of the research, the focus was on three main questions: "What creates true community safety? What creates true community health? And what do you need to thrive?" The researchers doing this work included youth, elders, people with criminal records, and people experiencing homelessness; over 70 percent were people of color. Severe explained that the Project looked for researchers who were representative of directly impacted neighborhoods because participatory research in targeted places helps get better, more holistic information: "If you're not living those experiences and being impacted by the things we're trying to change, then there's a lot of things you miss [in your research]. Having people who live that gets you better information."

In February 2021, the months of research culminated in a report of nearly 1,300 pages, submitted to the city council and released to the public via virtual teach-ins and podcasts. Bringing together themes from speaking with thousands of Seattle residents, the report called for the city of Seattle to invest in five general areas of service: housing and physical spaces, mental health, youth and children, economic development, and crises and wellness. In contrast to these buckets, the report concluded that "most people are not interested in continuing to invest in policing. They are interested in learning how to keep each other safe without police, coercion, or the threat of systemic violence and oppression."[40] Focusing on self-governance both inside and outside of city government, the budget called for $2.8 million to go toward Indigenous sovereignty, allowing the Duwamish Tribe to expand its own social, educational, health, and cultural programs. In addition, the report called for the continued growth of city-led participatory budgeting. LéTania Severe reflected on these experiences and demands: "We're in a stage of experimentation, and we have to try out all the different modes of self-governance and solidaristic community governance."

Throughout 2021, using analysis from the Black Brilliance Research Project report, the Solidarity Budget coalition created working groups that met regularly to develop detailed budgetary proposals in different areas—proposals that they could then bring together as one. Cházaro told me, "A city where policing is obsolete is also a city where everyone is housed, where we have a climate resilience plan, where Indigenous sovereignty is respected, where we have sidewalks in every neighborhood. Those fights are inextricable." A working group on municipal courts, for example, began to imagine how closing half of criminal courtrooms might open up funding for new diversion programs, which in turn could be run by community groups rather than the district attorney's office. Proposals such as this became part of the budgetary proposal generated collectively.

In September 2021, the coalition formally released its Solidarity Budget for the 2022 budget year. Now a coalition of more than two hundred community groups, the Seattle Solidarity Budget, as Cházaro explained, aimed to show that "there are two competing visions:" the budget proposed by the mayor, which largely stuck to existing budget priorities; and the one proposed by the Solidarity Budget, which broke down in detail the ways that the police budget could be reduced by 50 percent while money was instead invested in transportation, childcare, housing, and other initiatives—all via participatory budgeting processes.

In response, Seattle once again reduced its spending on its police department—the only major U.S. city to do so in both 2020 and 2021—and allocated hundreds of millions of dollars to new support and services outside of policing and courts, including restorative justice in schools and community safety initiatives outside of the system. The city also promised, and provided, $30 million in funding for an expanded, formal participatory budgeting process for future years.[41]

In these same months in the fall of 2021, Seattle experienced tremendous backlash against the Solidarity Budget from those resistant to reducing police funding. Backed by police unions, but also supported by some Democrats worried that reducing police presence would lead to more violence, this backlash was successful outside of the budget fight. Most prominently, Seattle elected a pro-police mayor, as well as a council member who explicitly ran on a platform opposing the Solidarity Budget. In supporting these candidates, the *Seattle Times* issued an editorial describing the Solidarity Budget as "an agenda of magical irrationality."[42] And Seattle was not the only large city electing a mayor who supported an increase to police funding in November 2021: New York City, Atlanta, and Buffalo all elected Democratic mayors who promised to resist calls to defund the police.[43]

The central success of Seattle's Solidarity Budget was not, then, necessarily to change the ideas of a majority of Democratic voters. Instead, it was slowly to begin to infuse new ideas about safety into the everyday work of the city, and the everyday consideration of voters, who now had to decide which vision they sided with. Just as important, the Solidarity Budget began to weave participatory research and an attention to directly impacted populations into the actual fabric of city governance: the city funded the Black Brilliance Research Project, it took seriously the detailed proposals of the Solidarity Budget, and it funded an increase in participatory budgeting in the years ahead.

A.J. Williams of Durham Beyond Policing is a lead organizer in a city where, as in Seattle, groups have pushed for participatory budgeting both within and outside formal channels.

Williams has said of these efforts, "We're dismantling the system while we're functioning in it."[44] Never able to declare a complete victory, these rising movements gained energy instead through the knowledge that it would be impossible to disentangle the power-building process of generating budgets from the budgets themselves.[45]

Budgets as Moral Documents

In the fall of 1965, civil rights leaders Bayard Rustin and A. Philip Randolph convened a group of activists, economists, and political scientists to put together a proposed federal budget to deliver to Congress, which they titled "A Freedom Budget for All Americans."[46] These leaders hoped to mobilize a cross-racial coalition around this detailed plan to fund a federal jobs guarantee, universal health care, public education, and a basic income—a "step-by-step plan for wiping out poverty in America during the next 10 years."[47]

Rustin and Randolph conceived of the Freedom Budget as a tool of organizing, a spark for mass struggle. Organizers gathered more than one hundred prominent endorsements, ranging from civil rights leaders to professors to labor leaders.[48] By 1968, they had distributed more than 100,000 copies of a twenty-page pamphlet summarizing the budget, with a foreword by Martin Luther King Jr. Rustin wrote a separate pamphlet for organizers, with strategies for creating study groups, events, and debates at college campuses around the country. One well-attended debate at UCLA pitted liberal economist Leon Keyserling against conservative Milton Friedman.[49]

The Freedom Budget was not as successful as its creators had hoped, even as an organizing tool. Its demands were never taken up in Congress, which instead headed in an increasingly conservative direction in both its rhetoric and its spending.

The Freedom Budget's underwhelming impact is likely due in part to criticism from the left of the budget's failure to call for a reduction in defense spending, at a time when war in Vietnam—and the anti-war movement—were ramping up.[50] (For that reason, neither the Student Non-Violent Coordinating Committee nor the Congress of Racial Equality endorsed the budget.) Randolph himself attributed the Freedom Budget's defeat to the rise of neoconservatism, what he described as the ascendancy of "the market economy" and the prizing of "profit [over] social justice."[51] As a result, the Freedom Budget is not remembered by many as a central aspect of the 1960s civil rights movement, and its impact pales in comparison to so many other collective actions that we celebrate today: sit-ins, freedom rides, boycotts, voting drives, the work of the Mississippi Democratic Freedom Party, the March on Washington.

But the Freedom Budget also showed how a budgetary document, when generated collectively, can make moral claims about the state. Indeed, it is sometimes cited as a source of the idea that a "budget is a moral document."[52] By calling itself the "Freedom Budget for All Americans," the document situated budgets as collective projects, something that should be "for all" in the context of a federal government that was budgeting for only the few. Thinking of "the people" in explicitly cross-racial terms, for example, Martin Luther King Jr. wrote in the forward to the budget: "We shall eliminate slums for Negroes when we destroy ghettos and build new cities for all."[53] The Freedom Budget was not on its face about "criminal justice" or "safety," but that is part of what is notable: it highlighted poverty and not a lack of policing or incarceration as the cause of harm, stating that "poverty and want breed crime, disease and social unrest." The complex budgetary document evokes both these big ideals and the concrete possibilities for attaining them. As Randolph wrote in the introduction to the budget,

"[The Freedom Budget] is not visionary or utopian. It is feasible. It is concrete. It is specific. It is quantitative. It talks dollars and cents. It sets goals and priorities. It tells how these can be achieved."[54]

Since the time of the Freedom Budget, the U.S. federal government has consistently increased its funding of local and state policing efforts, no matter the political leaning of the administration. Indeed, a steady stream of Democratic administrations—under Presidents Johnson, Carter, Clinton, Obama, and now Biden—turned to funding policing as part of larger pushes to combat poverty, disorder, and violence. Of particular note was the Violent Crime Control and Law Enforcement Act of 1994, also known as the '94 Crime Bill, which was signed by President Bill Clinton and authored, in part, by then-Senator Joe Biden. Among other provisions, the '94 Crime Bill allocated billions of dollars to states to build more prisons and hire 100,000 new police officers. It also established the Office of Community-Oriented Policing, which in years since has funneled tens of billions of dollars to local and state governments for policing initiatives.[55]

In the spirit of the Freedom Budget, national coalitions have not stopped pushing back against this form of spending in the name of safety. In late 2019, a national coalition of grassroots groups led by people who were formerly incarcerated, the People's Coalition for Safety and Freedom, took the twenty-fifth anniversary of the 1994 Crime Bill as an opportunity to present a vision of national legislation that could replace that much-maligned bill. The new legislation would require the federal government to reduce its spending on the criminal legal system and invest instead in health, education, housing, and infrastructure. The People's Coalition insisted that new national policies be generated by "join[ing] forces with the people most harmed by policing, criminalization and incarceration."[56]

The result is a call for a "People's Process," in which federal legislators would be required to conduct town halls, workshops, and peoples' assemblies on the impact of mass criminalization; hold in-district congressional hearings on the impact of the 1994 Crime Bill; and, ultimately, draft legislation based on the priorities of directly impacted people.[57]

These ideas gained steam in the summer of 2020, as the Movement for Black Lives proposed national legislation to divest from policing and invest in other forms of safety.[58] When President Biden's administration increased funding to local policing via federal grants and aid in 2021 and 2022, the People's Coalition went ahead with its own People's Processes, supporting town halls, workshops, surveys, and people's assemblies around the country in partnership with dozens of local grassroots groups.[59]

People's Budgets and other People's Processes present ways to participate in the justice system without participating in what we think of as "the justice system," without setting foot in a criminal courthouse. Part of the power of this tactic is that it reminds participants and, ideally, neighbors and elected officials that the problems of the criminal system are not just about what we do, but also about what we don't do. A group such as a community bail fund, which has experienced the day-to-day work of helping people within the criminal court system, is able to be a part of collectively articulating where the government's money, attention, and resources could be going instead. When the Philadelphia Bail Fund surveys people to ask for their ideas of safety, those people open their thinking to demands beyond "end cash bail." The demands expand beyond endings, to imagine new beginnings and ways to construct justice.

6

Practicing Justice and Safety

In mid-October of 2021—in the midst of a national health pandemic—the Boston Municipal Court announced a plan to address homelessness in Boston: the court would place an American flag inside a vacant room in the local county jail and declare the room to be a courtroom. In the new courtroom, officials would process the cases of people arrested after sweeps of a homeless encampment at the center of the city. Members of CourtWatch MA called this room simply "jail court." There were no judges inside jail court; instead, a television screen covering the sole window in the room showed a live feed of a judge inside one of Boston's actual criminal courthouses, seated at the front of a courtroom next to clerks and other personnel. The judge's screen showed the jail court, where each unhoused person sat, in handcuffs, at a small table next to lawyer, while a district attorney sat on the other side and two armed guards stood watch.

The sweeps were taking place in an area at the intersection of Massachusetts Avenue and Melnea Cass Boulevard—known as Mass and Cass—where dozens of people without permanent housing had set up tents and were living on a piece of land owned by the city. As a twenty-two-year-old regular of the area explained, "It's almost become a community within the city."

County Sheriff Steve Tompkins told a reporter, "We're looking to help the people who right now are on my doorstep, who are engaged in a humanitarian crisis."[1] The sheriff's claim was that by prosecuting people, the city would be able to connect those people to mandatory drug treatment or other resources, many of which were located inside the jail itself. The sheriff did not mention that his department was under a federal investigation for a string of deaths in the local jail—the same building in which the new courtroom would be placed. Four people had died in the sheriff's custody between July and September 2021 alone. At least one had been in withdrawal from drugs or alcohol when they died—a particular worry for many unhoused people who were living in the Mass and Cass area.

To Katy Naples-Mitchell, an organizer with CourtWatch MA, one of the most striking things about the jail court was the amount of official planning that went into it: multiple city and state agencies had come together to coordinate the best way to clear the Mass and Cass area. Naples-Mitchell told me, "They planned for months, and then they just built a special jail to process these poor and sick people. And then they called it humanitarianism!"

CourtWatch MA had for years been pushing back against the use of the city's criminal courts and jails to "solve" the problem of houselessness, and they had conducted courtwatching efforts after a series of similar sweeps of encampments in 2019. During the COVID-19 pandemic, CourtWatch MA had been working alongside the Massachusetts Bail Fund, the participatory defense group of Families for Justice as Healing, Black and Pink MA, and a score of other local groups to provide support and advocacy for people jailed or otherwise marginalized during the pandemic. These groups were horrified by the announcement of the jail court, but they had also developed an arsenal of tactics and relationships after years of collective action.

And so when the jail court opened on November 1, Court-Watch MA was ready. Because jail court took place inside a jail, at first the public could not go inside to watch. So court-watchers observed via a live Zoom feed, where they could see a video of the judge sitting in the actual criminal courthouse, as well as a video of the room inside the jail with the table and flag. The audio was garbled and uneven, but the courtwatchers could make out the basics. Eventually, the public was allowed to watch a video feed of proceedings from a room inside the jail.

Courtwatchers live-tweeted what they could see and hear. The first case was a man charged with misdemeanor drug possession, with open warrants from nearby counties related to other drug cases. The judge could have legally released the man to take care of his warrants, but the judge ordered him detained instead. CourtWatch MA wrote on Twitter, "This means he will most likely be held overnight to undergo painful, life-threatening withdrawal and be transported to [criminal court] tomorrow. This Court was created *to detain houseless people with substance use disorders* and don't let anyone tell you otherwise."[2] (Indeed, by the end of the day, the man had lost his place in a treatment facility and was sent to jail while in withdrawal.) The courtwatch tweeting continued for the next two cases, the only other ones that day. Officials had stated that this court would be reserved for people who were violent or created a public safety risk, but there was no mention of such risks in the court itself—instead, both sides spoke of drug charges, housing, and drug treatment. At the end of the day, the organizers summarized on Twitter, with their own emphasis: "2 of the 3 people arrested and prosecuted in the jail-court today created on Saturday to respond to an 'ongoing public health and humanitarian crisis' were SENT TO JAIL TO ENDURE FORCED WITHDRAWAL WITHOUT MEDICATION."[3] CourtWatch MA's Twitter account went on to link to articles and information about how tortuous, and sometimes deadly, drug withdrawal can be in a jail setting.

While courtwatchers observed and tweeted, outside of the jail building dozens of activists and organizers gathered with signs that said, "Stop the Sweeps" and "Close the Jail Court!" They chanted and protested as people entered and exited the building. The activists spoke to reporters who came to find out more about the new court. One group playing a leading role in the coalition, the Material Aid and Advocacy Program, had been organizing for years with people who were unhoused, and explained to reporters that the people who lived in the Mass and Cass encampment felt they had created a vibrant community and not a public safety hazard. The organizers voiced support for solutions to drug use and poverty that do not involve the police or criminal courts, such as the provision of clean water, affordable and accessible housing, safe consumption sites, and voluntary treatment or harm reduction programs. The advocates shared fears over the spread of COVID-19 in jails and crowded shelters. By the end of the first day, the experiences and stories from the courtwatchers, the Material Aid and Advocacy Program, the Massachusetts Bail Fund, and other coalition members began to make their way into the press and the public eye.

Energized and still angry, coalition members returned again the next day, using the same combination of strategies. The number of people protesting in solidarity with people being prosecuted grew each day. And the press continued to listen. When radio and local news reporters filed stories on the jail court, they declared it "controversial," or began their headlines with, "Despite criticism . . . ," and featured the quotes and stories of protesters outside, and the facts of cases inside that courtwatchers had shared. In the news, the jail court was a story of two contrasting ideas of how to approach housing insecurity and drug use during the pandemic—either criminalize it and force treatment using available space, even if that space is in a jail; or, in the alternative, allow people to stay in tents on public land while the state builds out more voluntary treatment, safe housing, and other forms of social support.

These conflicting understandings of health and safety were summed up by a sign held by one protester—and then included in news stories—which read, "A Tent Is Safer Than [Your] Jail." Janhavi Madabushi, the executive director of the Massachusetts Bail Fund, remembers feeling the power of groups coming together outside the jail to provide support in different ways. For the bail fund, this meant paying bail for some of the people who came through the jail court; but it also meant providing support and information in other ways: transportation and cell phones for people released, referrals to partners for those who needed services. Madabushi told me, "We were there every day, physically standing outside of jail court for every day it was open. And showing: you're not going to do this behind closed doors. We surfaced the atrocity: a targeted effort to surveil, incarcerate, and disappear our people." Through a combination of collective tactics, the coalition waged an ideological battle over the meaning of safety in the context of just one small, inaccessible room in the jailhouse.

And it worked: on November 19, 2021, the chief justice of Boston Municipal Court signed an order officially ending the jail court, just eighteen days after it had opened. During that time, the court heard only seventeen cases, and city officials pointed to that as the reason for its ending so soon after it started.[4] But coalition members experienced this as a victory:

they saw officials struggle to respond to reporters' questions, they watched the local district attorney try to backtrack on her support for the effort, and they felt that they had brought public attention to the relationship between houselessness and criminalization. More pointedly, these groups had exposed the hypocrisy of a liberal city's attempting a "humanitarian" approach to clearing a tent encampment while using the same old tools, and spaces, of the criminal system.

This is the work of such collective interventions in the criminal system: to help people while simultaneously holding out an alternative conception of what justice and safety can look like, one focused on the city providing housing, health care, and other support for people living in poverty. This battle of ideas cannot come just from protests. A sign saying "A Tent Is Safer Than [Your] Jail" articulates the ideological fight, but a public conversation about the meanings of justice and safety happens only when there has been collective action around the ideas over time. Had the broad coalition that included the Material Aid and Advocacy Program, CourtWatch MA, and the Massachusetts Bail Fund not already been in community together, they would not have been ready to branch out into their complementary tactics to counter what would otherwise have been an uncontroversial story of a new, humanitarian approach to clearing tents and people from public land. The organizers used the laws and tools of the system—the constitutional right to open courtrooms, the statutory right to post bail—to express how, to them, sticking an American flag inside of a jail does not make it a legitimate space of justice. The organizers worked within the rules of the system to put forth a collective idea of justice that cannot be reconciled with the dominant story the system tells itself.[5]

In this way, tactics such as bail funds and courtwatching are forms of collective *legal* thought, or "demosprudence."[6] When people reclaim legal language or concepts, they join in collective contestation of ideas that are integral to the legitimacy, and therefore the existence, of the criminal system and the statutes and practices that give it concrete power. No one tactic disables the system—in Boston, the end of the jail court did not signal the end of the criminalization of poverty, just of one tool of it. But the fight over the jail court did build power and organizing capacity in relation to the criminal system, dealing a blow to its ideas of justice and safety as much as to its methods of criminalization.

In the Interests of Justice

One indication of a genuine battle over legal ideology is when officials within the system are forced to name—and dismiss—new legal understandings that call into question the dominant ideas of justice and safety. This happened, for instance, in Tracy McCarter's homicide case, discussed in chapter 4, in which McCarter was charged with killing her estranged husband as he attacked her. In that case, the work of McCarter's collective defense campaign from Survived & Punished NY, as well as the swell of public support the campaign generated, made its way into a judge's decision on a motion to dismiss McCarter's case "in the interests of justice." In New York, the state criminal procedure law allows for such a dismissal when any number of ten factors are met, including "the impact of a dismissal upon the confidence of the public in the criminal justice system."[7] Although "evidence of guilt" in the case is relevant, it is merely one reason upon which a dismissal in the interest of justice can rest. Tracy McCarter certainly had plenty of evidence supporting the fact that she acted in self-defense. But much of the motion to dismiss from the defense focused instead on her life, her character, and the public support for her case.

At the time, in August 2022, Judge Diane Kiesel was already well aware of the public support for McCarter. At every single court date, for over two years, members of McCarter's Survived & Punished NY team and other supporters were in the audience—at first virtually, and then physically, many wearing red shirts that displayed McCarter's silhouette and said "Stand with Tracy." In recent months, over sixty organizations, institutions, and individuals had signed a public letter asking that McCarter's case be dismissed—including some victim's advocacy groups, such as Safe Horizon, that had historically acted in support of prosecutions in domestic violence cases. There was an additional letter of support from a collection of victim's and gender rights groups, and a letter from dozens of faith leaders that called McCarter's prosecution "the opposite of justice." And newspapers continued to cover the case from a critical angle, asking in particular why District Attorney Alvin Bragg was prosecuting the case despite having voiced support for McCarter on the campaign trail. Notably, Bragg's office also filed a motion to dismiss McCarter's murder charge in the interest of justice, although the district attorney's motion was a half-hearted one, using just one double-spaced page to make the argument to dismiss, and also asking that his office be able to charge her with the lower offense of manslaughter.[8]

Judge Kiesel denied the motion to dismiss McCarter's indictment in the interests of justice. But, as she did so, she was forced to reckon with the public support indicating that a significant number of people in the community—individuals, organizations, and faith leaders—believed that the interests of justice pointed to dismissal. In her written opinion, Judge Kiesel acknowledged this extensive public support for McCarter, and then proceeded to brush it off. The judge wrote that "public confidence," which is one factor that can lead to dismissal, was better served through a trial than a dismissal, because "public opinion, notoriously fickle, should not be mistaken for public confidence." She continued, "The defendant may indeed be a survivor, and her late husband may indeed have been a vicious, violent, and threatening man. If so, the trial will bear that out."[9]

Judge Kiesel's opinion was illogical and possibly disingenuous—after all, if the public's observation and opinions of a case do not matter, then the procedural rule would not explicitly list public confidence as a factor in the required analysis. The judge also cited two cases about the importance of having the public inside the courtroom—cases whose ideas would tend to support rather than undermine the legal importance of McCarter's supporters' appearing in court. The weak legal gymnastics of the judge in McCarter's case illustrated that, despite statutes and constitutional mandates requiring otherwise, the criminal system is not capable of limiting itself. Instead, Kiesel's opinion used the abstract idea of the "public" watching a hypothetical trial to reinforce the system's assumption that "justice" always requires prosecution and punishment, in the face of evidence—evidence sitting in her courtroom—that this is far from a universal sentiment. The judge gave no affirmative reason that this prosecution might further justice; she simply assumed it to be true.[10]

The motion to dismiss failed, but something powerful happened: the judge was forced to parse out the meaning of "justice" in the context of a visible and undeniable swell of support for McCarter. This support connected McCarter's prosecution to larger ideas: that Black women are too often the targets of criminalization; that the criminal system is not the best way to contend with trauma and harm; that prosecution and criminalization use resources that could be better spent on preventing domestic violence and supporting survivors. When the judge handed down her decision, there was more press coverage on that court date than ever before.[11] And so, despite the temporary legal loss, the work of McCarter's collective defense team as the case moved toward a possible trial was to continue, relentlessly, to connect McCarter's case to larger ideas about justice, and injustice, in criminal court.

When Judge Kiesel eventually dismissed the murder indictment against McCarter in December 2022, she did so reluctantly and with clear disdain for McCarter's collective defense. Emphasizing that the dismissal was still not within her understanding of "the interests of justice," the judge wrote, "The law must not apportion justice according to the size of one's advocacy group or the savviness of a media campaign." It was the act of dismissal, rather than the words of the court, that revealed the strength of the collective defense campaign.[12] Within a system committed to upholding itself, it is communal pressure such as that brought by Survived & Punished NY that can help the public see competing ideas of justice, and competing understandings of the will of "the people," even when the system doubles down on its circular justifications for its own existence.

Sometimes judges do adopt new understandings of who constitutes "the people." This happened, for instance, when in 2020 the American Civil Liberties Union of Pennsylvania and partner firms and organizations filed a federal class-action lawsuit on behalf of people incarcerated in unsanitary conditions in Philadelphia's city jail during the COVID-19 pandemic. Over the objections of the city's lawyers, the federal court designated Philadelphia's two bail funds, the Philadelphia Community Bail Fund and the Philadelphia Bail Fund, as the recipients of monetary fines that the city was required to pay to the court system because it was not complying with an order to reduce the jail population.[13] Neither bail fund was a party in the lawsuit; instead, they became stand-ins for representatives of communities affected by overincarceration. The fact that they could also literally pay bail made it come full circle: if the city was not going to protect people in the context of a bail statute meant to protect public safety, then the court system would give money to bail funds as representatives of the people, providing an alternative form of safety—the safety of freedom.

Explicit debate over the relationship between community bail funds and public safety has made its way into state legislative hearings and testimony too. In Kentucky, where a bill to ban bail funds outright was subject to debate, amendment, and ultimately failure, some state legislators in support of the ban painted a picture of bail funds as rogue groups or "cartels" that free people against the will of the system—an echo of the "fickle" public that the judge in Tracy McCarter's case described. In a 2022 debate on the Kentucky House floor, one representative, Jason Nemes, argued that only judges or the family of an accused should set or pay bail: "When you remove that human judgement . . . that doesn't comport with public safety."[14] At a Kentucky House Judiciary Committee hearing, organizers from both the Bail Project and the Louisville Community Bail Fund underscored the opposite view in public testimony. Carrie Cole, an operations manager from the Bail Project, described the organization's work as "designed to enhance the public safety . . . not undermine it;" and Chanelle Helm from the Louisville Community Bail Fund highlighted the work that the Bail Fund does in addition to freeing people: creating a grocery store in a food desert, buying an abandoned church to create a community center, helping connect people to emergency housing.[15] Taken together, bail fund testimony drew a different picture of "personal, human connection," a collective form of taking care of others and promoting safety in ways that the state neglects to do. The Kentucky bill did not pass, but similar efforts to limit the work of bail funds have succeeded in Indiana, Texas, and elsewhere. And, in each instance, the legislative debates were anchored by contrasting understandings of the relationship between public safety and the collective work of bail funds.

In Minnesota, a legislative debate over anti–bail fund legislation even took on religious undertones. The state legislature's attention in 2021 and 2022 was especially focused on trying to limit the work of the Minnesota Freedom Fund, which served as a national flashpoint during and after the 2020 uprisings. In both years, state legislators introduced a series of bills, some to regulate bail funds tightly, and some to allow for lawsuits against bail funds. In May 2021, one Minnesota state senator, Jennifer McEwan, speaking in opposition to the bills and in support of bail funds, stated on the Senate floor, "The Minnesota Freedom Fund is doing God's work . . . and I thank them." In response, another state senator, Andrew Mathews, countered in his own speech that bail funds "cause more crimes, and cause more harm in our community. If that's God's work, that's not the God of the Bible."[16]

Public disagreement over the meanings of "safety" and "justice" crystalizes in debates over "People's Budgets" generated by coalitions of groups in cities throughout the United States. Over three hours of public comments at a Nashville City Council budget hearing in 2021, each speaker began by clarifying whether they supported the budget of the mayor or that of the people. City council members in Los Angeles had to determine whether they would categorize "Public Safety" spending as going to jails and courts, or to mental health and wellness, restorative justice, and community empowerment initiatives. And in Seattle, these battle lines—Solidarity Budget or mayor's budget—became part of election campaigns and debates. These opposing ideas could not be reconciled, even if a complex budget can be.

In these public debates over legal concepts—the interests of "justice," the meaning of a budget for "public safety," and even the place of God in these laws and policies—there is no attempt at compromise. Some of the legislative fixes contain compromises, to be sure, such as a bill limiting bail fund actions to misdemeanor cases, or a complex budget that slightly reduces police funding in favor of public health initiatives. But the battle of ideas is uncompromisingly adversarial, whether inside or outside a courtroom—a collective push to reclaim the ideas of justice and safety that the system depends on for survival.

A New Source of Expertise

Another way in which these tactics chip away at the system's ideological foundations is by challenging the generation of expertise and data that the system uses to measure its progress. When the Black Brilliance Project in Seattle centers the generation of knowledge through complex participatory research processes that are conducted by directly impacted people, or when the Chicago Community Bond Fund helps collect missing data on how the criminal court's policies are playing out, they reset the terrain of the debate while filling in gaps in the public's knowledge. Conventional experts often come to parallel conclusions as these groups: for example, public health experts implore governments to stop relying on the criminal system to address harm and safety;[17] and sociologists and political scientists demonstrate how the criminal system harms entire neighborhoods and populations.[18] But decentering expertise away from ivory towers and think tanks also undermines the traditional hold that elites have over the criminal system and its understandings of truth and data.

In Fresno, California, participatory defense hub member

Marcel Woodruff has literally made this happen by testifying as a legal "expert" in court. In California, as in most criminal courts, testifying as an expert requires meeting technical legal requirements that are sometimes difficult to prove, including "special knowledge, skill, experience, training, or education."[19] These requirements are met routinely by police officers, medical examiners, and academics. Marcel Woodruff's "expertise," though backed up by a master's degree, centers around his personal experiences in a gang, doing violence prevention work, and engaging in participatory defense.

Woodruff, a native of Fresno, was in a gang from the age of eleven until he graduated from high school, as the valedictorian of his class. Woodruff's father was incarcerated on and off for much of his childhood, and Woodruff remembers that joining a gang felt like a requirement for survival, and, at times, an important source of support. After college in New Orleans, having broken all formal gang ties, Woodruff returned to Fresno and became involved in gang prevention and intervention work, including going into prisons to run workshops with incarcerated former gang members. As he repeatedly saw people given long sentences or having parole denied because of supposed gang involvement, he found himself asking, "What is the systemic role in perpetuating violence?" Woodruff then obtained a master's degree in divinity from Fresno Pacific University and began working with Advance Peace Fresno, a program engaged in violence prevention without the use of the police. It was around that time, in 2018, that Woodruff was part of a core group that started a participatory defense hub in affiliation with an organization called Faith in the Valley.

In 2019, Woodruff first began to take the witness stand as an official expert in the active cases of participatory defense hub members. Woodruff's testimony usually comes during hearings to determine whether a court will transfer the case of a young person charged as a juvenile into adult court, where they are subject to the same criminal records and punishments as an adult. Under California law, gang membership plays a formal role in charging and sentencing practice—if a judge finds that a felony was done "for the benefit of, at the direction of, or in association with any criminal street gang," the sentence can increase by decades.[20] And so Woodruff's expertise held legal import: being able to explain that a young person's gang involvement should not mean that what they do is done for the benefit of that gang, has life-altering significance.

Woodruff sees one essential insight of his form of legal expertise as bringing out the humanity in people who are labeled as criminals and gang members, categories that erase their membership in a broader community. These labels then make their way into the state's sentencing statutes and come to seem obvious: if someone has ever been in a gang, then surely they must deserve a long sentence in prison. In one case, for example, Woodruff testified how a seventeen-year-old's gang involvement stemmed from safety and survival needs, a membership "inherited" from his father and uncles rather than joined by choice. Once in the gang, membership "served as a vehicle to keep him and his siblings safe considering family history," and the young man spent most of his time with his girlfriend or playing sports or video games.[21] After Woodruff's formal "expert opinion" that this young person was not an active threat and had the potential to be integrated into a non-gang lifestyle, the judge determined that the case would not be transferred to adult court. Other participatory defense hubs have also brought members into courtrooms to testify as "experts" on gang involvement,[22] and Woodruff has conducted trainings for the National Participatory Defense Network on the tactic.

Like Woodruff and these participatory defense hubs, activists engaged in bail funds, courtwatching, and People's Budgets are also laying collective claims over the generation of expertise: by becoming the groups engaging in detailed research and analysis around budgets; by issuing reports about courtroom cases and outcomes when the system won't; by explaining to the public how courtrooms and sentencings work amid an otherwise opaque system. Some organizers, like Woodruff, do have advanced degrees or other traditional indicia of expertise. Or sometimes, the generation of data is done in collaboration with people with traditional elite credentials, such as lawyers or professors.[23] But it is the collectives that decide what to study and how to define and measure concepts such as safety and security. Black feminist theory, as well as various forms of critical legal scholarship, has long explored the relationship between the generation of knowledge and the legitimacy of the status quo, showing how claims of expertise *within* systems can raise existential questions about the systems themselves.[24] This is especially powerful within the criminal system, which isolates individuals and, by extension, entire neighborhoods and communities from the analysis of what "works" and what doesn't when it comes to keeping people safe.[25]

The work of these groups suggests that rather than looking for expertise only from social scientists or veterans on the police force, the people with expertise on what justice should be also include people who are subject to the domination of the criminal system on a regular basis.[26] Those who are harmed or neglected by the system, especially if they are members of racially or economically subordinated groups, can bring us knowledge that is missing, knowledge that is based on wisdom and experience but is just as real and true as the "facts" generated by the system itself.[27] And they generate this knowledge while demanding that we change the questions we're asking:

Do we measure safety by asking who has been arrested—often casually referred to as "crime rates"—or do we measure it by how people in particular neighborhoods feel about their own safety? Do we ask if justice has been served by thinking about whether an individual person has been appropriately punished, or do we ask if the state is working toward creating the conditions where people will harm each other less? To change the questions in this way begins to pull the rug out from under the system's foundations—explaining, perhaps, why the system is so resistant to these tactics in the first place.[28]

When a court qualifies someone such as Woodruff as an expert, he is able to use his formal qualifications—degrees and work experience—to bring collective ideas about gang membership and public safety into the courtroom. Along with this comes a concept of justice that clashes with the very idea of punishing people when they harm others. When I ask Woodruff to define "justice," he asks back, "How do you talk about justice without going backwards?" and illustrates what he means with an example from Faith in the Valley's hub:

> We have a guy we work with who watched his father get killed when he was in elementary school—he saw his father gunned down in the car, killed right in front of him. So, if you're eight years old, [then] ten years later, what happens? . . . you're eighteen, you're mad, so you go on a shooting spree. On one end, justice is: You went on a shooting spree, you shot four people, give you the chair. And at the other end, justice is: damn, we need to create a system that invests in the health and wellness and the healing of this eight-year-old child who saw his father killed. And beyond that, is: what are the conditions that created the environment where the father got killed? So,

justice looks backwards and says: where did that initial harm begin, and how do we restore, repair, and realign that.

This form of justice is no small task. But, for Woodruff, it happens in increments. In the courtroom, Woodruff testifies as to how past circumstances shape behavior that many want to punish. In Fresno's city budget meetings, Woodruff and his co-organizers demand funding for violence prevention programs. And in their participatory defense hub, they show each other what can be possible by looking out for each other. As Woodruff explains, "We can reimagine a new and different way of belonging and existing together that doesn't rely on dominance, exploitation, and oppression. . . . but it has to happen in ways that are digestible, which makes it incremental."

Part of what can make these incremental interventions disruptive is that they are collective, and so their lessons simply do not fit into the traditional calculus of individual rights and procedures. In a criminal courthouse, "justice" is dispensed in the form of punishment, at the direction of prosecutors and judges, as well as of the police officers who make arrests that generate prosecutions. This justice is well funded, at the expense of other forms of state support, and it cannot be separated from histories of racism and white supremacy in the United States.[29] It is also an understanding of justice that focuses on individuals: the mission of "criminal justice" is to figure out whether any one individual standing before the court is guilty or not, dangerous or not, worthy of freedom or not. If a court or legislature invokes the "public" or the "community," it is to protect an abstract collective from the threatening individual in handcuffs. This cuts off broader questioning of the structure of the system; as legal scholar Amna Akbar explains: "The blame is placed on individuals and groups, but never structures; the social, economic, and political landscape that renders particular identities as criminal is never implicated."[30]

When movement actors come together to bail someone out, to observe courtroom proceedings, or to create a video for their sentencing hearing, they enter the carceral space of the courtroom as a collective, as the community. The public becomes a concrete presence in contrast to the aggregated labels of "criminals" or "gangs." And the ideas generated by that public cannot be siloed into just one criminal case. This is true for the people engaging in the tactics themselves, who inevitably understand what they see and do from a collective perspective, especially when watching or intervening in multiple criminal cases over days, months, and years. Courtwatchers in Baton Rouge, Louisiana, for example, find themselves wondering about the policing practices that led to people's being in handcuffs before them, fined for failure to wear a seatbelt, charged with criminal abuse because a child did not go to school, or sent to jail despite a clearly visible mental disability. Rev. Alexis Anderson, co-founder of Court Watch Baton Rouge, explained to me that as she sits in court observing dozens of cases in a row, she feels emotionally connected to the people being prosecuted, but also finds her mind spinning, thinking about how the impact of what she's seeing reverberates within her largely poor and working-class Black community. Sitting in court with fellow courtwatchers, Rev. Anderson began to think, "It's not about the individual cases, and it's not about public safety. It's an economic system." As she thought about the state actors in the courtroom—lawyers, judges, clerks—she realized, "There are a lot of people invested in keeping the system exactly as it is."

Janhavi Madabushi, executive director of the Massachusetts Bail Fund, explained the development of this collective analysis in the bail fund's experience: "The ways that the bail fund has interacted with the system help us realize new things, because we are in the day-to-day work of bailing people—real-life humans—whose ransom we are paying. So it helps us see the individual ways that people experience carcerality. And then we see the ideologies that drive it, and then we see the cultures that drive it." As this collective analysis develops, the problem expands beyond just mass incarceration to include mass criminalization, an inevitable result of the institutions that we have created when we choose to "govern through crime."[31] And the solutions to this broader problem require new forms of ideation, measurement, and collectivity.

The Fuel for Everything

By all accounts, the American public's faith in the criminal system is as low as ever. A Gallup poll released in July 2022 shows that Americans have the lowest confidence in the "criminal justice system" in at least three decades—down to 14 percent of respondents who said they have a "great deal" or "quite a lot" of confidence in the institution. An August 2022 Pew Research Poll confirmed that this lack of confidence is especially high for Black people.[32] Institutional actors who work within criminal courts and state legislatures are well aware of this. But, in trying to renew confidence, their instinct is usually to double down on the existing ideas and stories about justice in the guise of something new. This is how, in places such as Boston, officials search for "humanitarianism" by creating a court within a jail rather than creating other kinds of structures of safety or justice.

It is through collective work to help each other within the system's existing rules that groups of people are able to live out other understandings of justice, ones that call into question the very existence of the system. Raj Jayadev of Silicon Valley De-bug explained to me the feeling of engaging in collective resistance on behalf of others this way: "It gives you a sense of faith or confidence that your imagination can go into places that you weren't initially conceiving. And get there."

These are not fleeting moments of faith. During one conversation that I had with Jayadev in November 2021, he told me that just that morning, De-bug's participatory defense hub, the Albert Cobarrubias Justice Project, had gathered in criminal court in San Jose. The hub members were supporting Barrett, a hub member and video artist who was living on an ankle monitor pending sentencing for a felony involving a car accident. The morning of the day that Jayadev and I spoke, Barrett was scheduled to appear in court and "step in" for a forty-five-day jail sentence. Weeks earlier, Barrett's experienced attorney had told hub members that there was no chance of a sentence other than jail time; rather than advocate for an alternative to incarceration, the hub should prepare to support Barrett on the inside.

But the De-bug hub members had learned, over twenty years, that seasoned system players, even well-meaning defense attorneys, can often underestimate the power of the collective work of participatory defense. And so the hub pushed forward in Barrett's case, creating a binder that included written testimony about Barrett's community connections and letters from doctors stressing that Barrett had acute medical needs that would make jail an especially devastating place for him during the COVID-19 pandemic. When the hub members arrived in court for Barrett's sentencing, the judge had been in possession of the binder for a few weeks, and it had clearly had an effect on both the defense attorney and the judge. As Jayadev told me, "Just this morning . . . the defender changed his tone. Then made the argument. Then won the argument. And no more jail time." Jayadev was not surprised, but he was elated. Barrett's sentencing is just one relatively small case in over twenty years of organizing at Silicon Valley De-bug. But each time that someone's fate changes because of a communal act in a courtroom, it is newly energizing.

Practices such as this are sometimes described as *prefigurative* because people are working communally to live out on a small scale a vision of a society that does not yet exist. By acting out and experiencing alternative forms of justice, these groups are showing that they are possible. Reflecting on the win in Barrett's case, Jayadev told me, "That is the fuel for everything, this sense of hope, this sense of anything's possible. [That's] the only thing, the only way we move."[33]

Again and again, people taking part in participatory defense hubs, bail funds, People's Budgets, or other collective tactics of resistance find that their collective visions of what is possible conflict with even the most well-meaning institutional actors. Sharlyn Grace, former executive director of the Chicago Community Bond Fund, has reflected on how, when the bond fund first worked to form a coalition to abolish money bond in Illinois, most advocates for bail reform scoffed at the idea of demanding that the state fully abolish money bail. The Coalition to End Money Bond pushed forward anyway. They put pressure on local judges in Chicago to implement a new procedural rule in the face of a civil rights lawsuit around money bail. They trained courtwatchers to document the effects of the rule, which forbid judges from setting money bond beyond what someone could afford, to make sure that the rule led to decarceration. They pushed for, but did not get, a similar state court rule. All along, the Bond Fund continued to post bond for hundreds of people each year. And the coalition combined these tactics with lobbying days, with litigation, with protests. At each moment, this constellation of groups worked to further public consciousness of how money bond was impacting their communities.

In 2021, only five years after the launch of the coalition, the

Illinois state legislature passed a law eliminating money bail in the state. Grace has written of this five-year turnaround, "If there is one overarching lesson in what we accomplished in Illinois, it is this: Attorneys and other professional advocates must take seriously the 'unrealistic' goals of organizers and work in partnership to achieve them."[34]

We have underestimated social movement visions before. The ideas behind the U.S. civil rights movement of the mid-twentieth century, although recognized now by many as transformative, were not especially popular during the 1960s. More than 60 percent of Americans held unfavorable opinions of the March on Washington, and less than 30 percent approved of sit-ins as a means of change.[35] If we look back at the civil rights movement fondly, as bringing forth an optimistic set of ideas about justice and equality, then we are likely forgetting the radical strains of the movement that were rattling the basic structures of American society and turning people off in the process. When we do so, we miss out on transformative ideas that might help us now—more than that, we suppress the power of those ideas and the collectives who gave them to us. As Robin D.G. Kelley has written, "Too often our standards for evaluating social movements pivot around whether they 'succeeded' in realizing their visions rather than on the merits or power of the visions themselves." The best of these visions "do what great poetry always does: transport us to another place, compel us to relive horrors, and, more importantly, enable us to imagine a new society."[36]

In seeking out these visions, we cannot look at the words of movement leaders alone, for those words can too easily be packaged as simplified rhetoric that elides their deeper critiques. Similarly, if we look at collective actions as merely a series of tactics, we fail to see the bigger possibilities behind those actions. We miss their performative power. Martin

Luther King Jr.'s famous phrase (borrowed in part from minister Theodore Parker) that "the arc of the moral universe is long, but it bends towards justice," when taken out of context, can become a simple sound bite, encouraging complacency rather than action. And the meaning of this phrase depends almost entirely on how you define "justice."[37] The actions of the groups within which King organized and struggled show us fairly radical ideas about what justice might mean—such as universal employment and a living wage for all, to take just one example.[38] More important, King's ideas did not come from personal reflection, but from engaging in collective struggle, often in groups led by Black women such as Ella Baker, Diane Nash, and so many more.[39] When transformative thinkers and organizers harness the radical visions of the past today, they do so not just by reading words but also by looking at how groups of people engaged in acts in which they lived out new ideas about justice, equality, and freedom.

Similarly, as Elizabeth Hinton has shown in her history of Black rebellions from the 1960s through today, large-scale acts that were labeled as dangerous "riots" were in fact a broader, collective response to widespread racial violence and structural neglect by the state. Whether it was the small town of Cairo, Illinois, in the late 1960s and early 1970s, or the large city of Miami, Florida, in the 1980s, Black residents rebelled against police violence as a tangible representation of the wider violence visited upon their neighborhoods by state disinvestment from other forms of support. As with any tactic, it is not that a riot, a sit-in, or a protest is inherently radical, but, contextually, a riot becomes a rebellion when people act out collective understandings that push back against existing power relationships. What is seen as disorder, as destruction, can also bring forth a profound set of collective ideas to help us understand where we have gone wrong and how we might find a way out.[40]

This is true, too, of the work of groups engaged in mutual aid outside of the state, who turn actions that might otherwise be thought of as charity into forms of communal care and solidarity that help us imagine other ways of relating to each other.[41]

Much like a single rebellion or mutual aid project, the day-to-day work of the tactics described in this book may not seem big: to survey a handful of neighbors about their definition of public safety, or to sit around a table dissecting police reports in one misdemeanor case. And they may feel arbitrary and disruptive in comparison to the uniform daily grind of the criminal system in most courthouses. But these small moments, using the tools of the system, repeated over and over, swell to something bigger, with the potential to transform our collective understanding of where to locate justice and safety.

Prosecutors, private bail bondsmen, and other opponents of community bail funds often share a common refrain: that bail funds are a problem because they leave a person who is freed without "skin in the game." The ostensible worry behind this phrase is that, when the "community" rather than a family member posts bail, an accused person with an open criminal case will not be incentivized to come back to court out of fear that the money will be forfeited. Within the logic of existing legal procedures—within the game of the criminal system—this argument makes some sense: if requiring money in exchange for freedom is a fair and rational way to make sure that people come back to court, then the process is disrupted when a bail fund pays instead. Indeed, prosecutors have had some limited success in making "skin in the game" arguments in court to prevent bail funds or collectives from posting bail.

Community bail funds, though, are using the existing procedures of the criminal system to play a different game. It is not a game just about individual players and the need to treat them fairly or provide the correct incentives. Instead, it is a game about large-scale collective relationships, in which people do their best to take care of each other while trying to push the state to provide support systems in ways other than the criminal system. The criminal system retaliates with vigor against bail funds not just because they free people, but because in doing so they require the system to explain itself and its idea of justice in the face of an alternative. Community bail funds are putting a lot of skin in *this* game, and the people whom they free are too. We cannot underestimate the movement visions that emerge from these experiences, if for no other reason than because these visions are *possible*. They are the fuel for everything.

Afterword

This is a book about the transformation of collective thought through collective action, told through the experiences of individuals. Some organizers whom I interviewed for this book describe themselves as abolitionists, people who believe that prisons, criminal courts, and policing should not exist in a just society. Others are uncomfortable with the term, or with the idea, seeing a limited place for formal state punishment in the world around them. Most organizers did not start out thinking in abolitionist terms, but rather came to that set of beliefs through years of collective action within the criminal system, by participating in organizing that embodied alternative meanings of justice. Think, for instance, of groups such as Court Watch NYC or the Massachusetts Bail Fund, which over five or six years of collective work inside courts increasingly transitioned into explicitly abolitionist projects. The Massachusetts Bail Fund's slogan became "Free Them All," and Court Watch NYC developed a focus on "Breaking Down the New York City Punishment Machine." These organizers were, in the words of Mary Hooks, "transformed in the service of the work."[1]

Even for those who already held abolitionist beliefs, engaging in these tactics pushed their thinking further. Angélica Cházaro, reflecting on her work with the Seattle Solidarity Budget, told me how members of nearly two hundred groups came together to form the budget and meet over months and years to work through its details. "The ground completely shifted," she said. "Everything about our abolitionist analysis changed. . . . We always all showed up for each other's fights, but this was very different." Rather than organizing around discrete issues such as Indigenous sovereignty or pedestrian safety, or competing over pots of city funding, the coalition collectively imagined a complete reworking of how the city raises money and supports people. They would rename their 2023 Solidarity Budget as "A Budget to Live, A Budget to Thrive," reflecting this new vision.[2]

In my own way, I have also been transformed in the service of the work. As a public defender in the Bronx, I fought for five years against a system that I believed was profoundly immoral, one that cycled poor Black and Latinx New Yorkers through police precincts, courts, corrections vans, and cages as a way of keeping "order" for the more privileged. Recognizing my own privilege as a white cisgender lawyer, I did my best to treat my clients as partners in our fight against their prosecution. But I still fought within the ideology of the system, the game of "the People" vs. each individual client. Sparks of other possibilities came from collective action around me: the early work of the Bronx Freedom Fund to lay bare the punitive nature of money bail, or organized copwatchers documenting everyday police violence in opposition to the police department's claims of promoting safety.

It was not until I became a law professor in 2012 that I turned to studying and thinking alongside people working with bail funds, courtwatching groups, and copwatching groups. I wrote about the democratic potential of these collective tactics, about the ways these groups were redefining the idea of community. In the stretch of one day I might move from a meeting with bail fund organizers strategizing over how to define "public safety" in bail reform, to a classroom where, with my law students, I parsed through the constitutional rules surrounding bail and jail. I studied and wrote in community with other academics and organizers wondering how the new movements against police violence and criminalization swelling around us were shifting the terrain of concepts such as "police accountability" or "bail reform."

In the meantime, I saw the court system itself push back against the movement energy around it. I witnessed the way that, in my own backyard, New York City sponsored its own bail fund, the "Liberty Fund," which posted bail based on a set of criteria handed down by city agencies, with strict limits on the cases in which it could intervene. Claiming to be inspired by community bail funds, the Liberty Fund, which began operation in 2017, seemed instead to be diluting the power of outside groups to post bail based on their own understandings of safety.[3] This response from the city aimed to ensure the smooth operation of the city's criminal courts and jails, in contrast to the questions emerging from the work of community bail funds about whether pretrial detention can ever be just.

Within a few years, I was no longer writing about the potential for tactics such as bail funds to foster a more democratic criminal system, but instead was thinking about how their oppositional stances to traditional methods of reform were opening up new possibilities. I saw how, in response to the Liberty Fund, organizers within bail funds continued to move away from trying to demonstrate that courts were making the wrong assessments about who poses a threat to the community, and toward a broader sense that money bail, pretrial detention, and even jails themselves were not generating real safety. I came to believe that the criminal system is at its heart anti-democratic—stifling, in myriad ways, the ability of people, families, and entire neighborhoods to keep each other safe and help each other thrive. The system does this by removing people from their communities via criminal punishment. But it also inhibits democracy by weakening the political power of entire neighborhoods, whether through literal disenfranchisement or through practices of state violence that cause people to disengage from politics completely and methods of "participation" that fail to make room for dissenting views.[4] In the face of this, I continued to find inspiration in the ideas generated within the formations of people working to free and support each other using the existing rules of the system.

In late 2019, I moderated a panel featuring the leaders of bail funds in Connecticut, Colorado, Massachusetts, and Minnesota at the annual FreeHer conference, organized by the National Council for Incarcerated and Formerly Incarcerated Women and Girls. It was one of the last times for over two years that national gatherings such as this would be possible: a hotel ballroom filled, mostly with women of color in "FreeHer" T-shirts, clapping after nearly every sentence at every keynote panel. The bail fund directors on our panel, each of whose funds had been operating for three or more years, described their work as contributing to two complementary phenomena: the slow breaking down of the punitive jail apparatus and the equally slow, simultaneous building up of a new vision of the world and how people can keep each other safe. As we discussed on the panel, these are, in abolitionist theory, the two sides to abolition democracy: deconstructing the punitive criminal system, and reconstructing other forms of justice.[5]

The tactics described in this book are, on their face, about the deconstructive side of abolition—about saving people from cages and working collectively to prevent criminalization and punishment by using the tools of the system. But, by offering mutual support and by organizing for alternative ways that the state can keep people safe, they are also about reconstruction. They rewrite definitions of justice and safety, and prefigure through action a kind of democracy that the criminal system does not allow. If this organizing teaches us lessons, those lessons are not about what to think, or whether to embrace the idea of abolition, as much as about how to generate radical ways of thinking and relating to each other: collectively, alongside people directly affected by the criminal system rather than on behalf of them.

As bail funds and other tactics of collective resistance—courtwatching, participatory defense, People's Budgets—do their work, they channel the political fight against punishment and incarceration away from the criminal system, even as they work within it. These tactics are not perfect, nor can they be perfectly replicated. As with all tactics, they can be co-opted and used to legitimize the system. And they are always temporary. Thinking about bail funds and participatory defense hubs as part of a larger political struggle, Pilar Weiss and Raj Jayadev have written, "We often get pushed to declare tactical victories as the end instead of the means to the end. The world we are building, the one without incarceration and with true community power, will not contain the formations we had to try out to [get there]."[6]

For the most part, this book has told the story of organizing tactics that began to spread around the United States in 2015, as protests and social movement activity on the left reached a new size and strength. This book ends just seven years later, in 2022, when I last conducted interviews with organizers. Seven years is an incredibly short amount of time in the arc of any large-scale social and political change. These stories are still unfolding, the ideas evolving.

And new tactics are constantly emerging, often taking

inspiration from the ones that came before. In 2022, for instance, the Debt Collective, a leader in the push to cancel student debt, began a project to create a union of people with debt from bail and court fines and fees.[7] Public defender offices have begun to plan new partnerships with organizers to create "plea bargaining unions," with an eye toward "crashing the system."[8] And in the wake of the United States Supreme Court's 2022 decision overturning *Roe v. Wade*, abortion funds have taken off throughout the country as a tool of collective care and resistance, much as bail funds did during the uprisings in 2020.[9] When people think and act alongside groups experimenting with tactics such as this, then justice may not always require the word "criminal" before it: it is broader than that—it is full of possibility.

Acknowledgments

This book would not have been possible without the time and insights of the organizers and other participants in radical acts of justice who agreed to share their stories with me in interviews in 2021 and 2022, sometimes in multiple interviews over many months. When I have not cited a source for a quotation, it is because the words and stories come from them. They are: Zohra Ahmed, Rev. Alexis Anderson, Erica Bersin, Darrin Browder, Rebecca Brown, Mirella Ceja-Orozco, Angélica Cházaro, Judith Clark, Chris Comeau, Elizer Darris, Rachel Foran, Fred Gilyard, Sharlyn Grace, Raj Jayadev, Nina Luo, Janhavi Madabushi, Tracy McCarter, Jon McFarlane, Imani Mfalme-Shu'la, Katy Naples-Mitchell, Malik Neal, Angel Parker, Tiera Rainey, Atara Rich-Shea, Josh Saunders, LéTania Severe, Pilar Weiss, Adrienna Wong, and Marcel Woodruff. I have been in community with many of these brilliant minds for a long time, and I am so grateful for them. Special thanks to Imani, Katy, Pilar, Raj, Tracy, and Zohra for their careful reads of parts of the book. Thank you to Mary Hooks, who co-wrote a *New York Times* op-ed with me about community bail funds during the summer of

2020, and whose work has helped shape my thinking over the years. Thanks, as well, to all the unnamed organizers and activists whose collective work is represented throughout the book.

This book is a product of years of collaboration with others, and it would be impossible to name all of the people who have influenced my thinking and supported my work. I am forever indebted to the collaborative writing I have done with Amna Akbar, Sameer Ashar, Bill Quigley, and Sabeel Rahman. My thinking about the relationship between theory, practice, and justice would not exist without Nisha Agarwal. Jen Parker's feedback and wisdom helped me at multiple moments during the book-writing process. A writing group of amazing women—Amna Akbar, Tendayi Achiume, Monica Bell, Priscilla Ocen, and Matiangai Sirleaf—was an important source of support as I was developing the project. And thank you to Kelli Moore and Rachel Rebouche for productive writing sessions, to Valena Beety and Vaidya Gullapalli for pep talks that came when I needed them most, and to Susan Sturm for continued feedback and support.

I received essential support from Brooklyn Law School, including from Dean Michael Cahill and from the BLS book-writers group—Anita Bernstein, Heidi Brown, Steven Dean, and Andrew Gold. Thank you to a group of friends and incredible colleagues, many from Brooklyn Law School, who read and discussed a draft manuscript of this book: Monica Bell, Rick Bierschbach, Cynthia Godsoe, Susan Herman, Kate Levine, Kate Mogulescu, Janet Moore, Naomi Murakawa, Sasha Natapoff, Ngozi Okidegbe, Alice Ristroph, Anna Roberts, and Lisa Washington. Their critiques were invaluable. Premal Dharia and Erin Murphy each read a full draft of the manuscript and provided much-needed insights. I also received helpful feedback on portions of the book from David Ball, Erin Collins, Jessica Eaglin, Russell Gold, Aya Gruber, Sean Hill, Shaun Ossei-Owusu, and Vincent Southerland. I received comments on draft chapters from the faculties at Utah Law School, UC-Hastings School of Law, and Cardozo School of Law, as well as the Loyola Law School Race & the Law Colloquium and participants at the 2022 Annual Law and Society Conference.

Thank you to my former colleagues at the Bronx Defenders, where I worked from 2007 to 2012, and where I first saw the power of bail funds through the work of the Bronx Freedom Fund.

A number of the ideas in this book were developed in prior law review articles, including publications in the *California Law Review*, *Harvard Law Review*, *Michigan Law Review*, *Northwestern University Law Review*, *Stanford Law Review*, and *Yale Law Journal*. Student editors at each of these journals provided important editing and citation assistance. I received fantastic research assistance from Brooklyn Law students Octavia Ewart, Kaitlyn Pavia, Meredith Wiles, Justine Woods, and Regina Yu. And editors at the *Boston Review*, *The Nation*, the *New York Times*, and *n+1* helped me rearticulate these scholarly ideas for a wider audience.

I am so grateful for my agent, Lisa Adams, who helped at every point along the way. And endless thanks to everyone at The New Press, including Emily Albarillo, Rachel Vega DeCesario, and Diane Wachtell, as well as April Rondeau for the careful copyediting.

I wrote much of this book while in intense physical pain, and it would feel incomplete not to acknowledge that. Shoutout to everyone out there making it through chronic pain of all kinds.

Thank you to my family. My daughter, Ramona, my brother, Charlie, and my parents, Beth Lief and Michael Simonson, each supported me during the writing of this book in countless ways. And thanks most of all to Mike Grinthal, without whom none of this would be possible.

Notes

Introduction

1. Chicago Community Bond Fund, "Announcing the Rally to #End MoneyBail," Aug. 7, 2018, https://endmoneybond.org/2018/07/20/announcing-the-rally-to-endmoneybail/; Chicago Community Bond Fund, *Year End Report 2018*, Nov. 2018.

2. In this book, I use the full names of real people either after an interview and with their permission, or when their stories or words come from public, published documents or videos. For people whose stories I learned secondhand through unpublished sources, I use pseudonymous first names only. There is a list of people interviewed for this book in the Acknowledgments.

3. Rally to End Money Bail, Sept. 2018, livestream archived at https://m.facebook.com/ChicagoCommunityBondFund/videos/the-rally-to-endmoneybail/703764266648789/?_rdr.

4. For Lavette Mayes's written account of her experience, *see* Lavette Mayes, "I Was Locked Away from My Children for 14 Months Because I Couldn't Make Bail," *Vice*, Mar. 30, 2018.

5. *See* The Bail Project, *Annual Report 2021* (2021).

6. Tanya Watkins, Sharlyn Grace, Will Tanzman, and Sharone Mitchell Jr., "Illinois May Be First State to Eliminate Money Bail, but the Fight Isn't Over," *Truthout*, Feb. 2, 2021.

7. Survived & Punished NY, *No Good Prosecutors, Now or Ever* (2021).

8. *See generally* Angela Davis, *An Autobiography* (Haymarket Books, 3d ed, 2021), 53–56 (on the Women's Bail Fund); Daniel Farbman, "Resistance Lawyering," 107 *California Law Review* 1877, 1906–09 (2019) (on resistance

in the Fugitive Slave Act cases); James Goodman, *Stories of Scottsboro* (Knopf Doubleday, 1995); Rebecca N. Hill, *Men, Mobs and Law: Anti-Lynching and Labor Defense in U.S. Radical History* (Duke University Press, 2008), 228–40 (on Scottsboro); Hugh Ryan, *The Women's House of Detention: A Queer History of a Forgotten Prison* (Bold Type Books, 2022), 302–305 (on the Women's Bail Fund).

9. *See* Ujju Aggarwal, "Mayor Eric Adams Is Siphoning Funds from Public Schools to Fortify NYPD," *Truthout*, June 21, 2022.

10. *See* Musadiq Bidar, "San Francisco Votes Overwhelmingly to Recall Progressive DA Chesa Boudin," *CBS News*, June 8, 2022.

11. Florida, Georgia, and Texas enacted state laws in 2021 to curtail the reallocation of funds away from the police at the local level. See H.R. 1900, 87th Leg., Reg. Sess. (Tex. 2021); S.R. 23, 87th Leg., Reg. Sess. (Tex. 2021); H.R. 1, 123d Leg., Reg. Sess. (Fla. 2021); H.R. 286, 156th Gen. Assemb., Reg. Sess. (Ga. 2021).

12. *See* Watkins, Grace, Tanzman, and Mitchell Jr., "Illinois May Be First State to Eliminate Money Bail."

13. *See* Andrea Ritchie, *The Demand Is Still #DefundthePolice* (Interrupting Criminalization, January 2021); Katie Way, "Here's What the Movement to 'Defund the Police' Actually Won," *Vice*, May 25, 2021.

14. *See* Ta-Nehisi Coates, "Civil-Rights Protests Have Never Been Popular," *The Atlantic*, Oct. 3, 2017.

15. Angela Y. Davis, Gina Dent, Erica Meiners, and Beth Richie, *Abolition. Feminism. Now.* (Haymarket Books, 2021), 51.

16. On just some of these strategies, *see* Mariame Kaba and Andrea J. Ritchie, *No More Police. A Case for Abolition* (The New Press, 2022), 240–70; Deva R. Woodly, *Reckoning: Black Lives Matter and the Democratic Necessity of Social Movements* (Oxford University Press, 2022), 89–127.

1. Justice, Safety, and the People

1. Kimberlianne Podlas begins her article on the public perception of *Law and Order* with this quotation. *See* Kimberlianne Podlas, "Guilty on All Accounts: Law and Order's Impact on Public Perception of Law and Order," 18 *Seton Hall Journal of Sports & Entertainment Law* 1, 1–2 (2008); *see also* John Langbein, *The Origins of Adversary Criminal Trial* (Oxford University Press, 2003), 332–34.

2. Emphasizing a definition of ideology in which it is always problematic in this way, Tommy Shelby defines ideology as "a widely held set of associated beliefs and implicit judgments that misrepresent significant social realities and that function, through this distortion, to bring about or perpetuate unjust

social relations. Tommy Shelby, *Dark Ghettos* (Harvard University Press, 2017), 22. Thomas Piketty provides a useful formulation as well: "Every epoch . . . develops a range of contradictory discourses and ideologies for the purpose of legitimizing the inequality that already exists or that people believe should exist." Thomas Piketty, *Capital and Ideology* (Harvard University Press, 2020), 1. *See also* Terry Eagleton, *Ideology: An Introduction* (Verso, 2d ed, 2007), 27 (describing how ideologies can "serve to block off the possibility of a transformed state of affairs").

3. *See* Naomi Murakawa, "Mass Incarceration Is Dead, Long Live the Carceral State!" 55 *Tulsa Law Review* 251, 251–52 (2020).

4. *See* Ruth Wilson Gilmore, *Golden Gulag: Prisons, Surplus, Crisis, and Opposition in Globalizing California* (University of California Press, 2007); Heather Schoenfeld, *Building the Prison State: Race and the Politics of Mass Incarceration* (University of Chicago Press, 2018).

5. For more on the violence of the carceral state, or criminal system, *see, for example,* Robert M. Cover, "Violence and the Word," 95 *Yale Law Journal* 1601 (1986); Alice Ristroph, "Criminal Law in the Shadow of Violence," 62 *Alabama Law Review* 571 (2011); David Alan Sklansky, *A Pattern of Violence: How the Law Classifies Crimes and What It Means for Justice* (Harvard University Press, 2021); Alex Vitale, *The End of Policing* (Verso Books, 2d ed, 2021), 235–46.

6. *See generally* Alice Ristroph, "An Intellectual History of Mass Incarceration," 60 *Boston College Law Review* 1949 (2019); Jonathan Simon, "Law's Violence, the Strong State, and the Crisis of Mass Imprisonment (for Stuart Hall)," 49 *Wake Forest Law Review* 649 (2014).

7. Mariame Kaba, interview with John Duda, "Toward the Horizon of Abolition," *The Next System Podcast* (Nov. 2017).

8. On violence, *see, for example,* Ristroph, "Criminal Law in the Shadow of Violence"; Sklansky, *A Pattern of Violence.* On justice, *see, for example,* Kate Levine, "Police Prosecutions and Punitive Instincts," 98 *Washington University Law Review* 997, 997–98 (2021). On expertise, *see, for example,* Erin Collins, "Abolishing the Evidence-Based Paradigm," *B.Y.U. Law Review* (forthcoming 2022); Benjamin Levin, "Criminal Justice Expertise," 90 *Fordham Law Review* 2777 (2022); Ngozi Okidegbe, "Discredited Data," 107 *Cornell Law Review* (forthcoming 2023); on safety, *see, for example,* Barry Friedman, "What Is Public Safety?" 102 *Boston University Law Review* 725 (2022); Brandon Hasbrouk, "Reimagining Public Safety," 117 *Northwestern University Law Review* 685 (2022); on criminal, *see, for example,* Alice Ristroph, "Farewell to the Criminal" (working paper); Anna Roberts, "Convictions as Guilt," 88 *Fordham Law Review* 2501, 2501–48 (2020); on felon, *see, for example,* Alice Ristroph,

"*Farewell to the Felonry*," 53 *Harvard Civil Rights-Civil Liberties Law Review* 563 (2018); on victims, *see, for example,* Cynthia Godsoe, "The Victim/Offender Overlap and Criminal System Reform," 87 *Brooklyn Law Review* 1319 (2022); Anna Roberts, "Victims, Right?" 42 *Cardozo Law Review* 1449 (2021).

9. *See* Bernard E. Harcourt, "The Systems Fallacy: A Genealogy and Critique of Public Policy and Cost-Benefit Analysis," 47 *Journal of Legal Studies* 419, 419–47 (2018); Sara Mayeux, "The Idea of 'The Criminal Justice System,' " 45 *American Journal of Criminal Law* 55 (2018).

10. *See generally* Khalil Gibran Muhammad, *The Condemnation of Blackness* (Harvard University Press, 2010), 277 (telling the history of the "invisible layers of racial ideology packed into the statistics, sociological theories, and the everyday stories we continue to tell about crime in modern urban America"). For just a few explorations of this ideology of white supremacy in various parts of the criminal system, *see, for example,* Devon Carbado, *Unreasonable: Black Lives, Police Power, and the Fourth Amendment* (New Press, 2022); I. India Thusi, "The Pathological Whiteness of Prosecution," 110 *California Law Review* 795 (2022); Yolanda Vazquez, "Constructing Crimmigration: Latino Subordination in a 'Post-Racial' World," 76 *Ohio St. Law Journal* 599 (2015).

11. *See, for example,* Anonymous, "How Many Lives?," *off our backs* (1971), in *Remaking Radicalism*, eds. Dan Berger and Emily K. Hobson (University of Georgia Press, 2020), 168–70 (critiquing idea of "rehabilitation"); Black Liberation Army Coordinating Committee, Special communique on the freeing of sister Assata Shakur (1979), in *Remaking Radicalism*, eds. Berger and Hobson, 182 (critiquing concept of "criminal").

12. Angela Y. Davis, Gina Dent, Erica Meiners, and Beth Richie, *Abolition. Feminism. Now.* (Haymarket Books, 2021), 43.

13. For even more on the ideology of criminal procedure, *see* Mirjan Damaška, "Structures of Authority and Comparative Criminal Procedure," 84 *Yale Law Journal* 480 (1975); Sharon Dolovich, "Exclusion and Control in the Carceral State," 16 *Berkeley Journal of Criminal Law* 259, 265 (2011); Malcolm M. Feeley and Jonathan Simon, "The New Penology: Notes on the Emerging Strategy of Corrections and Its Implications," 30 *Criminology* 449 (1992); David Sklansky, *Democracy and the Police* (Harvard University Press, 2008), 1–13; Carol S. Steiker and Jordan M. Steiker, "Lessons for Law Reform from the American Experiment with Capital Punishment," 87 *Southern California Law Review* 733, 783 (2014); Michael Tonry, "Evidence, Ideology, and Politics in the Making of American Criminal Justice Policy," 42 *Crime & Justice* 1, 8 (2013).

14. Night Out for Safety and Liberation, *Organizing Toolkit* (2021).

15. Rebecca Morris, "National Night Out: Building Police and Community Partnerships to Prevent Crime," *Bulletin from the Field: Practitioner Perspectives*, Bureau of Justice Assistance, Department of Justice (May 2000).

16. Night Out for Safety and Liberation, 2021 Livestream (Aug. 3, 2021), https://www.youtube.com/watch?v=qa7AnptwI7E; *See also* "Safety Beyond Police, Prisons and Punishment," *Ella's Voice Podcast* (Aug. 18, 2021) (featuring interviews with NOSL organizers Denise Ruben, Women on the Rise (Atlanta); Diana Williams, Texas Advocates for Justice (Houston); Nicole LaPorte, Equity and Transformation (Chicago) and Yvonne Yen Liu, Solidarity Research Center (Los Angeles)).

17. Zach Norris, *Defund Fear: Safety Without Policing, Prisons, and Punishment* (Beacon Press, 2021).

18. *See* Mariame Kaba and Andrea J. Ritchie, *No More Police. A Case for Abolition* (The New Press, 2022), 248–51.

19. *See generally* Kelly Lytle Hernández, *City of Inmates: Conquests, Rebellion, and the Rise of Human Caging in Los Angeles* (University of North Carolina Press, 2017); Elizabeth Hinton, *From the War on Poverty to the War on Crime: The Making of Mass Incarceration in America* (Harvard University Press, 2016); Naomi Murakawa, *The First Civil Right: How Liberals Built Prison America* (Oxford University Press, 2014).

20. *See* 18 U.S.C.A. § 3142 (West); Nev. Rev. Stat. Ann. § 178.484 (LexisNexis, 2011); Jocelyn Simonson, "Bail Nullification," 115 *Michigan Law Review* 585, 612–16 (2017).

21. *See* Monica C. Bell, "Safety, Friendship, and Dreams," 54 *Harvard Civil Rights-Civil Liberties Law Review* 703, 719–20 (2019).

22. Santera Matthews, Project NIA, *Two Sides of Justice: A Curriculum Resource* (Jan. 2020).

23. For more on transformative justice and restorative justice, *see* Kaba and Ritchie, *No More Police*, 255–64; Mia Mingus, *Transformative Justice: A Brief Description* (2019); Cameron Rasmussen and Sonya Shah, "Growing Justice," *Inquest*, Sept. 9, 2022; Danielle Sered, *Until We Reckon: Violence, Mass Incarceration, and a Road to Repair* (The New Press, 2019).

24. On the Second Amendment, *see, for example, District of Columbia v. Heller*, 554 U.S. 570, 625 (2008) (limiting the meaning of "the People" in the Second Amendment to "law-abiding citizens"). On "the people" in the Fourth Amendment, *see, for example, United States v. Verdugo-Urquidez*, 494 U.S. 259, 265 (1990) (defining "the People" in the Fourth Amendment as "a class of persons who are part of a national community or who have otherwise developed sufficient connection with this country"). On "We, the People," *see* Sanford Levinson, "Who, If Anyone, Really Trusts 'We the

People'?" 37 *Ohio N.U. Law Review* 311, 317 (2011); Michael Perry, *We the People: The Fourteenth Amendment and the Supreme Court* (Oxford University Press, 1999), 15–32; David A. Strauss, "We the People, They the People, and the Puzzle of Democratic Constitutionalism," 91 *Texas Law Review* 1969, 1973–77 (2013).

25. *See* Wendy Sawyer, Infographic, "What Do Victims Really Want?" *Prison Policy Institute*, 2022 (*citing* Alliance on Safety and Justice, *Crime Survivors Speak: The First-Ever National Survey on Victims' Views on Safety and Justice* (2016)).

26. American Bar Association, *Criminal Justice Standards for the Prosecution Function* (ABA, 4th ed, 2017).

27. Audre Lorde, "The Master's Tools Will Never Dismantle the Master's House," in *Sister Outsider: Essays and Speeches* (Crossing Press, Reprint ed., 2007), 110–12.

28. Paul Butler recently counted more than two hundred law review articles invoking the phrase. *See* Paul Butler, "Progressive Prosecutors Are Not Trying to Dismantle the Master's House, and the Master Wouldn't Let Them Anyway," 90 *Fordham Law Review* 1983, 1985 (2022).

29. Kimberlé Williams Crenshaw, "Race, Reform, and Retrenchment: Transformation and Legitimation in Antidiscrimination Law," 101 *Harvard Law Review* 1331, 1367–68 (1988).

30. *See* Chantal Mouffe, *Agonistics: Thinking the World Politically* (Verso, 2013), 5–9. For more on agonism in the criminal system, *see* Philip Goodman, Joshua Page, and Michelle Phelps, *Breaking the Pendulum: The Long Struggle Over Criminal Justice* (Oxford University Press, 2017), 3, 123–40; Jocelyn Simonson, "Copwatching," 104 *California Law Review* 393, 435–37 (2016).

31. *See* Rachel Elise Barkow, *Prisoners of Politics: Breaking the Cycle of Mass Incarceration* (Harvard University Press, 2019), 4–6; William J. Stuntz, "The Pathological Politics of Criminal Law," 100 *Michigan Law Review* 505, 506–11 (2001).

32. *See* Marie Gottschalk, *Caught: The Prison State and the Lockdown of American Politics* (Princeton University Press, 2015); Erin Collins, "Abolishing the Evidence-Based Paradigm," draft, at 22–46; Harcourt, "The Systems Fallacy," 432–33.

33. *See* Hannah L. Walker, *Mobilized by Injustice: Criminal Justice Contact, Participation, and Race* (Oxford University Press, 2020), 5; Okidegbe, "Discredited Data"; Vincent Southerland, "The Master's Tools and a Mission: Using Community Control and Oversight Laws to Resist and Abolish Police Surveillance Technologies," *U.C.L.A. Law Review* (forthcoming 2023).

34. *See, for example,* Mari J. Matsuda, "Looking to the Bottom: Critical Legal Studies and Reparations," 22 *Harvard Civil Rights-Civil Liberties Law Review* 323 (1987).

35. Lani Guinier and Gerald Torres, "Changing the Wind: Notes Toward a Demosprudence of Law and Social Movements," 123 *Yale Law Journal* 2740, 2768–80 (2014).

36. Taylor Branch, *Pillar of Fire: America in the King Years, 1963–65* (Simon & Schuster, 1998), 474, cited in Guinier and Torres, "Changing the Wind," 2768.

37. For more on the radical thinking of Fannie Lou Hamer, *see* Keisha Blain, *Until I Am Free: Fannie Lou Hamer's Enduring Message to America* (Beacon Press, 2021).

38. *See* Guinier and Torres, "Changing the Wind," 2799.

39. On this long history, *see* Guy-Uriel E. Charles and Luis E. Fuentes-Rohwer, "Slouching Toward Universality: A Brief History of Race, Voting, and Political Participation," 62 *Howard Law Journal* 809 (2019).

2. Community Bail Funds

1. *See* Pennsylvania Crim. Code R. 523I(1). For more on this process, see Malik Neal and Christina Matthias, "Broken Promises: Larry Krasner and the Continuation of Pretrial Punishment in Philadelphia," 16 *Stanford Journal of Civil Rights & Civil Liberties* 543, 544 (2021); Crystal S. Yang, "Toward an Optimal Bail System," 92 *N.Y.U. Law Review* 1399, 1452–58 (2017).

2. Co-sponsoring groups included ACLU-PA, the #No215Jail Coalition, POWER Interfaith, Live Free, Philly We Rise, and more. Philly We Rise LiveStream, People's Hearing on Bail and Pretrial Punishment (Jan. 20, 2020), https://www.facebook.com/phillywerise/videos/2507744875991167/.

3. See Aurélie Ouss and Megan Stevenson, "Does Cash Bail Deter Misconduct?" (Jan. 2022) (empirical study finding "no evidence that financial collateral has a deterrent effect on failure-to-appear or pretrial crime").

4. See Wendy Sawyer and Peter Wagner, "Mass Incarceration: The Whole Pie 2022," *Prison Policy Initiative,* Mar. 14, 2022 (showing that approximately 445,000 people were detained pretrial in the United States in 2021).

5. These numbers are from 2002 and 2000, the last available data at the time of this writing. See Wendy Sawyer, "How Race Impacts Who Is Detained Pretrial," *Prison Policy Institute,* Oct. 9, 2019; Wendy Sawyer, "New BJS Data Reveals a Jail-building Boom in Indian Country," *Prison Policy Institute,* Oct. 30, 2020.

6. See Paul Heaton, Sandra Mayson, and Megan Stevenson, "The Downstream Consequences of Misdemeanor Pretrial Detention," 69 *Stanford Law Review* 711 (2017); Yang, "Toward an Optimal Bail System," 1417–25.

7. *See* Neal and Matthias, "Broken Promises," 544.

8. Chase Strangio and Rage M. Kidvai, "Support Black Trans Women Fight for Survival," *Sylvia Rivera Law Project*, Aug. 15, 2015 ("The [Lorena Borjas Community] fund exists precisely to support transgender women of color . . . who because of systemic discrimination and profiling, are less likely to be able to pay bail and face particularly harsh abuses while incarcerated.").

9. For more on this history in 2015 and 2016, see Jocelyn Simonson, "Bail Nullification," 115 *Michigan Law Review* 585, 599–610 (2017).

10. *See WCNC News Charlotte*, "Moms Bailed Out of Jail for Mother's Day," May 13, 2017, https://www.youtube.com/watch?v=Hkj82BDiWjw; *News One Now*, "National Mama's Day Bailout," May 12, 2017, https://www.youtube.com/watch?v=tBoESjkYvUk.

11. National Bailout Collective, "What We Do and History," https://www.nationalbailout.org/history.

12. "Free Black Mamas with Veronica Rex," *Strong Feelings Podcast*, May 8, 2019.

13. Bronx Freedom Fund, *Second Annual Report* (2015), 2 ("97% of our clients returned to all of their court appearances"); Brooklyn Community Bail Fund, *2015–2016 Annual Report* (2016), 9 ("95% of clients return for all required court appearances. . . ."); Massachusetts Bail Fund: Campaign Details, Classy.org, https://perma.cc/WCP4-2L6G (last visited Oct. 7, 2016) ("Over 90% of our clients come back to court as required.").

14. Bronx Freedom Fund, *Second Annual Report*, 3.

15. *See, for example*, "Lippman Lauds Bronx Group's Nonprofit Approach to Bail Defenders," *New York Law Journal*, Oct. 2013; Pete Barrett, "Bronx Freedom Fund Seeks to Show Other Groups How to Post Bail for Needy Defendants," *New York Daily News*, July 14, 2014; Website of the City of New York, Press Release, "Mayor de Blasio Launches Bail Lab to Safely Reduce Overreliance on Money Bail," Oct. 13, 2015 (describing success of the Bronx Freedom Fund); David Howard King, "Bronx Program Serves as Inspiration for Mark-Viverito's City-Wide Bail Fund Proposal," *Gotham Gazette*, Feb. 20, 2015.

16. Believers Bail Out, "Video: Believers Bail Out Ramadan 2018," Apr. 23, 2020, https://www.youtube.com/watch?v=lBVieIGMxJA.

17. In its year-end report, the Bond Fund reported that it had paid more than $350,000 in bond to free sixty-eight people between November 2017

and October 2018. The rally was in September 2018. *See* Chicago Community Bond Fund, *Year End Report 2018* (2018).

18. Chicago Community Bond Fund, "Announcing the Rally to #End MoneyBail," Aug. 7, 2018, https://endmoneybond.org/2018/07/20/announcing-the-rally-to-endmoneybail/.

19. Chicago Community Bond Fund, *Year End Report 2018*.

20. Pilar Weiss, Welcome, 2021 National Bail Fund Network convening, Sept. 13, 2021.

21. *See* The Bail Project, *Annual Report 2021* (2021).

22. In particular, there is a rich history of bail funds run by Catholic charities and other religious institutions. *See, for example,* Zach Ezor, "Sister Sue, The Nun at County Jail," *WBUR News*, Feb. 26, 2015 (profiling a nun who administers a longstanding bail fund).

23. Arthur J. Sabin, *In Calmer Times: The Supreme Court and Red Monday* (University of Pennsylvania Press, 1999), 49–50 (describing bail fund set up by the Civil Rights Congress).

24. Robin Steinberg, Lillian Kalish, and Ezra Ritchin, "Freedom Should Be Free: A Brief History of Bail Funds in the United States," 2 *U.C.L.A. Criminal Justice Law Review* 1 (2018).

25. Resources for Community Change, *Women Behind Bars: An Organizing Tool* (1975).

26. Marc Mauer, *Bail Out: The Community Bail Fund Organizing Manual* (American Friends Service Committee, 1980).

27. Angela Davis, *An Autobiography* (Haymarket Books, 3d ed, 2021), 53–56; Hugh Ryan, *The Women's House of Detention: A Queer History of a Forgotten Prison* (Bold Type Books, 2022), 302–305; Women's Area Women's Center, 2 *Off Our Backs* 9, 15 (1972).

28. Angela Y. Davis, Gina Dent, Erica Meiners, and Beth Richie, *Abolition. Feminism. Now.* (Haymarket Books, 2021), 43.

29. Davis, Dent, Meiners, and Richie, *Abolition. Feminism. Now.*, 32.

30. Weiss, Welcome, 2021 National Bail Fund Network convening.

31. N.Y. C.P.L. § 510.30 (McKinney 2022).

32. The author was an attorney at the Bronx Defenders at the time and present for some of the hearings in this case, but the details come from court documents and the following sources: Email from Robyn Mar, Attorney, Bronx Defenders, to Jocelyn Simonson (Aug. 30, 2016) (on file with author); Andrea Clisura, "Note, None of Their Business: The Need for Another Alternative to New York's Bail Bond Business," 19 *Journal of Law & Policy* 307, 326–30 (2010) (describing the case of *People v. Miranda*, No. 012208C2009,

2009 WL 2170254 (Bronx Cty. Sup. Ct. June 22, 2009)); Nick Pinto, "Making Bail Better," *The Village Voice*, Oct. 12, 2012.

33. Philadelphia Bail Fund and Pennsylvanians for Modern Courts, *Philadelphia Bail Watch Report: Findings and Recommendations based on 611 Bail Hearings* (2018), 28.

34. On this history of bail in the United States, *see* Kellen Funk and Sandy Mayson, "Bail at the Founding" (2022) (draft paper on file with author, showing how, at the founding, a two-tiered system of bail existed, so that poor and marginalized people were regularly detained for inability to pay bail); Shima Baradaran Baughman, *The Bail Book: A Comprehensive Look at Bail in America's Criminal Justice System* (Cambridge University Press, 2018), 18–28.

35. Caleb Foote, "Compelling Appearance in Court: Administration of Bail in Philadelphia," 102 *University of Pennsylvania Law Review* 1031, 1037–43 (1954).

36. Roy B. Flemming, *Punishment Before Trial: An Organizational Perspective of Felony Bail Processes* (Longman Publishing, 1982), 18 (describing how a judge setting bail and worrying about future criminal conduct may be thinking, "How large a bail will assure his detention while still not appearing excessive or unreasonable?"); Ronald Goldfarb, *Ransom: A Critique of the American Bail System* (Harper & Row, 1965), 46–9 (describing the widespread practice of setting bail so as to give defendants "a taste of jail"); Wayne Thomas Jr., *Bail Reform in America* (University of California Press, 1976), 245–46 (describing tacit understanding of "sub rosa" pretrial detention by setting bail higher than defendants can pay).

37. See *People v. Miranda*, No. 012208C2009, 2009 WL 2170254, at *1 (Bronx Cty. Sup. Ct. June 22, 2009).

38. Pinto, "Making Bail Better"; Tana Geneva, "The Fight to End Cash Bail," *Stanford Social Innovation Review* (Spring 2019).

39. *Miranda* at *2.

40. *Miranda* at *4.

41. For more on "community ties," see Simonson, "Bail Nullification," at 616–21.

42. *United States v. Salerno*, 481 U.S. 739, 750 (1987).

43. *See* Kellen Funk, "The Present Crisis in American Bail," 128 *Yale Law Journal Forum* 1098 (2019).

44. Fla. Stat. Ann. § 903.046(1) (West 2016); Wis. Stat. Ann. § 969.01 (West 2015); Nev. Rev. Stat. Ann. § 178.484 (LexisNexis, 2011). For a full list of state bail statutes referencing community, *see* Simonson, "Bail Nullification," at 613–14.

45. *See* Eric Reinhart, "How Mass Incarceration Makes Us All Sick," *Health Affairs*, May 28, 2021.

46. Office of New York City Comptroller Scott Stringer, *The Public Cost of Private Bail: A Proposal to Ban Bail Bonds in NYC* (Jan. 2018).

47. People's Hearing on Bail and Pretrial Punishment (Jan. 20, 2020).

48. National Bailout Collective, *The Black Codes of Bail* (2019).

49. KXCI Community Radio, "Tucson Second Chance Community Bail Fund, Interview with Lola Rainey," Jan. 26, 2020.

50. On this unique Massachusetts system, *see* Thomas, Jr., *Bail Reform in America*, 214–17.

51. *See* Erin Collins, "Abolishing the Evidence-Based Paradigm;" Ngozi Okidegbe, "Discredited Data," 107 *Cornell Law Review* (forthcoming 2023); Anna Roberts, "Arrests as Guilt," 70 *Alabama Law Review* 987 (2019). For more on the fallacy of "failure to appear" statistics, see Lauryn Gouldin, "Defining Flight Risk," 85 *University of Chicago Law Review* 677 (2018); Puck Lo and Ethan Corey, "The Failure to Appear Fallacy," *The Appeal*, Jan. 9, 2019.

52. *See* Kay Whitlock and Nancy A. Heitzeg, *Carceral Con: The Deceptive Terrain of Criminal Justice Reform* (University of California Press, 2021), 102–25; Sean Allan Hill II, "Bail Reform and the (False) Racial Promise of Algorithmic Risk Assessment," 68 *U.C.L.A. Law Review* 910, 912 (2021); Sandra G. Mayson, "Bias in, Bias Out," 128 *Yale Law Journal* 2218 (2019).

53. Maya Schenwar and Victoria Law, *Prison by Any Other Name* (The New Press, 2020), 25–114.

54. Weiss, Welcome, 2021 National Bail Fund Network convening.

55. Davis, *An Autobiography*, 56.

56. Brett Davidson, Elisabeth Epps, Sharlyn Grace, and Atara Rich-Shea, "Moving from Ending Money Bail to Demanding Pretrial Freedom," *Law and Political Economy Blog*, Feb. 12, 2020.

57. Chicago Community Bond Fund, *Punishment Is Not a "Service": The Injustice of Pretrial Conditions in Cook County* (Oct. 24, 2017).

58. Lola Rainey, Tucson Second Chance Community Bail Fund, *Pretrial Injustice: How the Pima County Judiciary Is Using Pretrial Risk Assessments to Cage People* (Jan. 2021).

59. Brooklyn Community Bail Fund/Envision Freedom Fund, *Community Bail Funds and the Fight for Freedom* (Sept. 27, 2019).

60. Connecticut Bail Fund, "#SurvivingInside," http://www.ctbailfund.org/surviving-inside.

61. *See* Peter Eisler, Lindo So, Jason Szep, Grant Smith, and Ned Parker, "Dying Inside: The Hidden Crisis in America's Jails," *Reuters*, Oct. 16, 2020.

62. *See* Brendan Saloner, Kalind Parish, Julie A. Ward, Grace DiLaura and Sharon Dolovich, "COVID-19 Cases and Deaths in Federal and State Prisons," 324 *Journal of the American Medical Association* 602 (2020).

63. Chicago Community Bond Fund, Open Letter, "People Should Be Released from Cook County Jail to Support Public Health During Coronavirus Outbreak" (Mar. 6, 2020).

64. *See* Chicago Community Bond Fund, *Overview of CCBF's Work in 2020* (2020); Chicago Community Bond Fund, *Statement on the Solidarity Caravan Calling for Mass Release of Incarcerated People in the Name of Public Health* (April 7, 2020).

65. *See* Jia Tolentino, "Where Bail Funds Go from Here," *The New Yorker*, June 23, 2020.

66. Elisabeth Epps (@elisabeth), Twitter (June 4, 2020, 8:32 pm), https://twitter.com/elisabeth/status/1268702166287613953.

67. Nicholas Kulish, "Bail Funds, Flush with Cash, Learn to 'Grind Through This Horrible Process,' " *New York Times*, June 25, 2020.

68. Faith Miller, "Elisabeth Epps Wins Colorado District 6 Primary Race," *Colorado Newsline*, June 30, 2022; Denver Election Results, 2022 General Election—November 8, 2022, https://www.denvergov.org/electionresults#/results/20221108.

69. Tanya Watkins, Sharlyn Grace, Will Tanzman, and Sharone Mitchell Jr., "Illinois May Be First State to Eliminate Money Bail, But the Fight Isn't Over," *Truthout*, Feb. 2, 2021.

70. Chicago Community Bond Fund, "Update on Bonds Paid in 2022" (May 11, 2022).

71. Kamala Harris (@kamalaharris), Twitter (June 1, 2020, 4:34 pm), https://twitter.com/kamalaharris/status/1267555018128965643.

72. Paul Flahive, "Senate Bill 6 Signed Into Law, Cash-Bail Opponents Question Its Impact on Public Safety," *KSTX Tex. Pub. Radio*, Sept. 14, 2021.

73. *See Actions for House Bill 1300*, Ind. Gen. Assemb., http://iga.in.gov/legislative/2022/bills/house/1300#digest-heading; Lawrence Andrea, "Indiana Lawmakers Pass Legislation Restricting Bail Organizations, Targeting Crime in Indy," *IndyStar*, Mar. 9, 2022.

74. *See* Andrea Estes, "Sex Offender, Free on Bail, Is Charged with New Violent Rape," *Boston Globe*, Aug. 6, 2020; Andrea Estes, "Supporters Pull Back After Massachusetts Bail Fund Posts Bail for Registered Sex Offender Who Had Pending Rape Charges," *Boston Globe*, Aug. 11, 2020.

75. Boston Area Rape Crisis Center, *Statement: BARCC Responds to Bail in McClinton Case* (Aug. 11, 2020).

76. Boston Area Rape Crisis Center, *Statement: Following Up on McClinton Case* (Sept. 4, 2020).

77. National Council for Incarcerated and Formerly Incarcerated Women and Girls, Families for Justice as Healing, Black and Pink Massachusetts, and the Massachusetts Bail Fund, *Coalition Bail Statement* (2020).

3. Courtwatching

1. For more on the architecture and iconography of contemporary courthouses such as this, see Judith Resnik and Dennis Curtis, *Representing Justice* (Yale University Press, 2015), xv. They explain, "Most . . . new courthouses, often clad in glass to mark justice's transparency, celebrate courts without reflecting on the problems of access, injustice, opacity, and the complexity of rendering judgments."

2. Prison Policy Institute, Louisiana Profile (2022).

3. *See* "Background," Safety & Justice Challenge, East Baton Rouge Parish, LA, https://safetyandjusticechallenge.org/our-network/east-baton-rouge-parish-la/.

4. *See* Matt Sledge and Bryn Stole, "Supreme Court Panel Urges Revamp of Louisiana's 'User Pay' Criminal Justice System, but Implementing It Will Be Hard," *The Advocate*, Apr. 29, 2019.

5. Nineteenth Judicial District Court Building Commission, Baton Rouge, Louisiana, *Financial Report* (June 30, 2020).

6. Ruth Wilson Gilmore, *Golden Gulag: Prisons, Surplus, Crisis, and Opposition in Globalizing California* (University of California Press, 2007), 87–128.

7. *See* Stephanos Bibas, *The Machinery of Criminal Justice* (Cambridge University Press, 2012), 1–30.

8. *See* Louisiana Act No. 252 (2021) (amending Louisiana Criminal Procedure Rule 701(B) to require that charges be filed within thirty days of an arrest for a misdemeanor).

9. Bryce Covert, "The Court Watch Movement Wants to Expose the 'House of Cards,' " *The Appeal*, July 16, 2018.

10. Legal Momentum, "A Guide to Court Watching in Domestic Violence and Sexual Assault Cases" (2005).

11. The Fund for Modern Courts, "Citizen Court Monitoring," https://moderncourts.org/citizen-court-monitoring/ (summarizing its Citizen Court Monitoring program).

12. Robert M. Cover, "Violence and the Word," 95 *Yale Law Journal* 1601, 1608 (1986).

13. Philadelphia Bail Fund and Pennsylvanians for Modern Courts, *Philadelphia Bail Watch Report: Findings and Recommendations based on 611 Bail Hearings* (2018).

14. *See, for example,* "The Eye of Power," in Michel Foucault, *Power/Knowledge: Selected Interviews and Writings*, Colin Gordon, ed. (Pantheon Books, 1980), 146–66.

15. Professor Steven Mann, who coined the term, describes sousveillance as a technique "for uncovering the Panopticon and undercutting its primary purpose and privilege." Steve Mann, Jason Nolan, and Barry Wellman, "Sousveillance: Inventing and Using Wearable Computing Devices," 1 *Surveillance & Society* 331, 333 (2003).

16. Courtwatch-LA training slides, 2020.

17. For more on the complications with romanticizing transparency, *see* Community Justice Exchange, *Transparency Is Not Enough* (2019); Kate Levine, "Discipline and Policing," 68 *Duke Law Journal* 839 (2019); David Pozen, "Transparency's Ideological Drift," 128 *Yale Law Journal* 100 (2018).

18. Louis Brandeis, *Other People's Money: And How the Bankers Use It* (Frederick A. Stokes, 1914), 92.

19. Browder's case was eventually dismissed for lack of evidence. *See* Jennifer Gonnerman, "Kalief Browder, 1993–2015," *NewYorker.com*, June 7, 2015; Alysia Santo, "No Bail, Less Hope: The Death of Kalief Browder," *The Marshall Project*, June 9, 2015.

20. New York City Council Speaker Melissa Mark-Viverito, State of the City Address 2016 (Feb. 11, 2016), transcript available at http://council.nyc.gov/html/pr/021116mj.shtml.

21. James C. McKinley Jr., "Some Prosecutors Stop Asking for Bail in Minor Cases," *New York Times*, Jan. 9, 2018.

22. Court Watch NYC (@CourtWatchNYC), Twitter (4:33 PM Jan. 24, 2018), https://twitter.com/CourtWatchNYC/status/956278825427591174.

23. Joan Vollero (@JoanVollero), Twitter (3:17 PM Jan 26, 2018), https://twitter.com/JoanVollero/status/956984406094307328.

24. Beth Schwartzapfel, "[Eyes on] The Prosecutors," *The Marshall Project*, Feb. 26, 2018.

25. Court Watch NYC, Last Week in Court, March 13–March 20 (March 26, 2018).

26. Issa Kohler-Hausmann, *Misdemeanorland* (Princeton University Press, 2019), 60–98.

27. Alexandra Natapoff, *Punishment Without Crime* (Basic Books, 2018), 7.

28. Court Watch NYC, *Broken Promises: A CWNYC Response to Drug Policing and Prosecution in New York City*, October 2018.

29. Harry DiPrinzio, "Manhattan Pot Prosecutions," *City Limits*, Nov. 2, 2018.

30. *In re Oliver*, 333 U.S. 257, 270 (1948).

31. *Richmond Newspapers, Inc. v. Virginia*, 448 U.S. 555 (1980); *Waller v. Georgia*, 467 U.S. 39 (1984).

32. The other is the jury trial right. For more on the constitutional right to access criminal courtrooms, see Jocelyn Simonson, "The Criminal Court Audience in a Post-Trial World," 127 *Harvard Law Review* 2173 (2014).

33. Ted Passon, Yoni Brook, and Nicole Salazar, "Episode 8," *Philly D.A.*, Independent Lens, PBS: April 21, 2021.

34. Sharlyn Grace, "In Chicago and Beyond, Bail Reformers Win Big in Fight to End Money Bail," *Truthout*, July 25, 2017.

35. The Coalition to End Money Bond, *Monitoring Cook County's Central Bond Court: A Community Courtwatching Initiative, August–October, 2017* (2018).

36. Bryce Covert, "One Year After Cook County's Bail Reform," *The Appeal*, October 5, 2018.

37. Measures for Justice, *The Power and Problem of Criminal Justice Data: A Twenty State Review* (June 2021).

38. MacArthur Foundation's Safety and Justice Challenge, https://safetyandjusticechallenge.org/finding-solutions/.

39. *See* Christina Koningsor, "Public Undersight," 106 *Minnesota Law Review* 2221 (2022); Ngozi Okidegbe, "Discredited Data," 107 *Cornell Law Review* (forthcoming 2023).

40. Megan Hadley, "Can 'Court Watchers' Help Reform America's Flawed Justice Systems?," *The Crime Report*, Apr. 11, 2018.

41. Derrick Bell, "Racism in American Courts: Cause for Black Disruption or Despair?," 61 *California Law Review* 165 (1973).

42. Bell, "Racism in American Courts"; *see also* Alexandra Natapoff, "Speechless: The Silencing of Criminal Defendants," 80 *N.Y.U. Law Review* 1449 (2005).

43. Bell, "Racism in American Courts" 105 ("Regrettably, the much discussed revolution in criminal procedure has changed the actual plight of the average criminal defendant so little that black defendants have not been given reason to alter their conception of the criminal justice system."); Paul Butler, "Poor People Lose: *Gideon* and the Critique of Rights," 122 *Yale Law Journal* 2176 (2013).

44. Court Watch Los Angeles (@CourtWatchLA), Twitter (3:00 PM Feb. 6, 2021), https://twitter.com/CourtWatchLA/status/1358143601071378432.

45. CourtWatch PG, Let's Talk About Court Watch—Episode #1—May 2021, https://www.youtube.com/watch?v=Qu6eJKWsAek.

46. Baltimore Courtwatch (@bmorecourtwatch), Twitter (9:00 AM Nov. 5, 2020), https://twitter.com/bmorecourtwatch/status/1324351005354582022?s=20.

47. Baltimore Courtwatch (@bmorecourtwatch), Twitter (10:10 AM Apr. 15, 2021), https://twitter.com/bmorecourtwatch/status/1382697764216315920?s=20.

4. Participatory Defense

1. This description of the training combines information from an interview with Imani Mfalme-Shu'la and a video of a training done by the National Participatory Defense Network at a different location in the same year, available at https://www.youtube.com/watch?v=RbfQY3DLCnY.

2. On "contempt of cop," see Jamelia N. Morgan, "Rethinking Disorderly Conduct," 109 *California Law Review* 1637, 1652–54 (2021); Alexandra Natapoff, "A Stop Is Just a Stop: Terry's Formalism," 15 *Ohio St. Journal of Criminal Law* 113, 120 (2017).

3. Points of Unity, Community Defense of East Tennessee.

4. *See, for example,* Community Defense East TN (@CDET_), Twitter (4:21 PM July 22, 2020), https://twitter.com/CDET_/status/1286033635095830528.

5. Scott Herhold, "Ferguson Case Calls to Mind a San Jose Shooting from 2004," *Mercury News*, Nov. 29, 2014.

6. Blanca Bosquez, "Freeing My Son from the Hall," Albert Cobarrubias Justice Project, https://acjusticeproject.org/keycases/the-police-took-him-from-school-we-freed-him-from-the-hall/.

7. Gail Noble, "Standing Up to the Court," Albert Cobarrubias Justice Project, https://acjusticeproject.org/keycases/standing-up-to-a-racist-court/.

8. Charisse Domingo, "How the Undeniable Force of Family Won Unprecedented Change in California's Justice System—From the Streets to the Courts," *Silicon Valley De-bug* (Oct. 3, 2018); Raj Jayadev and Janet Moore, "Participatory Defense as an Abolitionist Strategy," in *Transforming Criminal Justice: An Evidence-based Agenda for Reform*, ed. Jon B. Gould and Pamela Metzger (NYU Press, 2022), 71–96.

9. *See* Silicon Valley De-bug, "Letter of Opposition to California's False Bail Reform Bill (SB10)," *Silicon Valley De-bug* (Aug. 14, 2018).

10. *In re Humphrey*, 482 P.3d 1008 (Cal. 2021); *see also* "Recent Cases, Criminal Law—Money Bail—California Supreme Court Holds Detention Solely Because of Inability to Pay Bail Unconstitutional—*in Re Humphrey*, 482 P.3d 1008 (Cal. 2021)," 135 *Harvard Law Review* 912 (2022).

11. *See* A Day in California Court, "Court Doing: For Participatory Defense Organizers and Families" (2018).

12. Ray Jayadev, "The Future of Pretrial Justice Is Not Money Bail or System Supervision—It's Freedom and Community," *Silicon Valley De-bug* (Apr. 4, 2019).

13. As Jayadev explained in more detail in one of our interviews, the county request required that the group tell the court if the person was not participating in the community support. In large part because of this requirement, no community groups applied, and the county gave up on the project.

14. Jayadev, "Freedom and Community."

15. *See* Natapoff, "Speechless."

16. Michelle Alexander, "Go to Trial: Crash the Justice System," *New York Times*, Mar. 11, 2012, SR5; Andrew Manuel Crespo, "No Justice No Pleas: Subverting Mass Incarceration Through Defendant Collective Action," 90 *Fordham Law Review* 1999 (2022); Oren Bar-Gill and Omri Ben-Shahar, "The Prisoners' (Plea Bargain) Dilemma," 1 *Journal of Legal Analysis* 737 (2009); Jenny Roberts, "Crashing the Misdemeanor System," 70 *Washington and Lee Law Review* 1089 (2014).

17. *See* James M. Anderson, Maya Buenaventura, and Paul Heaton, "The Effects of Holistic Defense on Criminal Justice Outcomes," 132 *Harvard Law Review* 819 (2019); Emily Galvin-Almanza, "Public Defenders Can Do More for Public Safety—If We Let Them," *Washington Post*, July 23, 2021.

18. Matthew Clair, *Privilege and Punishment: How Race and Class Matter in Criminal Court* (Princeton University Press, 2020), 24.

19. Nicole Gonzales Van Cleve, *Crook County: Racism and Injustice in America's Largest Criminal Court* (Stanford University Press, 2016), 157–81.

20. Paul Butler, "Poor People Lose: *Gideon* and the Critique of Rights," 122 *Yale Law Journal* 2176, 2194 (2013).

21. For a critical analysis of the myth of autonomy in the Sixth Amendment right to counsel and choice of counsel doctrines, *see* Zohra Ahmed, "The Right to Counsel in a Neoliberal Age," 69 *U.C.L.A. Law Review* 442 (2022); Alexis Hoag, "Black on Black Representation," 96 *N.Y.U. Law Review* 1493 (2021); Kathryn E. Miller, "The Myth of Autonomy Rights," 43 *Cardozo Law Review* 375, 377 (2021); Janet Moore, "Isonomy, Austerity, and the Right to Choose Counsel," 51 *Indiana Law Review* 167 (2018).

22. Although a sleeping defense attorney can be a reason to grant a defendant a new trial, many appellate federal courts have held that such conduct is only "prejudicial" enough under the Sixth Amendment when the lawyer sleeps through a "substantial portion" of the trial. *See, for example, Javor v. United States*, 724 F.2d 831, 834 (9th Cir. 1984); *Muniz v. Smith*, 647 F.3d 619, 623 (6th Cir. 2011) (collecting cases).

23. Eve Brensike Primus, "Defense Counsel and Public Defense," in *Academy for Justice, A Report on Scholarship and Criminal Justice Reform*, ed. Erik Luna (2017); A.B.A. Standing Committee on Legal Aid and Indigent Defense, *Gideon's Broken Promise: America's Continuing Quest for Equal Justice* (2004).

24. *Powell v. Alabama*, 287 U.S. 45, 68–69 (1932).

25. Lani Guinier and Gerald Torres, "Changing the Wind: Notes Toward a Demosprudence of Law and Social Movements," 123 *Yale Law Journal* 2740, 2768 (2014).

26. Janet Moore, Marla Sandys, and Raj Jayadev, "Make Them Hear You: Participatory Defense and the Struggle for Criminal Justice Reform," 78 *Albany Law Review* 1281 (2015).

27. *See, for example,* Black Public Defender Association, *Disrupting Carceral Systems: BPDA's Recommendations to the Biden-Harris Administration* (2021) (describing the importance of "centering Black communities in our work.").

28. Jayadev and Moore, "Participatory Defense as an Abolitionist Strategy."

29. Cynthia Godsoe, "Participatory Defense: Humanizing the Accused and Ceding Control to the Client," 69 *Mercer Law Review* 715 (2018).

30. Moore, Sandys, and Jayadev, "Make Them Hear You," 1300.

31. Some public defender offices even host or lead participatory defense hubs themselves, although locating a lawyer's office as the center of the hub can make it hard to develop the leadership and agency of those coming from outside of the office. *See* Liana Pennington, "An Empirical Study of One Participatory Defense Program Facilitated by a Public Defender Office," 14 *Ohio State Journal of Criminal Law* 603, 612 (2017).

32. Mariame Kaba, "Free Us All: Participatory Defense Campaigns as Abolitionist Organizing," *New Inquiry*, May 8, 2017; on participatory defense campaigns, *see also* Sophia Curule, Rosie Rios, and Mon M., *Participatory Defense: Re-defining Defense and Using People Power as a Tool for Liberation* (2022).

33. "#SurvivedandPunished: Survivor Defense as Abolitionist Praxis, A Collaborative Toolkit created by Love and Protect and Survived and Punished" (June 2017), 2–5.

34. Free Marissa Now, "Art Is a Core Part of the Movement to Free Marissa Alexander" (Visual Art slideshow), https://www.freemarissanow.org/art-for-marissa.html.

35. "#SurvivedandPunished: Survivor Defense as Abolitionist Praxis," 1.

36. Leigh Goodmark, *Imperfect Victims: Criminalized Survivors and the Promise of Abolition Feminism* (University of California Press, 2023), 12.

37. *See, for example,* Monica Cosby, *Intimate Partner Violence and State Violence Power and Control Wheel*, reprinted in Angela Y. Davis, Gina Dent, Erica Meiners, and Beth Richie, *Abolition. Feminism. Now.* (Haymarket Books, 2021), 113. For more on this, *see* Davis, Dent, Meiners, and Richie at 108–22.

38. *See, for example,* Daniel Farbman, "Resistance Lawyering," 107 *California Law Review* 1877, 1906–09 (2019).

39. Mariame Kaba, Keynote lecture, "Free Them All: Defending the Lives of Criminalized Survivors of Violence, Brooklyn Law School" (Mar. 19, 2019); *see also* "#SurvivedandPunished: Survivor Defense as Abolitionist Praxis," 8.

40. *See generally* Glenda Elizabeth Gilmore, *Defying Dixie: The Radical Roots of Civil Rights, 1919–1950* (W.W. Norton & Co., 2008), 118–28; James Goodman, *Stories of Scottsboro* (Knopf Doubleday, 1995); Rebecca N. Hill, *Men, Mobs and Law: Anti-Lynching and Labor Defense in U.S. Radical History* (Duke University Press, 2008), 228–40. On Louise Thompson Patterson, *see* Asha Futterman and Mariame Kaba, *Black Radical Women of Harlem Walking Tour* (2019) (with designs by Arrianna Planey and Neta Bomani).

41. Gilmore, *Defying Dixie*, 118–28; Goodman, *Stories of Scottsboro*, 233–41; Hill, *Men, Mobs and Law*, 232–36; Shaun Ossei-Owusu, "The Sixth Amendment Façade: The Racial Evolution of the Right to Counsel," 167 *University of Pennsylvania Law Review* 1161, 1190–97 (2019).

42. Langston Hughes, *Scottsboro Limited, Four Poems and a Play in Verse* (1932).

43. "#SurvivedandPunished: Survivor Defense as Abolitionist Praxis," 8.

44. Emily L. Thuma, *All Our Trials: Prisons, Policing, and the Feminist Fight to End Violence* (University of Illinois Press, 2019), 15–54.

45. Angela Davis, "Joan Little: The Dialectics of Rape," *Ms. Magazine*, 1972.

46. For more on this history of Survived & Punished, see Keynote Panel, "Participatory Defense Campaigns as a Strategy for Freedom," with Cherelle Baldwin, Ceyenne Doroshow, Michelle Horton, Ny Nourn, Kelly Savage, and Hyejin Shim, Columbia Law School (Mar. 2019), available at https://www.youtube.com/watch?v=Dx008vt4rMM.

47. *See* Kathy Boudin, Judith Clark, Michelle Fine, Elizabeth Isaacs, Michelle Daniel Jones, Melissa Mahabir, Kate Mogulescu, Anisah Sabur-Mumin, Patrice Smith, Monica Szlekovics, María Elena Torre, Sharon White-Harrigan, and Cheryl Wilkins, "Movement-Based Participatory Inquiry: The Multi-Voiced Story of the Survivors Justice Project," 11 *Social Sciences* 129 (2022).

48. Whether it is the hubs in the National Participatory Defense Network or the collective defense campaigns, including those of Survived & Punished

and Love & Protect, the work is not confined to criminal court cases. In both cases, the work extends into immigration court, family court, and housing court. For an example of an immigration defense campaign, *see* Curule, Rios, and M., *Participatory Defense* (describing the campaign for Ousman Darboe in immigration court).

49. *See, for example,* "Free: Survivors," *Survived & Punished Newsletter,* Issue 4, 2020.

50. McCarter generously agreed to talk with me about her experience with S&P NY. We spoke while her case was pending. We did not discuss the specifics of the death of Murray—those facts, and some details of her experiences on Riker's Island, are taken from public news accounts and public interviews with family members. Articles describing McCarter's case in the first two years include Victoria Law, "After Six Months on Rikers, a Nurse Stands Accused of Murder in a Case She Says Was Self-Defense," *Gothamist,* Sept. 9, 2020; Tamar Serai, "Pressure Mounts for Manhattan District Attorney to Drop Charges of Criminalized Survivor Tracy McCarter," *Prism,* Mar. 29, 2022; Brea Baker, "Who Is Safer When We Criminalize Domestic Violence Survivors?" *Elle,* Mar. 29, 2022.

51. "Good Nurse Practitioner," interview with Ariel Robbins, *Good Nurse Bad Nurse Podcast* (Dec. 28, 2021).

52. "Good Nurse Practitioner," interview with Ariel Robbins.

53. Alvin Bragg (@AlvinBraggNYC), Twitter (8:29 PM Sept. 10, 2020), https://twitter.com/AlvinBraggNYC/status/1304215413761413120 ("I #Stand WithTracy. Prosecuting a domestic violence survivor who acted in self -defense is unjust.").

54. Alvin L. Bragg, Jr., Letter to the Court, People v. McCarter, Ind. No. 746 /2020 (N.Y. Supreme Ct., Nov. 18, 2022).

55. Decision and Order, People v. McCarter, Ind. No. 746/2020 (N.Y. Supreme Ct., Dec. 2, 2022).

56. Tracy McCarter (@McCarter_Tracy), Twitter (12:43 on Nov. 19, 2022), https://twitter.com/mccarter_tracy/status/1594023572493713409.

57. Mariame Kaba, "Free Us All."

58. Taylor Blackston and Sojourner Rivers, "To Confront Sexual Violence, We Don't Need Better Prosecutors, We Need to Abolish Them," *Truthout,* June 17, 2021.

5. People's Budgets

1. Philadelphia Bail Fund, "Ransom and Freedom: Ending Cash Bail in Philly" (Aug. 2022).

2. Survived & Punished NY, *No Good Prosecutors, Now or Ever* (2021).

3. *See* Eddie Ellis, Center for NuLeadership, *The Seven Neighborhood Study Revisited* (1996); Orisanmi Burton, "Attica Is: Revolutionary Consciousness, Counterinsurgency and the Deferred Abolition of New York State Prisons" (2016) (Ph.D. dissertation, University of North Carolina at Chapel Hill).

4. For more on the Think Tank, *see* Burton, "Attica Is"; Seema Saifee, "Decarceration's Inside Partners," 91 *Fordham Law Review* 53 (2022).

5. Burton, "Attica Is," at 153, citing "Green Haven Seminar Part 2," Eddie Ellis, 1990.

6. *See* Alexandra Marks, "N.Y. Prison Religion Program Helps Turn Lives Around," *Christian Science Monitor*, Mar. 11, 1997.

7. Burton, "Attica Is"; Saifee, "Decarceration's Inside Partners."

8. Crips and Bloods, "Plan for the Reconstruction of Los Angeles: Give Us the Hammer and the Nails, We Will Rebuild the City" (1992), reprinted in *Remaking Radicalism*, eds. Dan Berger and Emily K. Hobson (University of Georgia Press, 2020).

9. Elizabeth Hinton, *America on Fire: The Untold History of Police Violence and Black Rebellion Since the 1960s* (Liveright, 2021), 229–57.

10. Ruth Wilson Gilmore and Craig Gilmore, "Restating the Obvious," *in* Ruth Wilson Gilmore, *Abolition Geography: Essays Towards Liberation* (Verso, 2022), 275–80.

11. Movement for Black Lives, *Invest-Divest*, https://policy.m4bl.org/invest-divest; *see also* Amna A. Akbar, "Toward a Radical Imagination of Law," 93 *N.Y.U. Law Review* 405, 431–33 (2018) (analyzing the ideological importance of this demand).

12. *See* Amna A. Akbar, "Demands for a Democratic Political Economy," 134 *Harvard Law Review Forum* 90, 109–11 (2020).

13. Kristoffer Tigue, "Civil Rights Groups Come Together to Push for Legislative Agenda Addressing Minnesota's Racial Disparities," *MinnPost*, April 7, 2016.

14. Center for Popular Democracy, Law for Black Lives, and the Black Youth Project, "Freedom to Thrive: Reimagining Safety and Security in Our Communities" (2017); *see also* Mariame Kaba and Andrea J. Ritchie, *No More Police. A Case for Abolition* (The New Press, 2022), 248–51 (describing similar experiments in reimagining safety through budgets).

15. On the "deep history" of the demand to Defund the Police, *see* Kaba and Ritchie, *No More Police*, 22–26.

16. Mariame Kaba, *We Do This 'Til We Free Us: Abolitionist Organizing and Transforming Justice* (Haymarket, 2021), 172.

17. Nashville People's Budget Coalition, https://nashvillepeoplesbudget.org/about/ (last visited June 9, 2022).

18. Nashville People's Budget Coalition, *Invest/Divest: Building a Nashville People's Budget* (2020).

19. *See* Kamau Franklin, "The New Southern Strategy: The Politics of Self-determination in the South," in *Jackson Rising: The Struggle for Economic Democracy and Black Self-Determination in Jackson, Mississippi*, eds. Cooperation Jackson et al. (Daraja Press, 2017).

20. Nashville People's Budget Coalition, *Demands for a Nashville People's Budget 2021–2022* (2021), 8.

21. *See* Akbar, "Demands for a Democratic Political Economy," 107–11.

22. Ari Brielle, Angela Faz, Eva Arreguin, Jodi Voice Yellowfish, Kristian Hernandez, Mayra Fierro, Nora Soto, Pat Arreguin, and Sara Mokuria, *2020 Our City Our Future Budget Report: Building a Safer Future for All* (2020).

23. People's Budget Chicago, "What Do Our Communities Need to Be Safe and Thriving?" Workshop Guide 2021 (2021); People's Budget Chicago, *People's Budget 2021* (2021); People's Budget Chicago, "What Is the People's Budget?" https://www.peoplesbudgetchicago.com/our-budget (last visited June 9, 2022).

24. Grant Schwab, "City Struggles with Low Attendance and Protest at Budget Forums," *South Side Weekly* (Aug. 15, 2022).

25. The People's Budget, *Los Angeles, 2020–21* (June 2020).

26. The People's Budget, *Los Angeles, 2020–21*.

27. *See, for example,* Jason Corburn and Amanda Fukutome, U.C. Berkeley Center for Global Healthy Cities, "Advance Peace Stockton: 2018–2020 Evaluation," Jan. 2021; *see generally* Patrick Sharkey, "Why Do We Need the Police? Cops Prevent Violence. But They Aren't the Only Ones Who Can Do It," *Washington Post*, June 12, 2020.

28. Los Angeles County Office of Violence Prevention, "Overview" (2021).

29. *See* County Executive of Los Angeles County, "Measure J Background" (2021).

30. *See* Elizabeth Marcellino, "LA County Commits to Community Investment—to Match Measure J, Which Court Put on Hold," *Los Angeles Daily News*, Aug. 10, 2021; Eric Leonard, "Tentative Ruling Stops LA County's Most Ambitious Justice Reform Measure," *NBC News Los Angeles*, June 17, 2021.

31. *See* Rachel A. Harmon, "Federal Programs and the Real Costs of Policing," 90 *N.Y.U. Law Review* 870, 948 (2015); Rick Su, Anthony O'Rourke, and Guyora Biner, "Defunding Police Agencies," 71 *Emory Law Journal* 1197, 1201 (2022).

32. *See* #NoNewYouthJail Coalition, "About Us," https://nonewyouthjail.com/about/ (last visited Dec. 18, 2022); #NoNewYouthJail Coalition,

"VICTORY: Less Than a Year After Opening, County Announces Plans to CLOSE the Jail!!!," July 21, 2020.

33. Decriminalize Seattle, *Blueprint to Divestment* (June 2020).

34. Jenny Durkan, "My Community-Led $100 Million Plan for BIPOC Communities," *South Seattle Emerald*, Sept. 25, 2020.

35. Seattle City Council, Press Release, "Council Passes Mosqueda's JumpStart Seattle Progressive Revenue Plan to Address COVID Response, Essential City Services, Affordable Housing" (July 6, 2020).

36. Seattle Solidarity Budget, *Towards a Solidarity Budget, a Statement of Joint Principles for the 2021 Seattle City Budget Process* (Sept. 2020). On participatory budgeting, *see* Archon Fung, *Empowered Participation: Reinventing Urban Democracy* (Princeton University Press, 2004); Josh Lerner, *Everyone Counts: Could "Participatory Budgeting" Change Democracy?* (Cornell University Press, 2014).

37. For more on these critiques of focusing on budgets via Invest/Divest strategies, *see* Hadar Aviram, *Cheap on Crime: Recession-Era Politics and the Transformation of American Punishment* (University of California Press, 2015); Darryl K. Brown, "The Perverse Effects of Efficiency in Criminal Process," 100 *Virginia Law Review* 183, 220 (2014); Fanna Gamal, "The Miseducation of Carceral Reform," 69 *U.C.L.A. Law Review* 928 (2022); Marie Gottschalk, *Caught: The Prison State and the Lockdown of American Politics* (Princeton University Press, 2015); Allegra M. McLeod, "Beyond the Carceral State," 59 *Texas Law Review* 651 (2017).

38. *See* Alexandra Natapoff, "Criminal Municipal Courts," 134 *Harvard Law Review* 964, 980–85 (2021) (cataloging the vast array of fines and fees collected via municipal courts); Joshua Page, Victoria Piehowski, and Joe Soss, "A Debt of Care: Commercial Bail and the Gendered Logic of Criminal Justice Predation," 5 *Russell Sage Foundation Journal of Social Science* 150 (2019); Council of Economic Advisers, Executive Office of the President, *Fines, Fees and Bail: Payments in the Criminal System That Disproportionately Impact the Poor* (2015).

39. McLeod, "Beyond the Carceral State," 656.

40. Black Brilliance Research Project, *Black Brilliance Research Report* (2021).

41. *See* Seattle Solidarity Budget, Press Release, "Solidarity Budget Wins Divestment in Seattle Police Department for the Second Consecutive Year, Expanded Investments in Community Well-being, and More" (Nov. 22, 2021).

42. Editorial, "Nikkita Oliver's Disruptive Agenda a Poor Fit for Seattle," *Seattle Times*, Oct. 22, 2021.

43. Maya King and Lisa Kashinsky, "7 Big Cities Elected Mayors Tuesday. Crime and Policing Shaped the Results," *Politico*, Nov. 3, 2021.

44. People's Coalition for Safety and Freedom, Webinar, "This Is What Democracy Looks Like: A Teach-in on Participatory Democracy" (May 27, 2021).

45. *See* Maggie Blackhawk, "On Power and the Law: McGirt v. Oklahoma," 2020 *Supreme Court Review* 367, 372 (2020) (describing the relationship between demands for formal law-making power and changing dominant ideologies); K. Sabeel Rahman and Jocelyn Simonson, "The Institutional Design of Community Control," 108 *California Law Review* 679 (2020).

46. *See* A. Philip Randolph and Bayard Rustin, "A 'Freedom Budget' for All Americans: A Summary" (Jan. 1967); Paul L. Blanc and Michael D. Yates, *A Freedom Budget for All Americans* (Monthly Review Press, 2013), 89–127.

47. A. Philip Randolph, "Introduction," 7, in Randolph and Rustin, "A 'Freedom Budget.' "

48. The ideas emanated from discussions among larger groups of organizers during the buildup to the March on Washington. Although Randolph and Rustin explicitly name themselves as authors of the budget, Dona Cooper Hamilton and Charles V. Hamilton later attributed the report to "the movement" rather than individuals. Blanc and Yates, *A Freedom Budget*, 89–127.

49. Blanc and Yates, *A Freedom Budget*, 96–98.

50. Rustin biographer John D'Emilio writes that the Freedom Budget "failed . . . abysmally," saying that it is "because, even as Rustin gave birth to it, the opportunities for a progressive coalition were evaporating." John D'Emilio, *Lost Prophet: The Life and Times of Bayard Rustin* (University of Chicago Press, 2003), 430–38.

51. Black and Yates, *A Freedom Budget*, 145–78.

52. The quote is also attributed to one of King's last speeches about Vietnam. *Cf.* Jon Weiner, "Martin Luther King's Final Year: An Interview With Tavis Smiley," *The Nation*, Jan 18, 2016.

53. Martin Luther King Jr., "Foreword," 6, in Randolph and Rustin, "Freedom Budget."

54. A. Philip Randolph, "Introduction," 7, in Randolph and Rustin, "Freedom Budget."

55. *See* Elizabeth Hinton, *From the War on Poverty to the War on Crime: The Making of Mass Incarceration in America* (Harvard University Press, 2016); Naomi Murakawa, *The First Civil Right: How Liberals Built Prison America* (Oxford University Press, 2014), 69–112.

56. *See* Deanna Hoskins, Andrea C. James, and Kumar Rao, Op-Ed, "The '94 Crime Bill 25 Years Later: It's Time for a Reckoning," *Colorlines*, Sept. 30, 2019.

57. *See* Center for Popular Democracy, "Reckoning with Mass Criminalization and Mass Incarceration: A Proposal to Advance a New Vision of Public Safety and Dismantle the 1994 Crime Bill Through a Participatory People's Process," Sept. 2019, 5 (on file with author).

58. *See* Movement for Black Lives, *The BREATHE Act* (Jul. 2020), https://perma.cc/832D-SVZJ; People's Coalition for Safety and Freedom, *People's Process*, https://perma.cc/LQ24-5Z24.

59. *See* People's Coalition for Safety and Freedom, People's Process Launch, Oct. 21, 2021.

6. Practicing Justice and Safety

1. *See* Deborah Becker, "Suffolk County Sheriff Says Courtroom in His Jail Will Soon Open to Help Address 'Mass. And Cass' Addiction Crisis," *WBUR*, Oct. 25, 2021.

2. CourtWatch MA (@CourtwatchMA), Twitter (Nov. 1, 2021, 2:32 p.m.), https://twitter.com/CourtWatchMA/status/1455241442457276428.

3. CourtWatch MA (@CourtwatchMA), Twitter (Nov. 1, 2021, 4:56 p.m.), https://twitter.com/CourtWatchMA/status/1455277666186240024.

4. Tori Bedford, "Wu on the End of Mass. And Cass Jail Court: 'We Need to Keep Doing Better,' " *WGBH*, Nov. 22, 2021.

5. In other words, they were acting agonistically. *See* Philip Goodman, Joshua Page, and Michelle Phelps, *Breaking the Pendulum: The Long Struggle Over Criminal Justice* (Oxford University Press, 2017), 123–40; Chantal Mouffe, *Agonistics: Thinking the World Politically* (Verso, 2013), 5–9.

6. Lani Guinier and Gerald Torres, "Changing the Wind: Notes Toward a Demosprudence of Law and Social Movements," 123 *Yale Law Journal* 2740, 2768 (2014).

7. N.Y. C.P.L. § 210.40 (McKinney). For more on dismissals in the interest of justice, *see* Anna Roberts, "Dismissals as Justice," 69 *Alabama Law Review* 327 (2017).

8. *See* N.Y. C.P.L. § 210.40(1)(i) (McKinney); People's Motion to Dismiss in the Interests of Justice, *People v. McCarter*, Ind. No. 746/2020 (N.Y. Supreme Ct., Aug. 5, 2022); Affirmation of Sean Hecker in Support of People's Motion to Dismiss in the Interests of Justice, *People v. McCarter*, Ind. No. 746 /2020 (N.Y. Supreme Ct., Aug. 8, 2022).

9. Decision and Order, *People v. McCarter*, Ind. No. 746/2020 (N.Y. Supreme Ct., Oct. 30, 2022).

10. For more on this, *see* Jocelyn Simonson, "Tracy McCarter and the 'Interests of Justice,' " *New York Law Journal*, Sept. 11, 2022; Jocelyn Simonson,

"The Criminal Court Audience in a Post-Trial World," 127 *Harvard Law Review* 2173 (2014).

11. *See, for example,* Ben Kesslen and Elizabeth Rosner, "Despite Bragg's Campaign Promise, NYC Nurse Tracy McCarter to Be Tried for Murder," *New York Post,* Aug. 30, 2022; Molly Crane-Newman, "Manhattan DA Must Try Abused Nurse for Husband's Murder After Judge Denies Reduced Charge Request," *New York Daily News,* Aug. 30, 2022.

12. Decision and Order, People v. McCarter, Ind. No. 746/2020 (N.Y. Supreme Ct., Dec. 2, 2022).

13. Order Approving Settlement Agreement, *Remick v. City of Philadelphia,* No. 2:20-cv-01959 (E.D. Pa. Jun. 23, 2021); Defendants' Motion to Terminate Prospective Relief Ordered by the Court on September 14, 2021 Under the PLRA, *Remick v. City of Philadelphia,* No. 2:20-cv-01959 (E.D. Pa. Dec. 12, 2022); Defendants' Response in Opposition to Plaintiff's Motion for Contempt and Sanctions, *Remick v. City of Philadelphia,* No. 2:20-cv-01959 (E.D. Pa. Dec. 12, 2022).

14. 2022 Regular Sess., Kentucky House Chambers, Mar. 1, 2022 at 22:50–23:30.

15. Kentucky House Judiciary Committee, Feb. 23, 2022.

16. Minnesota Senate Floor Session, 2021 Leg., 92nd Sess., Minn., May 14, 2021.

17. *See, for example,* American Public Health Association, *Policy Statement: Advancing Public Health Interventions to Address the Harms of the Carceral System* (2021) (collecting research).

18. *See, for example,* Monica C. Bell, "Police Reform and the Dismantling of Legal Estrangement," 126 *Yale Law Journal* 2067 (2017); Jeffrey Fagan, Valerie West, and Jan Holland, "Reciprocal Effects of Crime and Incarceration in New York City Neighborhoods," 30 *Fordham Urban Law Journal* 1551, 1554 (2003); Amy E. Lerman and Vesla M. Weaver, *Arresting Citizenship: The Democratic Consequences of American Crime Control* (University of Chicago Press, 2014), 64–9; Dorothy E. Roberts, "The Social and Moral Cost of Mass Incarceration in African American Communities," 56 *Stanford Law Review* 1291–97 (2004).

19. *See* 2009 California Evidence Code §§ 720–723.

20. *See, for example,* California Penal Code § 186.22(b)(1).

21. Marcel Woodruff, Live Free Peacemakers/Advance Peace, Gang Affiliation and Risk Assessment (on file with author).

22. *See* Cynthia Godsoe, "Participatory Defense: Humanizing the Accused and Ceding Control to the Client," 69 *Mercer Law Review* 715, 722 (2018) (describing the impact of bringing lay expertise into the courtroom).

23. On the power-building potential of collaborations between movements and lawyers, *see* Michael Grinthal, "Power with: Practice Models for Social Justice Lawyering," 15 *University of Pennsylvania Journal of Law & Social Change* 25 (2011).

24. *See, for example,* Patricia Hill Collins, "Black Feminist Epistemology," in *Black Feminist Thought: Knowledge, Consciousness, and the Politics of Empowerment* (Routledge, 2000), 271; Mari J. Matsuda, "Public Response to Racist Speech: Considering the Victim's Story," 87 *Michigan Law Review* 2320, 2322 (1989) ("[O]utsider jurisprudence—jurisprudence derived from considering stories from the bottom—will help resolve the seemingly irresolvable conflicts of value and doctrine that characterize liberal thought."). For more on the importance of this tradition for scholarship today, see Amna Akbar, Sameer Ashar, and Jocelyn Simonson, "Movement Law," 73 *Stanford Law Review* 821, 832–43 (2021).

25. *See generally* Bell, "Legal Estrangement"; Vesla Weaver, Gwen Prowse, and Spencer Piston, "Too Much Knowledge, Too Little Power: An Assessment of Political Knowledge in Highly Policed Communities." 81 *Journal of Politics* 1153 (2019).

26. *See* Christina Koningsor, "Public Undersight," 106 *Minnesota Law Review* 2221 (2022); Benjamin Levin, "Criminal Justice Expertise," 90 *Fordham Law Review* 2777, 2779 (2022); Ngozi Okidegbe, "Discredited Data," 107 *Cornell Law Review* (forthcoming 2023); Susan P. Sturm and Haran Tae, "Leading with Conviction: The Transformative Role of Formerly Incarcerated Leaders in Reducing Mass Incarceration," Columbia Public Law Research Paper No. 14-547 (2017), 15–27; Hannah L. Walker, *Mobilized By Injustice: Criminal Justice Contact, Political Participation, and Race* (Oxford University Press, 2020).

27. On the shortcomings of data using the system's own parameters, *see* Erin Collins, "Abolishing the Evidence-Based Paradigm," *B.Y.U. Law Review* (forthcoming 2022); Jessica M. Eaglin, "Constructing Recidivism Risk," 67 *Emory Law Journal* 59 (2017); Cecelia M. Klingele, "The Promises and Perils of Evidence-Based Corrections," 91 *Notre Dame Law Review* 537 (2015); Megan Stevenson, "Assessing Risk Assessment in Action," 103 *Minnesota Law Review* 303 (2018).

28. *See* Alice Ristroph, "An Intellectual History of Mass Incarceration," 60 *Boston College Law Review* 1949, 2009 (2019) ("Were we to seek a different paradigm [for criminal law], the first step would be to describe criminal law more accurately.").

29. It is impossible to summarize the intersections between white supremacy, racism, and the carceral state in one short footnote, but some touchstones

for me are Kelly Lytle Hernández, *City of Inmates: Conquests, Rebellion, and the Rise of Human Caging in Los Angeles* (University of North Carolina Press, 2017); Khalil Gibran Muhammad, *The Condemnation of Blackness* (Harvard University Press, 2010); and Naomi Murakawa, *The First Civil Right: How Liberals Built Prison America* (Oxford University Press, 2014).

30. Amna A. Akbar, "An Abolitionist Horizon for (Police) Reform," 108 *California Law Review* 1781, 1824 (2020).

31. Jonathan Simon, *Governing Through Crime: How the War on Crime Transformed American Democracy and Created a Culture of Fear* (Oxford University Press, 2007).

32. Jeffrey M. Jones, "Confidence in U.S. Institutions Down; Average at New Low," *Gallup News*, Jul. 5, 2022; Black Kiana Cox and Khadijah Edwards, "Americans Have a Clear Vision for Reducing Racism but Little Hope It Will Happen," *Pew Research Center*, Aug. 30, 2022.

33. *See* Sameer Ashar, "The Pedagogy of Prefiguration," *Yale Law Journal* (forthcoming 2022); Carl Boggs, "Marxism, Prefigurative Communism, and the Problem of Workers' Control," 11 *Radical America* 100 (1977); Amy J. Cohen and Bronwen Morgan, "Prefigurative Legality," *Law & Social Inquiry* (forthcoming 2022); David Graeber, "'You're Creating a Vision of the Sort of Society You Want to Have in Miniature,' Interview with Ezra Klein," *Washington Post*, Oct. 3, 2011; Deva R. Woodly, *Reckoning: Black Lives Matter and the Democratic Necessity of Social Movements* (Oxford University Press, 2022), 70–71, 208.

34. Sharlyn Grace, "Organizers Change What's Possible," *Inquest*, Sept. 23, 2021.

35. Ta-Nehisi Coates, "Civil-Rights Protests Have Never Been Popular," *The Atlantic*, Oct. 3, 2017; Elahe Izadi, "Black Lives Matter and America's Long History of Resisting Civil Rights Protesters," *Washington Post*, April 19, 2016.

36. Robin D.G. Kelley, *Freedom Dreams: The Black Radical Tradition* (Beacon Press, 2002), ix, 9; *see also* Erin R. Pineda, *Seeing Like an Activist: Civil Disobedience and the Civil Rights Movement* (Oxford University Press, 2020), 21; Amna A. Akbar, "Toward a Radical Imagination of Law," 93 *N.Y.U. Law Review* 405, 479 (2018) ("Progressive wins have been hard fought by social movements—often with more radical visions than what we now see.").

37. Tommy Shelby and Brandon M. Terry, "Introduction," in *To Shape a New World: Essays on the Political Philosophy of Martin Luther King, Jr.*, eds. Shelby and Terry (Harvard University Press, 2020), 3–4, 6.

38. *See generally* "Fifty Years Since MLK," *Boston Review*, ed. Brandon Terry (Feb. 2018); Martin Luther King, Jr., *The Radical King*, ed. Cornel West (Beacon Press, 2016).

39. *See* Barbara Ransby, "We Must Not Sanitize King," *Boston Review*, Sept. 10, 2018.

40. Elizabeth Hinton, *America on Fire: The Untold History of Police Violence and Black Rebellion Since the 1960s* (Liveright, 2021), 1–19.

41. *See* Dean Spade, *Mutual Aid: Building Solidarity During This Crisis (and the Next)* (Verso, 2020), 31–45; Woodly, *Reckoning*, 89–126.

Afterword

1. Gabrielle Hernandez, Interview with Mary Hooks, "If We Can Dismantle Patriarchy and Capitalism, We Might Be onto Something," *Scalawag*, Jan. 28, 2020.

2. *See* Seattle Solidarity Budget, *Solidarity Budget 2023: Budget to Live, Budget to Thrive* (Oct. 2022).

3. *See* Teresa Mathew, "Why New York City Created Its Own Fund to Bail People Out of Jail," *Bloomberg News*, Dec. 1, 2017.

4. For more on these anti-democratic elements of the criminal system, *see* Monica C. Bell, "Police Reform and the Dismantling of Legal Estrangement," 126 *Yale Law Journal* 2067 (2017); Amy E. Lerman and Vesla M. Weaver, *Arresting Citizenship: The Democratic Consequences of American Crime Control* (University of Chicago Press, 2014), 64–9; Dorothy E. Roberts, "Democratizing Criminal Law as an Abolitionist Project," 111 *Northwestern University Law Review* 1597 (2017).

5. Angela Y. Davis, *Abolition Democracy* (AK Press, 2005), 95–6; Allegra M. McLeod, "Envisioning Abolition Democracy," 132 *Harvard Law Review* 1613, 1617–18 (2019).

6. Raj Jayadev and Pilar Weiss, "Organizing Towards a New Vision of Community Justice," *Law & Political Economy Blog* (May 9, 2019).

7. Debt Collective, "Cancel Carceral Debt," https://cancelmybaildebt.org/ (last visited Oct. 26, 2022).

8. Michelle Alexander, "Go to Trial: Crash the Justice System," *New York Times*, Mar. 11, 2012, SR5; Andrew Manuel Crespo, "No Justice No Pleas: Subverting Mass Incarceration Through Defendant Collective Action," 90 *Fordham Law Review* 1999 (2022).

9. National Network of Abortion Funds, https://abortionfunds.org/ (last visited Oct. 26, 2022).

Index

About the Author

A former public defender, **Jocelyn Simonson** is professor of law at Brooklyn Law School. Her work has been cited by the Supreme Court and discussed in *The Atlantic*, the *New Yorker*, and the Associated Press, and she has written for the *New York Times*, *The Nation*, *n+1*, the *Washington Post*, and others. She lives in New York City.

Publishing in the Public Interest

Thank you for reading this book published by The New Press; we hope you enjoyed it. New Press books and authors play a crucial role in sparking conversations about the key political and social issues of our day.

We hope that you will stay in touch with us. Here are a few ways to keep up to date with our books, events, and the issues we cover:

- Sign up at www.thenewpress.com/subscribe to receive updates on New Press authors and issues and to be notified about local events
- www.facebook.com/newpressbooks
- www.twitter.com/thenewpress
- www.instagram.com/thenewpress

Please consider buying New Press books not only for yourself, but also for friends and family and to donate to schools, libraries, community centers, prison libraries, and other organizations involved with the issues our authors write about.

The New Press is a 501(c)(3) nonprofit organization; if you wish to support our work with a tax-deductible gift please visit www.thenewpress.com/donate or use the QR code below.

[redacted]